150
Things
to Make with
Roast
Chicken
And 50 Ways to Roast It

TONY ROSENFELD

150 Things to Make with Roast Chicken

And 50 Ways to Roast It

The Taunton Press

The Taunton Press
Inspiration for hands-on living®

The Taunton Press, Inc.,
63 South Main Street, PO Box 5506,
Newtown, CT 06470-5506
e-mail: tp@taunton.com

Editor: Pam Hoenig
Jacket/Cover design: Suzanne Heiser
Interior design: jennykate.com
Layout: Lissi Sigillo and Cathy Cassidy
Illustrators: Robert DeMichiel and Christine Erikson

LIBRARY OF CONGRESS CATALOGING-IN-PUBLICATION DATA
ROSENFELD, TONY.
   150 THINGS TO MAKE WITH ROAST CHICKEN (AND 50 WAYS TO ROAST IT) /
AUTHOR: TONY ROSENFELD ; PHOTOGRAPHER: SCOTT PHILLIPS.
      P. CM.
   INCLUDES INDEX.
   ISBN-13: 978-1-56158-845-9
   ISBN-10: 1-56158-845-8
   1. COOKERY (CHICKEN) I. TITLE. II. TITLE: ONE HUNDRED AND FIFTY THINGS
TO MAKE WITH ROAST CHICKEN (AND 50 WAYS TO ROAST IT).

TX750.5.C45R663 2007
641.6'65--DC22

                                                    2006032139

The Taunton Press publishes *Fine Cooking*, the magazine for people who love to cook.

For Marguerite, Mom, and Dad,
who have fed me much love and inspiration over the years

Acknowledgments

There are a lot of people who ate a lot of chicken for the sake of this book—I'm talking about a *lot* of chicken, on many nights past the point of fullness, all in the name of culinary advancement. To the friends, family members, and colleagues who endured this substantial chicken diet, I am eternally grateful (and more than a little impressed).

I'm indebted to my friends at *Fine Cooking*. With great generosity, Susie Middleton has continually opened up new doorways for me—it's my version of a winning lottery ticket, perhaps undeserved but greatly appreciated. Before Susie, Martha Holmberg was the first to let me into the *Fine Cooking* club. Kim Masibay cleaned up this book's science text, Jennifer Armentrout and Sarah Jay cleared out the test kitchen so we could shoot the book's photos, Deanah Kim helped style the food, and Molly Stevens and Abby Dodge offered good, practical advice. And everybody else on the *FC* staff was there to cheer me along the way.

A diligent crew helped test the recipes and wordsmith the language for this book. Andrew "Moneyman" Pease is as caring and thoughtful a cook as he is a best friend. Practiced recipe tester Christine Merlo gave me wonderful feedback on many dishes. Paula Figoni was the first to refine the science content in the first chapter. And Richard Lobb at the National Chicken Council provided plenty of data and poultry information.

Of course, I am most grateful to those who worked directly on this book. Pam Hoenig came up with the concept and then oversaw its development decisively and with great vision. Tammy Mitman undangled the dangling modifiers and matched up all the cross-referencing throughout the recipes, no small feat. Katie Benoit helped with all facets of organization while Nicole Radder enthusiastically headed up the marketing. And even-tempered Scott Philips, an artist without the ego, did beautiful work despite the rigors of the shooting schedule.

And finally, thanks to all the members of the b.good team who were flexible with my roasting hours over the last couple of hectic years.

Contents

Roast Your Way to Weeknight Meal Magic

Cooking every night isn't easy. Little things like hunger and fatigue and junk food can get in the way (tortilla chips are my kryptonite). And on those occasions when you do get to the stovetop, clear-headed and skillet in hand, the rut of routine can ensnare you, making tonight's meal a lot like the one from last night or last week or last year. It's the culinary equivalent of writer's block, and your spouse and/or kids are always ready to call you on it with the cry that haunts every hard-working home cook: "Again?!?!"

Of course, you can just give in: throw your hands up in the air and call for pizza. *Or*, you can get hip to the concept of meal planning. It may sound like something out of home economics class, but it just means getting organized: Go to the store with a plan, then prepare the foundation for a couple of meals back at home. In the coming nights, that jump-start can be the beginning of all sorts of new meals. Sounds good, right?

There are many things you can use as a base. A pot roast, a pot of marinara sauce, or even a large batch of grilled vegetables will do. But absolutely nothing matches the versatility and simplicity of a roast chicken. The fact is, it's dead easy to roast a chicken. And it takes no extra effort at all to set another bird in the pan to roast along with the first one. By doing this, you've got the lovely makings of at least one, if not a few, weeknight meals. I'm talking about dishes with vibrant flavors that go beyond your basic chicken à la king. With some spice, a well-stocked pantry, and a little imagination, leftover chicken can be dressed up in a world of ways: bright salads, crisp stir-fries, warming baked pastas, creamy casseroles, or satisfying soups.

And that's as complicated as it gets. Roast two medium birds (or you could make it a big roaster), enjoy one for dinner tonight and the other in any of 150 different dishes. To keep things interesting, I've also given you more than 50 ways to roast your chicken—you can hit it with a spice or herb rub before roasting, brush it with a glaze so it gets browned and sweet, or surround it with vegetables to roast alongside it in the pan. You also can play around with the roasting method: use a low fire on the grill to grill-roast a bird or sear it in a skillet before roasting to intensify and brown the crust.

I must add one final note: Not only am I the author of this book, but I'm also a member of the leftover chicken fan club. When somebody first suggested the idea to me, I had never really approached a roast bird as a way to create other meals. But now, many hundreds of chickens later, I am still playing around with different roasting pairings and leftover dishes. It simply is a great way to get dinner to the table. I think you will agree.

How to Use This Book

The one item you may need to invest in for this book is a large roasting pan (one big enough to cook two medium birds at the same time—you probably already have a pan that size for the Thanksgiving turkey). Beyond that, pick your roast chicken recipe and have at it. I've tried to make my roast chicken recipes flexible, since no two nights or two families are ever the same. Maybe you're only cooking for one or two people and one bird will be enough for dinner and leftovers. Or maybe you don't need the leftovers and you simply want to roast a bird for dinner tonight. Whatever the case, each of the roast chicken recipes has ingredient lists for preparing one or two birds at a time so you can make what you need.

Some nights you may just want to skip the roasting step and get straight to the leftovers. In that case, grab a rotisserie chicken at the market and turn it into a casserole, salad, or soup the same night. And if you've got lots of leftover turkey from Thanksgiving, don't hesitate to give these recipes a whirl.

The remaining chapters contain 150 ways to enjoy the fruits of your forethought. For each second-time-around recipe, I've suggested particular roast chicken recipes that will pair well with it—for instance, a roast chicken with curry powder in its spice rub would go nicely in a chicken curry stew. The truth is that the external flavorings you add to roast chicken often don't get too far past the skin, so feel free to use whatever roast chicken you have on hand in whatever dish you're in the mood for.

Chapter 1

Roasting 101

When I began my research for this book,

I turned to cooks whose opinions I trust and asked them their favorite way to roast a bird. I wasn't looking for anything in particular. Rather, I just hoped to gather a little consensus and make sure my own method matched up favorably with theirs.

Alas, my experiment did not go as planned. My cooking friends wildly differed on most every aspect of their preparations. Some favored large birds, while others preferred small, tender chickens. Roasting temperatures ranged from 350°F to 500°F. And almost every version included some unique combination of flipping, twisting, trussing, brushing, or basting.

Instead of consensus, I was left with a confusing and contradictory culinary roadmap. What to make of all these differing viewpoints? Something very simple: There is no one way to properly roast a chicken. Roasting a chicken isn't so much about finding the "perfect" method as it is about your own preferences and taste buds.

For this reason, to determine your own preferred way for roasting a bird, you need to focus on how you like your chicken, and then cook it accordingly. If you like a bird that's well browned with crisp skin, high heat is the route for you. If you're more partial to a chicken that's moist and juicy, more moderate heat would be the way to go. Of course, that's not to say you can't have it all—you could brine the bird to make sure it stays juicy or slip it under the broiler at the end to ensure it browns.

This chapter covers the pertinent information on all things chicken, starting at the poultry case and ending at the dinner table. Quite simply it's a compilation of what I've found works best for me, but you should feel free to take what you like and leave the rest.

At the Market

Not long ago, picking up a chicken at the market demanded little thought. One or two brands filled the case and the only major decision concerned the size of the bird. Now, there are many types and brands of chicken from which to choose. This larger selection is an exciting development, though it does mean you have to wade through all the offerings to find the best bird for you.

To start off, it's important to note that the focus of this book is roasting whole birds. It's not that I don't love the ease and flexibility of chicken parts. It's just that a whole chicken satisfies both those who prefer white meat and those who prefer dark, and still yields plentiful leftovers (which is the aim of this book). Thus we can narrow our search down to whole chickens.

Size. Step up to the poultry case and one of the first things you'll notice is the different sizes of birds. This characteristic is directly related to age—the smaller the chicken, the younger it is and vice versa. Birds of different sizes also tend to have different characteristics. Smaller birds, often labeled broilers or fryers, usually have a tender texture and mild flavor. Larger birds, generally labeled roasters, have a more pronounced flavor and slightly tougher texture.

While there are merits to both groupings, I prefer a 3½- to 4-pound chicken, which occupies a happy middle ground. It's small enough to be tender and cook quickly in a hot oven. At the same time, this size is large enough to feed four—but not so large that you can't fit two birds in a roasting pan.

National brand vs. free range/organic vs. kosher. Whole chickens can be broken down into a few simple groupings. There are the national brands sold by well known companies such as Tyson® or Perdue®, which produce staggering quantities of birds and attempt to keep their products uniform and affordable. Then there are free-range and organic birds, which can be one and the same. The term "free range" refers to the animal's living conditions. Whereas large-scale producers raise chickens in close quarters, free-range farms allow the birds more space to roam, often in large pens, ideally providing healthier living conditions, which in turn presumably produces a more flavorful chicken. Some of these free-range birds are also "organic," a term that connotes that they've been raised on organic feed and have not been injected with antibiotics or growth hormones. The last group is kosher chickens, which are butchered according to Jewish law using a process that sanitizes the birds with plenty of salt. This quick salt bath gives the meat a well-seasoned flavor similar to brining. (The salt bath also helps remove blood and any impurities.)

Which chicken to buy? My advice, quite simply, is to pick out the best one you can find (and afford). Indeed, quality and expense are often intertwined. Free-range, organic birds are more expensive, but I do find their flavor and texture to be superior to national brands. Ultimately, there is no better test than your own taste buds, so try the different birds at the market to find what you like best.

HOW TO PICK A BIRD

No matter what size or type of bird you buy, there are a few things you should look for at the poultry case. These visual tests, though simple and obvious, can help you avoid a bad experience:

* Look for smooth, unblemished skin and a well-shaped bird with plump legs. Crusted skin is a sign of freezer burn.

* Make sure that the packaging has no tears or holes (and definitely no off odors).

* Try to find a bird with the most distant sell-by date. I'm sure I don't make any friends with the butchers who stock the case, but I like digging to the back of the cooler to find the freshest bird. This area also is generally the coolest, ensuring another level of freshness.

Flavoring the Bird

Once you've picked up a bird and brought it home, it's time to get started. As with most things in life, the more time you have to prepare, the better. For roasting chicken, this is true not because the process is complicated, but rather because seasoning the bird ahead of time allows the flavors to soak in.

Of all the different seasonings, salt is the most important. Not only does it enhance a chicken's flavor, but it also helps cleanse the bird of any bacterial impurities.

THE BEST TYPES OF CHICKEN FOR ROASTING AND LEFTOVERS

NAME	SIZE (POUNDS)	AGE OF BIRD	CHARACTERISTICS	APPROXIMATE COOKING TIME	SUGGESTED ROASTING TEMPERATURE
Broiler (or fryer)	2½ to 4½	Around 2½ months old	Tender, quick-cooking; as its name indicates, perfect for high heat methods	45 to 60 minutes	425°F
Capon	4 to 7	Up to 10 months old	Neutered male bird; tender, light meat	1 to 1¾ hours	375°F
Roaster	5 to 7	3 to 5 months old	Less tender but flavorful; holds up well to roasting	1¼ to 1¾ hours	375°F

Brining

Though I love marinating chicken, when it comes to whole birds, a brine is my first choice. It soaks in the flavors like a marinade but it also adds moisture, which will keep the chicken (particularly the lean breast meat) from drying out during roasting. A brined bird also makes for juicier leftovers.

A brine is a mix of salt and water, with sugar and additional seasonings often tossed in. (I like to use about 1 cup of salt and 1 cup of sugar for every gallon of liquid.) To brine a bird, set a whole chicken with its brine in a large container (I use a large Tupperware® container) and let it sit in the refrigerator for at least 4 and up to 12 hours before roasting.

Brining does have drawbacks. You need to plan ahead, and the container can take up quite a bit of space in your refrigerator, especially if you're preparing two birds at a time. Finally, if you brine a chicken for too long, the saltwater solution firms up the meat's protein strands, creating a rubbery texture similar to bad deli meat. For this reason, don't brine your bird more than 24 hours.

The brining ratio I use is standard for a soaking period of between 4 and 12 hours. Some people like increasing the amounts of salt and sugar for a shorter soak. I find that these quick brines produce unpredictable and largely ineffective results for whole birds. If you only have an hour or two, you're best off just salting the bird or hitting it with a vibrant spice rub instead of using a brine.

Basic Brine

For a basic brine, I simply whisk salt and sugar together with cold water. For flavored brines, though, it's necessary to heat the mixture up to properly infuse all the different flavors. I hold back a little cool water during this heating stage, then whisk it into the mix afterwards to help it cool down at least to room temperature for brining. (If you're in a rush, you can use ice to further speed up the process.)

Enough for 1 or 2 chickens

FOR 1 BIRD	FOR 2 BIRDS	
½ cup	I cup	kosher salt
½ cup	I cup	sugar
2 quarts	I gallon	water

Add the salt and sugar to a container large enough to comfortably hold the chicken. Whisk in half of the water and continue whisking until the salt and sugar are dissolved. Add the remaining water and stir well. Submerge the chicken completely in the brine and refrigerate for at least 4 and up to 12 hours prior to cooking.

Soy-Ginger Brine

Enough for 1 or 2 chickens

FOR 1 BIRD	FOR 2 BIRDS	
1½ quarts	3 quarts	water
¼ cup	½ cup	kosher salt
½ cup	1 cup	firmly packed light brown sugar
1 cup	2 cups	soy sauce
2 tablespoons	¼ cup	peeled and coarsely chopped fresh ginger
4 cloves	8 cloves	garlic, smashed
1 tablespoon	2 tablespoons	toasted sesame oil

1. Combine half the water with the remaining ingredients in a large saucepan and bring to a boil, whisking occasionally.

2. Remove from the heat, stir in the remaining water, and let cool to room temperature before using. Submerge the chicken completely in the brine and refrigerate, uncovered, for at least 4 and up to 12 hours prior to cooking.

Cinnamon and Cider Brine

Enough for 1 or 2 chickens

FOR 1 BIRD	FOR 2 BIRDS	
1 quart	2 quarts	water
1 quart	2 quarts	apple cider or apple juice
½ cup	1 cup	kosher salt
½ cup	1 cup	firmly packed light brown sugar
3	6	cinnamon sticks

1. Combine half the water and cider with the remaining ingredients in a large saucepan and bring to a boil, whisking occasionally.

2. Remove from the heat, stir in the remaining water and cider, and let cool to room temperature before using. Submerge the chicken completely in the brine and refrigerate, uncovered, for at least 4 and up to 12 hours prior to cooking.

Orange-Rosemary Brine

Enough for 1 or 2 chickens

FOR 1 BIRD	FOR 2 BIRDS	
1 quart	2 quarts	water
1/2 cup	1 cup	kosher salt
1/2 cup	1 cup	firmly packed light brown sugar
2 tablespoons	1/4 cup	chopped fresh rosemary
1 quart	2 quarts	orange juice

1. Combine the water, salt, sugar, and rosemary in a large saucepan and bring to a boil, whisking occasionally.

2. Remove from the heat, stir in the orange juice, and let cool to room temperature before using. Submerge the chicken completely in the brine and refrigerate, uncovered, for at least 4 and up to 12 hours prior to cooking.

Dry Rubs

Dry rubs forgo the liquid of a brine and instead focus solely on the flavoring component. A rub consists of herbs, spices, and aromatics mixed into a powder or paste. You can slather this mixture all over a bird right before cooking to form an intense crust—great on a harried weeknight —or sprinkle it on well before cooking to let the flavors soak into the skin. Spice rubs are an excellent choice for grill-roasts; the spices bloom and intensify, complementing the smokiness from the grill. They're also great for a simple oven-roasted chicken—I should know, as I was raised on my mom's Hungarian Roast Chicken (p. 40), served at least once a week. Herb-based rubs are more subtle and understated than spice rubs, though they still give a bird a wonderful aromatic essence, especially if you spread the rub between the skin and breast meat.

I'm including a few rub recipes here to get you started. With the exception of the herb rub, which is best used immediately, each of them will keep for up to a month, tightly covered, in your pantry.

All-Purpose Poultry Spice Rub

Enough for 1 or 2 chickens

FOR 1 BIRD	FOR 2 BIRDS	
2½ teaspoons	5 teaspoons	kosher salt
1 teaspoon	2 teaspoons	chili powder
1 teaspoon	2 teaspoons	freshly ground black pepper
1 teaspoon	2 teaspoons	light brown sugar
1 teaspoon	2 teaspoons	sweet paprika
½ teaspoon	1 teaspoon	dry mustard

In a small bowl, combine the ingredients. Sprinkle evenly all over the chicken, including the cavity, at least 30 minutes before cooking, or apply the rub up to 24 hours ahead and refrigerate.

Southwestern Chile Spice Rub

Enough for 1 or 2 chickens

FOR 1 BIRD	FOR 2 BIRDS	
2½ teaspoons	5 teaspoons	kosher salt
2 teaspoons	4 teaspoons	chili powder
1 teaspoon	2 teaspoons	ground cumin
1 teaspoon	2 teaspoons	ground chipotle powder
1 teaspoon	2 teaspoons	light brown sugar
1 teaspoon	2 teaspoons	garlic powder
¼ teaspoon	½ teaspoon	freshly ground black pepper

In a small bowl, combine the ingredients. Sprinkle evenly all over the chicken, including the cavity, at least 30 minutes before cooking, or apply the rub up to 24 hours ahead and refrigerate.

Sweet Southern Spice Rub

Enough for 1 or 2 chickens

FOR 1 BIRD	FOR 2 BIRDS	
2½ teaspoons	5 teaspoons	kosher salt
2 teaspoons	4 teaspoons	chili powder
1 teaspoon	2 teaspoons	sweet paprika
1 teaspoon	2 teaspoons	garlic powder
1 teaspoon	2 teaspoons	freshly ground black pepper
1 teaspoon	2 teaspoons	light brown sugar
¼ teaspoon	½ teaspoon	dry mustard
pinch	large pinch	cayenne pepper

In a small bowl, combine the ingredients. Sprinkle evenly all over the chicken, including the cavity, at least 30 minutes before cooking, or apply the rub up to 24 hours ahead and refrigerate.

Moroccan Spice Rub

Enough for 1 or 2 chickens

FOR 1 BIRD	FOR 2 BIRDS	
2½ teaspoons	5 teaspoons	kosher salt
2 teaspoons	4 teaspoons	ground cumin
1 teaspoon	2 teaspoons	ground coriander
1 teaspoon	2 teaspoons	freshly ground black pepper
1 teaspoon	2 teaspoons	light brown sugar
¼ teaspoon	½ teaspoon	ground cinnamon
¼ teaspoon	½ teaspoon	cayenne pepper

In a small bowl, combine the ingredients. Sprinkle evenly all over the chicken, including the cavity, at least 30 minutes before cooking, or apply the rub up to 24 hours ahead and refrigerate.

Lemon-Herb Rub

Enough for 1 or 2 chickens

FOR 1 BIRD	FOR 2 BIRDS	
2½ teaspoons	5 teaspoons	kosher salt
1	2	lemon(s), zest only, finely grated (I like using a microplane for this)
2 teaspoons	4 teaspoons	chopped fresh rosemary
1 teaspoon	2 teaspoons	chopped fresh thyme
1 teaspoon	2 teaspoons	freshly ground black pepper

In a small bowl, combine the ingredients. Sprinkle evenly all over the chicken, including the cavity, at least 30 minutes before cooking.

Glazes

Glazes are sugary mixtures that give grilled or roasted chicken a wonderful, browned crust. The flavor of a glaze is only skin deep, though, so it must be intense and concentrated to ensure that its presence is prominent. Glazes should be sweet, of course, but they also need some measure of heat and tang for complexity.

A glaze's texture also demands attention—it should be thick enough to brush on the bird and stick. While you can reduce a glaze to create this consistency, for the sake of speed and simplicity, I like using already thickened ingredients like jam, honey, or syrup so you can just whisk one of these glazes together, then brush it on the bird.

The other big question with glazes is when to add them. Sugar and roasting are a whimsical match—one moment you've got browned perfection, the next a charred mess. For this reason, I like roasting a bird almost halfway through before beginning to brush it with a glaze. This allows enough time for the mixture to brown and intensify, without burning.

Rosemary-Balsamic Glaze

Enough for 1 or 2 chickens

FOR 1 BIRD	FOR 2 BIRDS	
1½ tablespoons	3 tablespoons	balsamic vinegar
¼ cup	½ cup	honey
1 tablespoon	2 tablespoons	chopped fresh rosemary

Whisk all the ingredients together and use immediately, or store for up to 1 week, tightly covered, in the refrigerator.

Orange-Apricot Glaze

Enough for 1 or 2 chickens

FOR 1 BIRD	FOR 2 BIRDS	
3 tablespoons	6 tablespoons	orange marmalade
3 tablespoons	6 tablespoons	apricot preserves
3 tablespoons	6 tablespoons	honey
2 tablespoons	1/4 cup	orange juice
1 tablespoon	2 tablespoons	chopped fresh thyme

Whisk all the ingredients together and use immediately, or store for up to 1 week, tightly covered, in the refrigerator.

Maple-Mustard Glaze

Enough for 1 or 2 chickens

FOR 1 BIRD	FOR 2 BIRDS	
1/4 cup	1/2 cup	maple syrup
1/4 cup	1/2 cup	Dijon mustard
2 tablespoons	1/4 cup	light brown sugar
1 tablespoon	2 tablespoons	chopped fresh thyme

Whisk all the ingredients together and use immediately, or store for up to 1 week, tightly covered, in the refrigerator.

Asian Barbecue Glaze

Enough for 1 or 2 chickens

FOR 1 BIRD	FOR 2 BIRDS	
3 tablespoons	6 tablespoons	hoisin sauce
2 tablespoons	1/4 cup	light corn syrup
1 tablespoon	2 tablespoons	soy sauce
1 tablespoon	2 tablespoons	rice vinegar

Whisk all the ingredients together and use immediately, or store for up to 1 week, tightly covered, in the refrigerator.

Keeping It Simple

The simplest of all flavoring methods for chicken—and the one I use most often—is a generous sprinkling of plain old salt (kosher salt, that is), about 2½ teaspoons, up to 24 hours ahead of time. I follow this approach when I'm not sure how I want to prepare a bird, but I know I want to cook one (or two) the following night. When I get home from the market, I sprinkle the chicken generously with salt, then let it sit on a rack, uncovered, in the refrigerator overnight. Seasoning the bird ahead of time allows the salt to penetrate beyond the skin. Leaving it uncovered helps dry out the skin so it becomes extra crisp during roasting. I'll often embellish this salting with some fresh herbs or spices (upgrading the mixture to a rub) if I have the foresight or inspiration.

While these seasonings are most effective when added well in advance, spontaneous cooks need not be scared off. If you can't season a bird ahead of time, simply do so just before cooking, but make sure to sprinkle it with salt to taste after cooking as well.

Chicken Safety

People seem to be ever more aware of the importance of working cleanly and safely with chicken. Salmonella is the primary enemy you need to guard against as you prepare and cook raw chicken. During prep time, your biggest risk is cross-contamination. If you think of all the things you do while getting a bird ready to cook—grab spices and herbs out of the pantry, pick up the salt crock and the pepper mill, twist the oven knobs to the proper setting—you can see how easy it is to contaminate other ingredients or items in the kitchen after touching the raw chicken. The simplest solution is to pay attention and take extra precautions: Set some salt aside in a separate, small container just for seasoning the bird. Keep on hand a cutting board for use with raw chicken only. Make sure to wipe down the countertops well after working with raw chicken. And, of course, wash your hands often.

Salmonella is effectively killed at 160°F (though for the sake of caution it's best to roast a chicken to 165°F which is the temperature I call for in the recipes in this book). Though there are all sorts of visual tests for telling when a chicken is done, the safest and most certain way is to measure the bird's internal temperature. The best tool for this is an instant-read thermometer, which gives a reading in a matter of seconds. Running between $10 and $20, these small, pen-sized probes are a worthwhile investment: they not only ensure that you cook a chicken sufficiently, but also that you don't overcook it, either. Insert an instant-read thermometer into the thickest part of a thigh without touching the bone. When the thermometer registers 165°F, you know the entire chicken is done.

Finding the Right Roasting Pan

Successful roasting starts with the pan and a good one will last a lifetime. It will cost quite a bit, too (between $150 to $200), so it's worth spending time to make sure you pick out a winner (if you don't already own one).

A roasting pan should be sturdy and flame-proof, so that you can put it over your stovetop burners to make a pan sauce. The heavier the base of the pan, the more evenly it transfers heat. This heavy base helps brown (not burn) the bird and any accompaniments (be they stuffing or vegetables) that come into contact with the pan. A sturdy pan also ensures that the browned bits and chicken drippings form a rich base for a sauce; in more flimsy pans, these drippings can burn and become acrid, which will make a nasty-tasting sauce.

For this book, it's important to have a pan large enough to comfortably cook two birds at a time. Of course, you can roast the birds in two separate pans, though it's hard to fit two pans on the same shelf in most ovens.

Of the roasting pans large enough to accommodate two birds at once, most are either made of stainless steel or are lined with a nonstick surface. (Enameled cast-iron roasting pans are great but generally on the small side.) Of the two options, I prefer sturdy, stainless steel pans. They heat up steadily and evenly, hold up well over time, and will produce the beautifully browned and caramelized makings for a great pan sauce.

On the other hand, nothing sticks to the surface of a nonstick roasting pan, which is both a good and a bad thing. On a positive note, this makes for quick clean-up. But the browned bits don't form the same bond with the pan's bottom and fail to caramelize in the way they do with a stainless steel pan. Furthermore, nonstick surfaces tend to break down with frequent use and exposure to high heat.

You're best off picking out a pan that's well built and, of course, large enough to roast two birds at once. Whichever type of pan you select, do make sure to purchase one with sturdy handles, to make transfers to and from the oven easier.

To Rack or Not to Rack?

A roasting rack lifts a bird off the bottom of a roasting pan so that air can circulate evenly underneath, crisping the bottom of the chicken as it does the top. The rack provides kind of a rotisserie effect, allowing the juices to drip off the bird as it slowly browns.

Of course, you can roast a bird just fine without a rack. The major drawback is that the bottom of the bird won't crisp up. It this isn't a problem for you, go rackless (see "No Rack?" on p. 19). If you like maximum crispness, read on.

There are all sorts of roasting racks on the market. Most of them work well with one bird, but they're put to the test when you try to roast two birds at a time. What follows is a quick run-down of the roasting racks you're likely to find:

MY TAKE ON RACKING

For roasting two birds at a time, I like using two small v-racks—preferably non-adjustable. If you go this route, make sure the racks fit side by side in the roasting pan. If you prefer to go with one large rack instead, pick up a sturdy nonadjustable v-rack or a basket rack, both of which will do a fine job with two birds (and even better with one). In a pinch, you can most certainly make due with a flat rack. This rack offers plenty of space for roasting two birds at once, though it won't do so as delicately as the other racks.

Flat rack: A flat rack looks like a cooling rack, with long ridges running along its length. For lifting a bird off the bottom of a pan, a flat rack achieves mixed results. While it does raise the bird up, it only does so by about 1 inch, which isn't ideal for crisping the bottom of the bird. This small space isn't sufficient for sliding vegetables under the roasting bird either. Finally, the flat rack's shape isn't well suited to cradling a bird—the chicken always is perched at a somewhat wobbly angle.

Nonadjustable v-rack: Sturdy, with v-shaped ridges running along its length, this rack is great for roasting chicken. You can choose one large rack, or two small ones to fit within your roasting pan. Though the larger version of this rack can be a tight fit for two birds at a time, it is doable with two 4-pounders; flipping is the only tricky part. The tight spacing and the ridges of the rack make the task somewhat challenging. The smaller version of these racks is ideal for roasting two birds at a time (if you can find two of the small racks that will fit in your largest roasting pan).

Adjustable v-rack: Unlike the nonadjustable v-racks, these can be shifted to accompany large or small birds and will fold flat for easy storage. This flexibility comes at the expense of sturdiness, as the adjustable v-rack tends to be more fragile than the nonadjustable variety and, thus, for my tastes not as desirable. The smaller versions of this rack are fine for cooking two birds at a time, though you will need to make sure the two racks fit side by side in your roasting pan. Adjustable v-racks don't offer much space for setting vegetables underneath a bird, and any vegetables or potatoes you scatter around the chicken can knock the legs of the rack out from under, collapsing it.

Vertical rack: As the name implies, a vertical rack roasts a chicken at an upright angle. This makes it easy to roast two birds at a time in the same pan, though the chickens tend to cook unevenly on these racks (the bottom of the bird doesn't brown as nicely as the top). Vertical racks demand a relatively spacious oven as they stretch upward from the pan about 6 inches.

Basket rack: Many cooks swear by these racks, but they can be hard to find. This type is similar to a nonadjustable v-rack, only instead of a v-base, it has a rounded "basket" full of small holes, almost like a strainer. Basket racks are sturdy and well suited to roasting one large or two small birds at a time; their one advantage over a large v-rack is the ease of flipping the bird. In a basket rack, the wings and legs don't get caught.

Roasting the Bird

All of the roasting recipes in this book follow one of these basic roasting methods. Rather than repeat these instructions in each of the roasting recipes in the following chapters, I've put all the information here, explaining each step. Think of this section as your cheat sheet for roasting chicken.

Roasting Temperature

While arguments can be made for roasting at all sorts of temperatures, the issue is simple: High heat (450°F to 500°F) cooks chicken quickly and gives the skin plenty of color and crispness.

It can cook a bird unevenly, though, drying out the outside before the inside cooks through. Conversely, low heat (325°F to 350°F) cooks chicken evenly, but it doesn't brown or crisp the skin quite as effectively.

So what temperature should you go with? The size of the bird may best determine this. Smaller birds are better suited to high heat. They cook through quickly, so there's less worry of drying out. On the other hand, slow, even cooking is the thing for large birds (think how long it takes to roast a turkey on Thanksgiving).

Because the size of the bird I favor (about 4 pounds) occupies the middle ground between large and small chickens, the temperature I like to use to roast a chicken, 425°F, is also somewhere in between—hot enough to brown a medium bird, but gentle enough to cook it evenly.

No Truss, No Fuss

I generally don't a truss chicken for roasting, even though the technique makes for a beautiful bird at the dinner table. Trussing, like tying a necktie, can be done many ways, though all methods include some form of binding the wings and legs closer to a bird's frame to make it more compact and shapely.

The primary benefit of trussing a chicken is presentation—the bird holds its tight shape during roasting instead of the legs and wings splaying out. Trussing also ensures that the wings and drumsticks don't burn—a common occurrence during roasting, as these appendages jut out and up from the rest of the bird. Finally, if you stuff a bird, trussing helps hold the dressing inside during roasting.

Trussing does have its drawbacks. First, it adds preparation time, not a good thing on a busy week-night. Second, this method can prevent a chicken from cooking evenly. Tightly bound together, the slowest-cooking parts of a bird (most notably the thighs) can take even longer to cook through, increasing the likelihood that the rest of the chicken will dry out before the thighs are done. For this reason, trussing generally works best with large birds that are cooked at low temperatures. Slow cooking helps even out any imbalances in the make-up of the bird.

The recipes in this book are intended for fast-paced weeknights where time is of the essence. Trussing's tendency to prolong the cooking time of thighs doesn't pair well with the high heat I favor for roasting. So my suggestion? Save trussing for the Thanksgiving bird.

ROASTING WITH CONVECTION HEAT

If you live in a cold climate, you're probably familiar with the meteorological expression "windchill." This weather catchphrase expresses a relatively simple concept: When it's cold and it's windy, it feels even colder than the thermometer would indicate. The same principle applies to convection heat in an oven. A convection oven has a fan that circulates the air, in a sense making the oven hotter. This blowing heat cooks food more quickly and efficiently so that it browns and crisps uniformly.

A convection oven does wonders with roast chicken. The blowing air dries out the skin and browns it handsomely. It also cooks a bird more quickly than a standard oven, helping to keep the chicken moist. Because the heat of a convection oven is quite strong, when following the recipes in this book, decrease the temperature by about 25°F if you are using the convection feature in your oven. Even with this decreased temperature, the bird still may cook through more quickly than one cooked in a standard oven, so start checking it early.

Oven-Roasted Chicken

Most every time I roast chicken, I follow this basic method, sometimes embellishing it with a glaze, rub, or some other sort of flavoring or accompaniment. It's as simple a bird as you can make, but sometimes the easiest preparations are the best.

FOR 1 BIRD	FOR 2 BIRDS	
1	2	3½- to 4-pound chicken(s)
		Kosher salt and freshly ground black pepper
2 tablespoons	¼ cup	unsalted butter, melted
1 tablespoon	2 tablespoon	chopped fresh herbs, such as rosemary or thyme

NO RACK? ALTER THE BASIC ROASTING METHOD A BIT

While I am a big proponent of using a rack for roasting chicken (see "My Take on Racking" on p. 16), I understand that you may not have one but still want to roast. If this is the case, I would suggest inverting the order for flipping in my method. When oven-roasting a chicken without a rack, I like to start the bird breast side down (for about 20 minutes) and then finish it breast side up so that the skin on the breasts is crisp and browned upon serving. Or, if you prefer, you can just use the flavorings from any of the roasting recipes in this book and simply use your own favorite roasting technique.

1. Wash and rinse each bird. Rinsing washes off any odors and surface bacteria.

2. Pat dry. Use a wad of paper towels to dry each bird. It's important to remove as much moisture as you can, as it creates steam during roasting, which will prevent the skin from properly browning and crisping.

3. Trim off any excess fat. While fat is flavor, a whole chicken has more than enough of it. I like to remove the heavy pockets of fat near the tail and neck of the bird. This ensures that the pan drippings are clearer and easier to incorporate into a pan sauce.

4. Sprinkle 2½ teaspoons of salt and ½ teaspoon of black pepper all over each bird and inside the cavity, to season it.

5. Set on a rack (over a sheet pan or in the roasting pan itself) and, if you have the time, let sit, uncovered, in the refrigerator for up to 24 hours. Allowing the chicken to sit for at least a couple of hours ensures that the seasonings soak into the meat. Leaving the chicken uncovered in the refrigerator (as well as setting it on a rack) helps dry out the skin so it crisps up during roasting.

6. About 45 minutes prior to roasting, preheat the oven to 425°F. For the oven to come fully to temperature, you may need to heat it longer than you think. Mod-

continued

ern digital ovens often will indicate they've hit the desired roasting temperature after only 15 or 20 minutes of preheating, though it actually takes most ovens about 45 minutes. The best way to ensure that your oven hits the proper temperature is an oven thermometer.

7. Brush each chicken evenly with the butter and sprinkle with the herbs and more salt. While butter may diminish the crispness of the skin, it gives the roasted bird a wonderful browned sheen. This final sprinkling of salt, as well as the fresh herbs, season the skin.

8. Set each chicken on a rack breast side up in a large roasting pan and cook until well browned, about 35 minutes. The rack helps keep the skin crisp (rather than let it become soggy by touching the bottom of the pan). Starting the chicken breast side up ensures that the breast browns properly before flipping (the next step). If you were to start roasting with the thighs facing up, the bird may cook through before the breasts properly brown.

9. Flip and cook until an instant-read thermometer inserted into the thickest part of the thigh registers 165°F to 170°F (check the breast as well)—this should take another 15 to 20 minutes.

10. Remove from the oven and let rest for 5 to 10 minutes, uncovered, breast side facing up. This allows the juices in the bird to settle. If you carve the bird immediately, many of these juices will run off onto the cutting board rather than stay in the meat. Use this resting period to finish up any final dinner preparations: whisk together a quick pan sauce, sauté some vegetables, or even set the table.

11. Carve the bird and serve (see "Carving Your Bird" on p. 25).

Brining: If you want to brine your chicken, use one of the brine recipes on pp. 8–10, and brine your bird for at least 4 and up to 12 hours before draining. Rinse the bird well and pat dry as instructed above. When seasoning the bird with salt, reduce the amount used to ½ teaspoon. Proceed as directed above.

ONE FLIP DOES THE JOB

In a perfect world, you would never have to flip a chicken during roasting, but a bird's rounded shape and uneven balance of white and dark meat make it far from perfect to cook. If you follow the traditional roasting positioning for a bird—breast side up—the breast meat will overcook long before the thighs hit the requisite 165°F. You can brine a bird to keep the breast meat moist, but without flipping the bird, the skin of the thighs and legs won't properly brown or crisp.

For these two reasons—even cooking and even browning—I like to flip a bird during roasting. (The only exception is when I butterfly, or spatchcock, a bird for roasting.) I start the bird roasting breast side up. Once the skin is nicely browned, I flip the bird so that the breast faces down, and roast until the chicken is just cooked through, at which point the thighs and legs should be nicely browned, too.

A roasting rack is important to this process, for it helps the crisped skin stay crisp (rather than sogging out from sitting on the bottom of the pan). A rack also helps hold the bird steady during roasting.

A partially cooked bird is hot, slippery, and full of juices, making it awkward to handle. There are a couple of different pieces of equipment you can use for the task. Turkey lifters, which look like small pitchforks, can be hard to maneuver. Some cooks use thick wads of paper towels or worn kitchen towels. I generally like to use a pair of sturdy tongs. I insert them into the cavity and around the side of the bird to avoid piercing the breast.

Using a dry rub: If you plan to use a dry rub, instead of seasoning with salt in step 4, use your chosen dry rub and omit the butter, herbs, and salt.

Glazing: Omit the herbs. Roast the chicken until it just starts to brown, about 25 minutes. Place two thirds of the glaze of your choice in a small bowl and the remainder in another small bowl. Using the large portion of glaze, generously brush it all over the top of bird and cook for 5 minutes, then brush the top of the bird with the glaze again and cook until nicely browned, about 10 minutes. Brush the top of the bird one more time with the glaze, flip, and brush the bottom of the bird with anything the remains of the larger portion of glaze. Cook 15 to 20 minutes or until an instant-read thermometer inserted into the thickest part of the thigh registers 165°F to 170°F, then brush both sides of the bird with the remaining glaze and let rest for 10 minutes, breast side up. If your glaze hasn't browned to the degree you prefer, you can pop the bird under the broiler for a minute or so, but not much longer to avoid burning.

Grill-Roasted Chicken

Spurred by the popularity of beer-can chicken, grilling chicken (especially whole birds) has become fashionable. While I do love beer-can chicken, I favor the simplicity and reliability of my technique below.

As its name implies, grill-roasting is a hybrid of grilling and roasting: the chicken cooks over a moderate gas or charcoal fire with the lid closed, so the bird cooks by even, indirect heat as well as by the heat coming up from the gas or charcoal below. My method for grill-roasting relies on spatchcocking, or cutting out the bird's backbone (p. 23), which helps it lie flat on the grill grates so it cooks evenly and quickly.

Grill-roasting is easier—but not necessarily better—on a gas grill than a charcoal fire. The heat of a gas grill is easy to adjust and thus easy to control. Charcoal fires have a tendency to hit more extreme temperatures (both high and low), so it's important to stay ever vigilant while the chicken roasts so the fire doesn't get either too hot or peter out. The benefit of a charcoal fire is the wonderful smoky flavor the bird acquires. On either type of grill it's best to be cautious and lean towards the cooler end of the heat spectrum. An even, low fire will properly brown and crisp up a bird without any worries of flare-ups.

FOR 1 BIRDS	FOR 2 BIRDS	
1	2	3½- to 4-pound chicken(s)
		Dry rub of your choice (pp. 11–13)

1. Spatchcock the chicken and flatten the bird (see "Spatchcock a Chicken for Stuffing or Grill-Roasting" on p. 23). This speeds up the cooking process, so the chicken cooks through before burning.

continued

2. Wash and rinse the bird. Rinsing washes off any odors and surface bacteria.

3. Pat dry. Use a wad of paper towels to dry each bird. It's important to remove as much moisture as you can, as it creates steam during grill-roasting, which will prevent the skin from properly browning and crisping.

4. Sprinkle with the spice rub, place in a zip-top plastic bag, and refrigerate for at least 2 and up to 24 hours.

5. Prepare a charcoal fire or heat up the gas grill (heat all the burners to medium-low). For a charcoal fire, pile a couple of layers of briquettes on one side and a sparse, single layer of charcoal on the other side of the grill so that you end up with a medium-hot zone and a moderate to cool zone. Your fire should be ready when the briquettes are mostly gray (or, if you're using hardwood, when they're red hot). Clean the grill grates with a wire brush to avoid any off flavors. Using an old dishtowel or a wad of paper towels, oil the grill grates to avoid sticking.

6. Grill the chicken skin side down until nicely browned, with good grill marks, 10 to 15 minutes. For a gas grill, set the chicken over the burners and close the lid. For a charcoal grill, set the chicken over the hot zone, and leave uncovered. Cook until the skin starts to brown (without blackening), about 15 minutes.

7. Flip the chicken. For the gas grill, reduce the heat to low. For a charcoal grill, move the chicken to the cool zone. In both cases, close the lid. Grill, checking occasionally to ensure that the chicken doesn't burn, until it's nicely browned all over and an instant-read thermometer inserted into the thickest part of the thigh registers 165°F to 170°F—this should take about 25 to 30 minutes.

8. Remove from the grill and let rest 5 to 10 minutes before carving.

9. Carve the bird and serve.

Brining: If you want to brine your chicken, use one of the brine recipes on pp. 8–10 and brine your bird for at least 4 and up to 12 hours before draining. Rinse the bird well and pat dry. When putting together your spice rub, reduce the amount of salt to ½ teaspoon. Proceed as directed above.

Glazing: To glaze, cook until step 7, then brush the top of the flipped bird with the glaze every 10 minutes or so until the bird is cooked through.

SPATCHCOCK A CHICKEN
FOR STUFFING OR GRILL-ROASTING

For certain preparations, most notably chickens roasted with stuffing or grill-roasted birds, I like to spatchcock, or butterfly, the bird before cooking it. According to Alan Davidson in *The Penguin Companion to Food*, the term, of Irish origin, is short for "dispatch cock," meaning to remove the backbone and flatten out the chicken. This technique accomplishes a number of things. It:

* makes it easy to season a bird all over, especially inside the cavity (which is now flattened and exposed);

* makes a chicken easier to grill (you can set a whole bird over moderate but direct heat and grill it quickly);

* helps a chicken cook more evenly. The three major parts of a bird—breast, thigh, and leg—all receive even heat.

* also is great for stuffing a bird. Obviously I don't mean "stuffing" in the traditional manner. With a spatchcocked bird, I put the stuffing in the bottom of a roasting pan, then set the butterflied bird on top. The stuffing still absorbs all of the juices from the roasting bird and, because it's not jammed inside the chicken, the stuffing cooks through more easily, avoiding food safety issues.

To butterfly or spatchcock a chicken, grab a pair of heavy kitchen shears, set the bird so it's facing breast side down, and cut along both sides of the backbone (it should be 1 to 2 inches wide). Remove the backbone. Then flip the bird and press down on the breasts and legs to flatten the chicken. The bird is now ready for grilling or roasting.

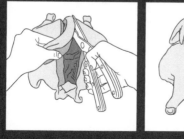 

Sear-Roasted Chicken

Why sear-roast a chicken? After all, searing adds an extra step to a basic roast chicken. The answer is that this extra work translates into intense flavor. Searing gives the skin a browned crust and crispness that roasting alone cannot achieve. It also gives the roasting process a running start so the chicken cooks more quickly.

While sear-roasting is the preferred manner for roasting chicken in a restaurant, the technique can be performed in the home kitchen without much trouble. Perhaps the only catch is sear-roasting two birds at once. The solution is simple—sear two birds in two pans at once—though it does demand your full attention (and a sturdy exhaust fan). For this reason, it's best to sear-roast a bird when you have a little extra time and energy for hands-on cooking. Otherwise, you're best off simply oven-roasting the chicken.

FOR 1 BIRD	FOR 2 BIRDS	
1	2	3½- to 4-pound chicken(s)
		Kosher salt and freshly ground black pepper
1 tablespoon	2 tablespoons	chopped fresh herbs, such as rosemary or thyme
1 tablespoon	2 tablespoons	olive oil
1 tablespoon	2 tablespoons	unsalted butter, softened

1. Spatchcock the chicken and flatten the bird (p. 23). This makes it easier to sear the chicken and also helps it cook through more quickly.

2. Wash and rinse the bird. Rinsing washes off any odors and surface bacteria.

3. Pat dry. Use a wad of paper towels to dry each bird. It's important to remove as much moisture as you can, as it creates steam during roasting, which will prevent the skin from properly browning.

4. Sprinkle each bird all over with 2½ teaspoons salt and fresh herbs and let sit on a large plate skin side up, uncovered, in the refrigerator for at least 30 minutes and up to 24 hours.

5. About 45 minutes prior to roasting, preheat the oven to 425°F.

6. Heat one or two 12-inch, heavy, ovenproof skillets (preferably cast iron) over medium-high heat. The pan needs to be well heated before adding the chicken, not only to brown it, but to make sure it doesn't stick to the pan. The pan is hot enough when a droplet of water instantly evaporates as it hits the surface. The pan is too hot if the droplet skitters around the pan's surface.

7. Add the oil and butter to the hot pan and cook until the foam from the butter subsides and the butter starts to brown, about 1 minute.

continued

CARVING YOUR BIRD

There are many ways to carve chicken. The method that follows is the way I prefer to do it. It creates a lot of evenly sized pieces so that everyone can have a bit of white and dark meat.
   Worth noting: Leftover chicken will keep best if left on the bone, uncarved. If you've cooked an extra bird, let it cool and then store it whole, tightly wrapped, in the refrigerator until you're ready to use it.

1. Slice off the legs. Gently pull the tip of the drumstick away from the bird and slide a large knife (preferably a chef's knife) between the body and the leg. Slice all the way down and around the bottom of the thigh to cut the leg from the bird. Repeat on the other side.

2. Split the drumsticks and thighs. Use your fingers to feel for the joint between the drumstick and the thigh. Gently slice through this joint to split the two. Repeat on the other side.

3. Slice the wings from the breasts. Slice the top of the breast towards the wing to expose the joint joining the two. Cut through the joint to remove the wing. Split the wing and drummette. Repeat on the other side.

4. Remove the ribcage and backbone from the breasts. Set the bird so its backbone faces up. Using kitchen shears, slice along both sides of the backbone—from the bottom of the bird all the way up to the neck—to remove a piece about 1 inch wide. Note: You won't need to follow this step for birds that have been butterflied.

5. Split the breasts. Flip the bird and press flat. Using a chef's knife and a little bit of force, cut through the breast bone to split the breasts. Slice each breast in half crosswise into two even pieces.

6. Halve the breasts. Slice each breast in half crosswise into two even pieces.

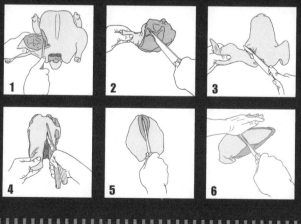

8. Carefully set the chicken in the pan skin side down and cook until the skin is nicely browned all over, about 5 minutes.

9. Using tongs and a spatula, carefully flip the chicken, transfer the pan to the oven, and cook until an instant-read thermometer inserted into the thickest part of the thigh registers 165°F to 170°F—this should take about 30 to 35 minutes.

10. Remove from the oven and let rest for 5 to 10 minutes before carving.

11. Carve the bird and serve.

Brining: If you want to brine your chicken, use one of the brine recipes on pp. 8–10 and brine your bird for at least 4 and up to 12 hours before draining. Rinse the bird well and pat dry as instructed above. When seasoning the bird with salt, reduce the amount used to ½ teaspoon. Proceed as directed above.

Using a dry rub: I don't recommend using rubs with this method, as the searing heat can burn the spices.

Tips for Making the Most of Your Roast Chicken Leftovers

There's no real science to cooking with leftovers, but there are a few tricks I have learned over the years (and during many rounds of recipe testing for this book) for getting the best results.

- Keep a cooked chicken intact (meaning, uncarved and on the bone) until you use it in leftovers. This prolongs the chicken's shelf life. A bird that hasn't been cut will keep up to 4 or 5 days, while sliced chicken only stays good for a couple of days.

- Discard the skin (unless it's from a grilled bird). Even crisp skin has a tendency to turn into a rubbery mass after being refrigerated. The one exception I make is grill-roasted chicken. Slow cooking on the grill has a tendency to render much of the fat in the skin, making it palatable in leftovers. The smoke also imparts the skin with a rich essence that works well in most leftover preparations.

- When taking meat off the bone, slice first, then pull. I like using a paring knife and my hand to remove the meat from the bones. I generally start with the knife to slice off the big pieces, then use my fingers to pull off whatever remains.

- As you roast your bird, think about what kind of leftovers it will go well in. Thinking ahead makes for good pairings (and also helps organize shopping at the market). You can use your own best judgment with the pairings, though I also have given you my favorite roast chicken for each dish.

- If you can, use dark meat for soups, stews, and casseroles, and white meat for sandwiches and salads. Dark meat holds up better to more cooking than white meat. For this reason, when I'm making a leftover dish using reheated chicken, I try to use dark meat. Conversely, the delicate flavor and texture of white meat chicken is better suited to no-cook preparations like sandwiches and salads.

WHAT YOUR ROAST CHICKEN GETS YOU

APPROXIMATE YIELD FROM 3½- TO 4-POUND CHICKEN

LEFTOVERS	YIELD WHEN DICED (CUPS)	YIELD WHEN THINLY SLICED (CUPS)	POTENTIAL LEFTOVER MEALS
1 whole chicken	5½	5	2 to 3
½ chicken	2¾	2½	1 to 2
1 breast	1¼	1	1
1 leg (thigh and drumstick)	1¼	1	1

STRIPPING YOUR CHICKEN CLEAN

I like to use my hands and a paring knife to remove leftover chicken from the bones, to ensure no meat is left behind. Also, I discard the skin from the chicken for leftovers unless it's from a grilled bird, which tends to be less fatty and more flavorful.

* **For the breast:** Using a paring knife, try to remove the breast from the bird in one piece. Use your fingers to pull any of the tenderloin that remains on the carcass or any meat running along the breastbone.

* **For the thighs:** Using a paring knife, slice off any large pieces of fat running along the sides. Slice along the bone running the length of the thigh and peel off the meat. Trim and discard any tendons or gnarly pieces of fat.

* **For the drumsticks:** Using a paring knife, slice to the bone and then peel off the meat. Trim and discard any tendon or gnarly pieces of fat.

* **For the back:** Using your fingers, pick at the bones to remove the pockets of meat. This yields a minimal amount of meat, but it is generally lean and quite flavorful.

* **For the wings:** While the little drumettes have some meat, you're best off sprinkling the wings with some salt and eating them cold while you prepare your leftovers.

Chapter 2

A World of Roast Chicken

Chicken's mild flavor makes it a blank

canvas for vibrant ingredients. Of course, you can sprinkle a bird with salt and pepper, cook it just right, and serve as is. Bright flavors add a little more complexity, though, without much extra work.

There are all sorts of ways to flavor a bird (see chapter 1 for recipes for spice rubs, brines, and glazes). Spice rubs are quick and effective, creating a flavorful crust. These rubs can hit many points on the culinary map, from an herb-and-garlic Italian mixture to a sweet and spicy Jamaican jerk crust. In contrast, marinades soak their flavors into the meat. Marinades can range from simple oil and herb mixtures to more exotic varieties like a curry-yogurt combination for an Indian tandoori-style roast chicken. Both spice rubs and marinades are best when added to a bird well before roasting.

For the time-challenged or more spontaneous cook, there are other ways to boost a chicken's flavor. Brush a sugary glaze on a bird while it roasts to give the skin a browned crust. Or whip together a tangy vinaigrette or a luscious compound butter for drizzling or melting over the bird once it finishes cooking. And then there are pan sauces, which are a snap to whisk together. The recipes in this chapter cover the flavor landscape of roast chicken and will give you plenty of inspiration for developing recipes of your own. And as dinner does not consist of roast chicken alone, I've provided you with lots of side dishes to choose from as well.

How to Use These Recipes

The recipes in this chapter list instructions and ingredients for roasting one or two birds, depending on how much chicken you want for leftovers and how many people you are feeding. In most cases, making two birds simply involves doubling the amount of ingredients you would use when making one. What isn't necessarily doubled are any vegetables and/or stuffing that are roasted along with the bird. The assumption is that the vegetables and sides are intended for eating with dinner tonight along with one of the birds, and not for leftovers with the second bird. If you want to double the vegetables or any of the other accompaniments, by all means, do (just double all of the ingredients).

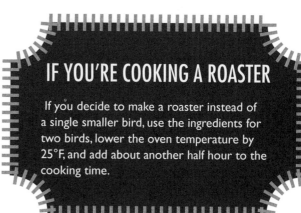

IF YOU'RE COOKING A ROASTER

If you decide to make a roaster instead of a single smaller bird, use the ingredients for two birds, lower the oven temperature by 25°F, and add about another half hour to the cooking time.

Roast Chicken with Rosemary-Mustard Crust and Browned Onions

If you don't have a roasting rack, you will need to alter the oven-roasting methods in the following recipes (see sidebar, p. 19).

Serves at least 4

Dijon mustard is at its best when you only get a hint of its spice and heat. In this roast chicken, the mustard coats the skin, along with chopped rosemary and a sprinkling of brown sugar, forming a rich browned crust. Scatter the onion slices under the chicken to catch the juices, a trick that *Fine Cooking* editor Susie Middleton taught me. The onions don't quite caramelize but they do brown and soak up all the richness of the roasting bird, becoming sort of a sharp onion jam (sherry vinegar gives them a tangy edge).

FOR 1 BIRD	FOR 2 BIRDS	
		Kosher salt and freshly ground black pepper
1	2	3½- to 4-pound chicken(s), rinsed and patted dry with paper towels
3 tablespoons	6 tablespoons	Dijon mustard
1 tablespoon	2 tablespoons	olive oil
1 tablespoon	2 tablespoons	chopped fresh rosemary
2 teaspoons	4 teaspoons	light brown sugar
2	2	large Spanish onions, thinly sliced
2 tablespoons	2 tablespoons	sherry vinegar

1. Sprinkle 2½ teaspoons salt and ½ teaspoon black pepper all over each chicken, including the cavity. Place a rack in a pan, put the chicken on top, and let sit for up to 24 hours, uncovered, in the refrigerator. (If you've brined the chicken, skip this step. Just sprinkle the bird with ½ teaspoon salt and ½ teaspoon black pepper and proceed with the rest of the recipe.)

2. Preheat the oven to 425°F. Set an oven rack to the middle position. Mix the mustard, oil, rosemary, and brown sugar together in a small bowl and brush all over the chicken and inside the cavity. Toss the onion with the vinegar and ½ teaspoon salt in a large roasting pan. Set a rack in the pan and the chicken breast side up on the rack.

3. Roast the chicken until the breasts are nicely browned all over, about 35 minutes. Gently flip the chicken (I like using tongs to clutch the inside of the cavity and the side of the bird) and cook until an instant-read thermometer inserted into the thickest part of the thigh registers 165°F to 170°F—this should take another 15 to 20 minutes.

4. Transfer to a cutting board and let rest for 10 minutes, breast side up. Meanwhile, return the pan to the oven to finish browning the onions for 10 minutes. Carve the chicken, drizzle with any juices accumulated on the cutting board, and serve with the onions.

On the Side: Rice Pilaf with Mushrooms (p. 64) and Snap Peas and Carrots with Lemon (p. 73).

The Second Time Around: The onions and this mustard-crusted bird pair nicely with saucy preparations like soups, stews, and braises.

CATCH THOSE JUICES

While I do love making pan sauces, I often go without. That's not to say I serve a bird without any adornment. I find that the juices that accumulate on the cutting board while the bird rests before carving are a light but adequate stand-in for a pan sauce. For the juices to properly accumulate, you'll need a carving board with grooved ridges running along its length to catch them.

MAKE A PAN SAUCE

There are two basic methods for making a pan sauce. You can prepare the sauce in a saucepan while the bird roasts, then stir in the cooking juices from the roasting pan at the end. Or, you can make the sauce in the roasting pan, setting it on the stovetop after removing the cooked bird, and scraping together a quick pan sauce. I prefer making the sauce in a separate pot because the quality of the drippings on the pan's bottom can wildly differ based on the roasting pan you use. For instance, large roasting pans have a large surface area, which cooks off (and sometimes burns) the juices as the bird roasts. A pan with a more snug fit tends to accumulate more drippings.

Shallot and Red Wine Sauce

Enough for 1 bird

1/4 cup unsalted butter
2 shallots, finely diced
Kosher salt
1 cup red wine
1 cup low-salt chicken broth
2 teaspoons chopped fresh thyme
Juices from the roasting pan
Freshly ground black pepper

1. Melt half the butter in a large saucepan over medium heat. Add the shallots, sprinkle generously with salt and cook, stirring often, until translucent and soft, about 6 minutes. Raise the heat to high, add the wine and cook, stirring, until reduced to a thick, glazy consistency (you should have 2 or 3 tablespoons), about 8 minutes. Add the broth and thyme and cook, stirring, until it again reduces by about half, about 5 minutes. Remove from the heat.

2. Once the chicken is done roasting, pour the juices from the pan off into a gravy separator or large measuring cup. Let sit for a couple of minutes, then pour or spoon off the layer of fat. Add these juices to the pan sauce, set over high heat, and cook for a couple of minutes to reduce again by half. Whisk in the remaining butter, season with salt and pepper to taste, and serve spooned over the roast chicken.

Orange-Rosemary Pan Sauce

Enough for 1 bird

1 large shallot, finely diced
2 tablespoons olive oil
1 cup orange juice
1 cup low-salt chicken broth
1 tablespoon brandy
1 tablespoon honey
1 teaspoon chopped fresh rosemary
Juices from the roasting pan
Kosher salt and freshly ground black pepper

1. Heat the shallot in the oil in a large sauté pan over medium heat until it sizzles steadily and becomes fragrant, about 1 1/2 minutes, stirring. Add the orange juice, broth, brandy, honey, and rosemary raise the heat to high, and cook, stirring, until reduced almost three quarters. Remove from the heat.

2. Once the chicken is done roasting, pour the juices from the pan into a gravy separator or large measuring cup. Let sit for a couple of minutes, then pour or spoon off the layer of fat. Add these juices to the pan sauce, set over high heat, and cook for a couple of minutes to reduce it to a thick, glazy consistency. Season with salt and pepper to taste and serve spooned over the roast chicken.

Wild Mushroom and Herb Jus

Enough for 1 bird

1 ounce dried shiitake mushrooms
1/2 ounce dried porcini mushrooms
2 cups boiling water
1 shallot, finely diced
2 tablespoons olive oil
1/4 cup dry sherry
1 tablespoon soy sauce
2 teaspoons fresh thyme
Juices from the roasting pan
Kosher salt and freshly ground black pepper

1. Soak the mushrooms in the boiling water until just tender, about 10 minutes. Strain the soaking liquid through a coffee filter or paper towels and set aside. Stem the shiitakes, discard the stems, and coarsely chop the mushrooms.

2. Heat the oil in a large sauté pan over medium heat and cook the shallot, stirring often, until translucent and soft, about 6 minutes. Raise the heat to high, add the sherry and cook, stirring, until almost completely reduced, about 2 minutes. Add the mushroom soaking liquid, soy sauce, and thyme and cook, stirring, until reduced by about half. Remove from the heat.

3. Once the chicken is done roasting, pour the juices from the pan into a gravy separator or large measuring cup. Let sit for a couple of minutes, then pour or spoon off the layer of fat. Add the juices to the pan sauce, set over high heat, and cook for a couple of minutes to reduce by about one half. Season with salt and pepper to taste and serve.

Chicken and Herb Gravy

Enough for 1 bird

2 tablespoons chicken fat from the roasting pan or unsalted butter
1 clove garlic, minced
1 1/2 tablespoons all-purpose flour
1 cup low-salt chicken broth
1 tablespoon balsamic vinegar
1 teaspoon chopped fresh thyme
Juices from the roasting pan
Kosher salt and freshly ground black pepper

1. Add the chicken fat to a large sauté pan set over medium heat. Add the garlic and cook, stirring, until it starts to sizzle, about 1 minute. Add the flour and cook, stirring often, until it starts to color a light mocha brown, about 3 minutes. Add the broth, vinegar, and thyme, raise the heat to medium-high, and cook, whisking often, until reduced by about half and thickened, about 5 minutes. Remove from the heat.

2. Once the chicken is done roasting, pour the juices from the pan into a gravy separator or large measuring cup. Let sit for a couple of minutes, then pour or spoon off the layer of fat. Add these juices to the pan sauce, set over high heat, and cook for a couple of minutes to thicken. Season with salt and pepper to taste and serve spooned over the roast chicken.

Bistro Roast Chicken with Lemon and Thyme

Serves at least 4

Everyone has a simple recipe for roast chicken and for good reason: a properly roasted bird needs little adornment. Here, the seasonings—lemon, thyme, salt, and butter—are basic but wonderfully vibrant.

FOR 1 BIRD	FOR 2 BIRDS	
		Kosher salt and freshly ground black pepper
1	2	3½- to 4-pound chicken(s), rinsed and patted dry with paper towels
1	2	lemon(s)
3 tablespoons	6 tablespoons	unsalted butter, melted
1 tablespoon	2 tablespoons	chopped fresh thyme

1. Sprinkle 2½ teaspoons salt and ½ teaspoon black pepper all over each chicken, including the cavity. Place a rack in a pan, put the chicken on top, and let sit for up to 24 hours, uncovered, in the refrigerator. (If you've brined the chicken, skip this step. Just sprinkle the bird with ½ teaspoon salt and ½ teaspoon black pepper and proceed with the rest of the recipe.)

2. Preheat the oven to 425°F. Set an oven rack to the middle position. Finely grate the zest of the lemon. Cut the lemon in half and set aside. In a small bowl, mix together the butter, chopped thyme, and lemon zest. Using a brush, dab the butter between the skin and breast meat, taking care not to rip the skin, then spread the remaining butter all over the bird and inside the cavity. Push a lemon half into the cavity of the bird. Reserve the remaining lemon.

3. Set the chicken breast side up on a rack in a large roasting pan. Roast until the breasts are nicely browned, about 35 minutes. Gently flip the bird (I like using tongs to clutch the inside of the cavity and the side of the bird) and cook until an instant-read thermometer inserted into the thickest part of the thigh registers 165°F to 170°F—this should take another 15 to 20 minutes.

4. Let rest for 5 to 10 minutes breast side up. Carve the chicken and serve immediately with a drizzle of any juices accumulated on the cutting board and a squirt of juice from the remaining lemon half.

On the Side: Simple Sautéed Spinach (p. 43), and Leek and Parmesan Mashed Potatoes (p. 85), or Potato and Scallion Cakes (p. 64).

The Second Time Around: The bright, citrusy flavor of this bird goes well with most all types of leftover preparations.

Jerrod's Roast Chicken with Vermont Maple Glaze, Sweet Potatoes, and Sage

Serves at least 4

As a card-carrying, full-fledged Vermonter, my good friend Jerrod Deshaw pushes tins of maple syrup from his home state onto me every chance he gets. But there's only so many pancakes and waffles a guy can make, so one night I prepared this glazed chicken with sweet potatoes and it's been part of my standard repertoire ever since.

FOR 1 BIRD	FOR 2 BIRDS	
		Kosher salt and freshly ground black pepper
1	2	3½- to 4-pound chicken(s), rinsed and patted dry with paper towels
2 tablespoons	¼ cup	unsalted butter, melted
2 tablespoons	¼ cup	chopped fresh sage
¼ cup	½ cup	maple syrup
2 tablespoons	¼ cup	light brown sugar
2 teaspoons	1 tablespoon	chili powder
¼ teaspoon	½ teaspoon	ground chipotle or cayenne pepper
1	1	large sweet potato, cut into 1-inch-thick rounds
1 tablespoon	1 tablespoon	olive oil

1. Sprinkle 2½ teaspoons salt and ½ teaspoon black pepper all over each chicken, including the cavity. Place a rack in a pan, put the chicken on top, and let sit for up to 24 hours, uncovered, in the refrigerator. (If you've brined the chicken, skip this step. Just sprinkle the bird with ½ teaspoon salt and ½ teaspoon black pepper and proceed with the rest of the recipe.)

2. Preheat the oven to 425°F. Set an oven rack to the middle position. In a small bowl, mix the butter with the sage, half of the maple syrup, half the brown sugar, about three quarters of the chili powder, and all of the chipotle powder until well combined. Using a brush, dab the butter mixture between the skin and breast meat, taking care not to tear the skin, then brush it all over the bird, including the cavity. Toss the sweet potatoes with the remaining chili powder, the olive oil and ½ teaspoon salt.

3. Set the sweet potatoes to the sides of a large roasting pan, leaving room for a rack. Set the chicken breast side up on the rack and roast until the breasts start to brown, about 25 minutes.

4. In a small bowl, mix together the remaining brown sugar and maple syrup, brush some of it over the top of the bird, and cook for 10 more minutes. Gently flip the chicken (I like using tongs to clutch the inside of the cavity and the side of the bird), brush with the rest of the maple mixture, and cook until an instant-read thermometer inserted into the thickest part of the thigh registers 165°F to 170°F—this should take another 15 to 20 minutes.

5. Transfer the chicken to a cutting board and let rest for 10 minutes breast side up. Meanwhile, return the pan to the oven to finish browning and crisping the potatoes, about 10 minutes. Carve the chicken and serve immediately with the potatoes and with any juices accumulated on the cutting board.

On the Side: Rice Pilaf with Mushrooms (p. 64) and Snap Peas and Carrots with Lemon (p. 73).

The Second Time Around: The sweet and spice of the maple glaze steer this chicken towards full-flavored salads, sandwiches, and casseroles.

Balsamic-Glazed Rosemary Chicken with Bacon and Pearl Onions

Serves at least 4

I love roasting pearl onions, though I realize they're a pain to peel, especially if you don't have the assistance of a restaurant prep cook. For this reason, I've stayed away from preparing these onions in my home kitchen. Recently, I realized there are decent frozen pearl onions out there and I've been adding them to all sorts of preparations ever since. In this dish, I toss the onions with some chopped rosemary and bacon and set them underneath a roasting bird. The onions soften and brown as they soak up the juices from the roasting chicken and bacon.

FOR 1 BIRD	FOR 2 BIRDS	
		Kosher salt and freshly ground black pepper
1	2	3½- to 4-pound chicken(s), rinsed and patted dry with paper towels
¼ pound	½ pound	bacon, cut into ¼-inch strips
2 tablespoons	¼ cup	unsalted butter, melted
1 tablespoon	2 tablespoons	chopped fresh thyme
2 tablespoons	¼ cup	balsamic vinegar
1 tablespoon	2 tablespoons	light brown sugar
3/4 pound	¾ pound	frozen pearl onions

1. Sprinkle 2½ teaspoons salt and ½ teaspoon black pepper all over each chicken, including the cavity. Place a rack in a pan, put the chicken on top, and let sit for up to 24 hours, uncovered, in the refrigerator. (If you've brined the chicken, skip this step. Just sprinkle the bird with ½ teaspoon salt and ½ teaspoon black pepper and proceed with the rest of the recipe.)

2. Preheat the oven to 425°F. Set an oven rack to the middle position. Slip about half the bacon beneath the skin of the breasts of the chicken. In a small bowl, stir together the butter, thyme, vinegar, and brown sugar. Brush three quarters of this mixture all over the chicken, including the cavity. Set the chicken breast side up on a rack in a large roasting pan. Toss the pearl onions with the remaining balsamic mixture and bacon and set under the bird on the bottom of the pan.

3. Roast the chicken until the breasts are nicely browned, about 35 minutes. Gently flip the chicken (I like using tongs to clutch the inside of the cavity and the side of the bird) and cook until an instant-read thermometer inserted into the thickest part of the thigh registers 165°F to 170°F—this should take another 15 to 20 minutes.

4. Let rest for 5 to 10 minutes breast side up, then carve the chicken and serve with the onions and bacon.

On the Side: Leek and Parmesan Mashed Potatoes (p. 85) and Garlicky Sear-Roasted Cauliflower (p. 51).

The Second Time Around: The sweetness of the balsamic glaze and the richness of the bacon goes well in basic pastas, salads, soups, and stews.

Roast Chicken with Caramelized Shallots and Fingerling Potatoes

Serves at least 4

Fingerlings are a variety of heirloom potato increasingly available at local markets. These tiny tubers (also referred to as Russian banana potatoes) have a thin, waxy skin and a soft buttery texture similar to Yukon Golds, only richer. They're great pan-fried or roasted, as in this dish.

FOR 1 BIRD	FOR 2 BIRDS	
		Kosher salt and freshly ground black pepper
1	2	3½- to 4-pound chicken(s), rinsed and patted dry with paper towels
2 tablespoons	¼ cup	unsalted butter, melted
2 tablespoons	3 tablespoons	chopped fresh rosemary
1½ pounds	1½ pounds	fingerling potatoes, cut on the diagonal into 1½-inch pieces
4	4	shallots, peeled
1 tablespoon	1 tablespoon	sherry vinegar

1. Sprinkle 2½ teaspoons salt and ½ teaspoon black pepper all over each chicken, including the cavity. Place a rack in a pan, put the chicken on top, and let sit for up to 24 hours, uncovered, in the refrigerator. (If you've brined the chicken, skip this step. Just sprinkle the bird with ½ teaspoon salt and ½ teaspoon black pepper and proceed with the rest of the recipe.)

2. Preheat the oven to 425°F. Set an oven rack to the middle position. In a small bowl, mix the butter with half the rosemary. Using a brush, dab the butter between the skin and breast meat, taking care not to rip the skin, and spread the remaining butter all over the bird, including the cavity. In a large bowl, toss the potatoes and shallots with the remaining rosemary, 1 teaspoon salt, and ½ teaspoon pepper. Set the chicken breast side up on a rack in a large roasting pan. Scatter the potatoes and shallots underneath the chicken and the rack.

3. Roast the chicken until the breasts are nicely browned all over, about 35 minutes. Gently flip the chicken (I like using tongs to clutch the inside of the cavity and the side of the bird) and cook until an instant-read thermometer inserted into the thickest part of the thigh registers 165°F to 170°F—this should take another 15 to 20 minutes.

4. Transfer the chicken to a cutting board and let rest breast side up for 10 minutes. Meanwhile, toss the potatoes and shallots with the vinegar and return the pan to the oven to continue browning them, another 10 minutes, tossing again once or twice.

5. Carve the chicken. Serve it with a drizzle of any juices accumulated on the cutting board and the shallots and potatoes.

Perk It Up: Serve with Shallot and Red Wine Sauce (p. 32); its sharpness cuts through the richness of the potatoes and chicken. This roast chicken is also delicious with Wild Mushroom and Herb Jus (p. 33).

On the Side: Prosciutto-Wrapped Asparagus with Mozzarella and Sun-Dried Tomatoes (p. 51), and Brussels Sprouts with Bacon, Apple, and Sage (p. 72).

The Second Time Around: This mildly flavored bird (and the shallots) is great in pastas and salads. I like stirring any leftover potatoes into soups, stews, and braises.

Mom's Hungarian Roast Chicken with Wild Mushrooms and Buttered Egg Noodles

Serves at least 4

My mom made this roast chicken so often (at least once a week) that we would groan when we saw it arrive at the dinner table. Kids are tough and my brothers and I were no different.

These days I actually miss it so much that I make it often. The spice rub is a nod to my family's Hungarian roots: a simple dusting of good paprika, salt, pepper, and garlic powder. I then roast the chicken along with mushrooms—though my mom never did—and make a quick pan sauce to serve over the buttered egg noodles.

FOR 1 BIRD	FOR 2 BIRDS	
		Kosher salt and freshly ground black pepper
2 teaspoons	4 teaspoons	Hungarian sweet paprika
2 teaspoons	4 teaspoons	garlic powder
1	2	3½- to 4-pound chicken(s), rinsed and patted dry with paper towels
10 ounces	10 ounces	white mushrooms, quartered
3½ ounces	3½ ounces	shiitake mushrooms, stemmed and cut into 1-inch pieces
2 teaspoons	4 teaspoons	chopped fresh thyme
2 tablespoons	2 tablespoons	all-purpose flour
¼ cup	¼ cup	dry sherry
1½ cups	1½ cups	chicken broth
¾ pound	¾ pound	egg noodles, cooked until just tender and drained
2 tablespoons	2 tablespoons	unsalted butter, cut into small pieces
2 tablespoons	2 tablespoons	thinly sliced fresh chives

1. In a small bowl, mix together 2½ teaspoons salt and ½ teaspoon pepper for each bird along with the paprika and the garlic powder, then sprinkle this mixture all over the chicken, including the cavity. Place a rack in a pan, put the chicken on top, and let sit for up to 24 hours, uncovered, in the refrigerator. (If you've brined the chicken, reduce the salt in the rub to ½ teaspoon and proceed with the rest of the recipe.)

2. Preheat the oven to 425°F. Set an oven rack to the middle position. In a large bowl, toss the mushrooms with the thyme and ¾ teaspoon salt. Set the chicken breast side up on a rack in a large flame-proof roasting pan. Scatter the mushrooms underneath the rack. Roast the chicken until the breasts are nicely browned all over, about 35 minutes. Gently flip the chicken (I like using tongs to clutch the inside of the cavity and the side of the bird) and cook until an instant-read thermometer inserted into the thickest part of the thigh registers 165°F to 170°F—this should take another 15 to 20 minutes.

3. Transfer the chicken to a cutting board and let rest, breast side up, for 5 to 10 minutes. Transfer the mushrooms to a large bowl. Pour off all but 1 tablespoon of the fat from the roasting pan (set aside the juices, pour off the top layer of fat, and reserve) and set the pan over medium heat. Add the flour and cook, stirring, until it starts to color a light brown. Add the sherry and cook, scraping the bottom of the pan with a wooden spoon to get up all the browned bits, until it's almost completely cooked off. Add the broth and degreased pan juices and cook, stirring, until the mixture thickens up considerably and reduces by about half. Stir in the mushrooms, season with salt and pepper, and remove from the heat. Toss the egg noodles with the butter.

4. Carve the chicken and serve with the egg noodles, a couple spoonfuls of the sauce, and a sprinkling of the chives.

On the Side: Creamed Spinach Gratin (p. 42) or Green Beans with Balsamic Vinegar and Almonds (p. 73).

The Second Time Around: The spice of this roast bird pairs well with hearty stews and braises.

GREAT GREENS

Greens provide healthy, instant gratification. They take little time to prepare and go great with whatever is for dinner, especially roast chicken. I generally like to treat greens simply, sautéing them with some garlic. I'll layer on a few basic flavors—sun-dried tomatoes, lemon zest, pine nuts, or olives—if I'm in the mood.

Spinach wilts quickly, so you can sauté it straight through. For slower cooking greens like Swiss chard or collard greens, turn down the flame, add a little liquid, and cook until tender. And if you're looking for a bit more substance, mix sautéed greens together with cream, cheese, and breadcrumbs for a quick gratin.

Creamed Spinach Gratin

Serves 4

2 cloves garlic, minced
3 tablespoons olive oil
1 pound spinach, heavy stems removed, washed, and spun dry
Kosher salt and freshly ground black pepper
2 tablespoons heavy cream
1/3 cup freshly grated Parmesan cheese
1 cup Garlic-Thyme Breadcrumbs (p. 205) or Homemade Breadcrumbs (p. 151)

1. Preheat the oven to 450°F.

2. Heat the garlic in 2 tablespoons of the olive oil in a 12-inch ovenproof skillet over medium-high heat until it sizzles steadily, becomes fragrant, and just begins to brown at the edges, about 2 minutes. Add the spinach, stir well, and sprinkle with salt and pepper, about 1/4 teaspoon each. Cook, tossing well, until the spinach wilts and becomes tender, about 3 minutes. Pour off most all of the liquid from the spinach, then stir in the cream and Parmesan.

3. Sprinkle the crumbs evenly over the spinach, transfer to the oven and cook until the breadcrumbs brown, about 10 minutes. Let rest for a couple of minutes, then serve.

Swiss Chard with Pancetta and Lemon

Serves 4

1/4 pound pancetta or bacon, cut into 1/2-inch strips
1 tablespoon olive oil
2 cloves garlic, minced
1 large bunch Swiss chard (about 1 1/2 pounds), stemmed, washed, patted dry, and cut into 3-inch lengths
Kosher salt
1/4 cup low-salt chicken broth
Grated zest of 1/2 lemon

1. Heat the pancetta with the oil in a large skillet over medium heat, stirring occasionally, until it renders much of its fat and browns, about 5 minutes. Transfer the pancetta to a large plate lined with paper towels.

2. Add the garlic to the skillet and heat until it sizzles steadily for about 30 seconds. Add the Swiss chard, sprinkle with salt (about 1/2 teaspoon) and cook, tossing well, until it just wilts. Add the broth, cover with the lid slightly askew, reduce the heat to medium-low and cook until the greens are just tender, about 3 minutes. Serve immediately with a sprinkling of the pancetta and lemon zest.

Simple Sautéed Spinach

Serves 4

2 cloves garlic, minced
2 tablespoons olive oil
1 pound spinach, heavy stems removed, washed, and spun dry
Kosher salt

Heat the garlic in the olive oil in a large skillet over medium-high heat until it sizzles steadily, becomes fragrant, and just begins to brown at the edges, about 2 minutes. Add the spinach and sprinkle generously with salt, about ½ teaspoon. Cook, tossing well, until the spinach wilts and becomes tender, about 3 minutes. Season with salt to taste and serve immediately.

Braised Garlicky Collard Greens

Serves 4

2 tablespoons olive oil
4 cloves garlic, thinly sliced
1 pound collard greens, washed and spun dry, stemmed, and cut into 3-inch pieces
Kosher salt
½ cup low-salt chicken broth

Heat the garlic in the olive oil in a large skillet over medium heat until it sizzles steadily and just begins to brown at the edges, about 3 minutes. Add the collard greens, sprinkle with salt (about ½ teaspoon), and cook, tossing well, until just wilted about 4 minutes. Add the broth, reduce the heat to medium-low, cover, and cook until the greens are just tender, about 10 minutes. Season with salt to taste and serve immediately.

Spinach with Raisins and Pine Nuts

Serves 4

2 cloves garlic, minced
2 tablespoons olive oil
1 pound spinach, heavy stems removed, washed, and spun dry
Kosher salt and freshly ground black pepper
¼ cup raisins
¼ cup pine nuts, toasted in a dry skillet over medium-low heat until lightly browned
½ cup Garlic-Thyme Breadcrumbs (p. 205)

Heat the garlic in the olive oil in a large skillet over medium-high heat until it sizzles steadily, becomes fragrant, and just begins to brown at the edges, about 2 minutes. Add the spinach and sprinkle generously with salt and pepper, about ½ teaspoon each. Cook, tossing well, until the spinach wilts and becomes tender, about 3 minutes. Toss with the raisins and pine nuts and serve immediately with a generous sprinkling of the breadcrumbs.

 A World of Roast Chicken   43

Roast Chicken with Rosemary-Garlic Croutons

Serves at least 4

I love stuffing. There simply is nothing like vegetables and bread that have been slowly cooked in or below a roasting bird. The stuffing in this recipe is very simple, consisting of little more than bread cubes and herbs so feel free to toss in some mushrooms, onions, sausage, or even apple. The croutons cooked directly under the bird become soft, soaking up the chicken juices while the bread to the sides becomes crisp and browned. I've doubled the amount of stuffing for two birds in this recipe because I love it so much and it reheats just fine.

FOR 1 BIRD	FOR 2 BIRDS	
		Kosher salt and freshly ground black pepper
1	2	3½- to 4-pound chicken(s), spatchcocked (p. 23), rinsed, and patted dry with paper towels
2 tablespoons	¼ cup	unsalted butter, softened
2 tablespoons	3 tablespoons	chopped fresh rosemary
1 tablespoon	2 tablespoons	sherry vinegar or balsamic vinegar
10 ounces	1¼ pounds	good crusty bread (like a baguette or a country bread), cut into 1-inch cubes
2	4	cloves garlic, minced
1 tablespoon	2 tablespoons	olive oil

1. Sprinkle 2½ teaspoons salt and ½ teaspoon black pepper all over each chicken, including the cavity. Place a rack in a pan, put the chicken on top, and let sit for up to 24 hours, uncovered, in the refrigerator. (If you've brined the chicken, skip this step. Just sprinkle the bird with ½ teaspoon salt and ½ teaspoon black pepper and proceed with the rest of the recipe.)

2. Preheat the oven to 425°F. Set an oven rack to the middle position. In a small bowl, mix the butter with half the rosemary and all of the vinegar. Using your fingers, spread some of the butter between the skin and breast meat, taking care not to rip the skin, then brush the remaining butter all over the bird, including the cavity. In a large bowl, toss the bread cubes with the remaining rosemary, the garlic, olive oil, 1 teaspoon salt, and ½ teaspoon black pepper.

3. Spread the croutons over the bottom of the roasting pan. Set the chicken on top of the croutons, skin side up, and roast until it's nicely browned all over and an instant-read thermometer inserted into the thickest part of the thigh registers 165° to 170°F, about 40 minutes.

4. Transfer the chicken to a cutting board and let rest for 10 minutes. Meanwhile, return the pan to the oven and continue to cook the croutons until browned and crisped a bit on top, about 10 minutes. Carve the chicken, drizzle with any juices accumulated on the cutting board, and serve with the croutons.

Perk It Up: This plain bird sparkles with the addition of Black Olive and Sherry Vinaigrette (p. 60), Rosemary-Balsamic Glaze (p. 13) or Chicken and Herb Gravy (p. 33).

On the Side: Brussels Sprouts with Bacon, Apple, and Sage (p. 72) or Roasted Fennel and Pears (p. 51).

The Second Time Around: This roast chicken is mild enough to use in most any type of leftover preparation. Any stuffing you have left over is great in sandwiches, simply reheated alone, or in Chicken and Stuffing Casserole with Sherry and Mushrooms (p. 202).

E.G.'s Curried Roast Chicken with Tarragon and Whole-Grain Mustard

Serves at least 4

Almost every restaurant has some form of "family meal" to feed the staff before the dinner service begins. One particularly grueling afternoon, Eric Gregory, sous-chef at Beacon Hill Bistro in Boston and one of my cooking mentors, threw together this curry, mustard, and tarragon rub, tossed it on some whole birds, and roasted them in a hot convection oven. The results were ethereal—crisp, spiced, and juicy—so much so that my notoriously fickle cooking colleagues nodded their approval (the culinary equivalent of a standing ovation).

FOR 1 BIRD	FOR 2 BIRDS	
¼ cup	½ cup	whole-grain mustard
3 tablespoons	⅓ cup	olive oil
3 tablespoons	⅓ cup	chopped fresh tarragon
1 tablespoon	2 tablespoons	curry powder
1 tablespoon	2 tablespoons	kosher salt
1 teaspoon	2 teaspoons	freshly ground black pepper
1	2	3½- to 4-pound chicken(s), rinsed and patted dry with paper towels

1. In a small bowl, mix together the mustard, olive oil, tarragon, curry powder, salt, and pepper, then rub this all over the bird, including the cavity. Transfer to a large zip-top bag and let sit for at least 1 hour and up to 24 hours in the refrigerator. (If you've brined the chicken, reduce the amount of salt to ½ teaspoon and proceed with the rest of the recipe.)

2. Preheat the oven to 425°F. Set an oven rack to the middle position. Set each chicken breast side up on a rack in a large roasting pan and roast until the breasts are nicely browned all over, about 35 minutes. Gently flip the chicken (I like using tongs to clutch the inside of the cavity and the side of the bird) and cook until an instant-read thermometer inserted into the thickest part of the thigh registers 165° to 170°F—about another 15 to 20 minutes.

3. Let rest for 5 to 10 minutes breast side up. Carve the chicken, drizzle with any juices accumulated on the cutting board, and serve.

On the Side: Roasted Acorn Squash with Maple Butter and Walnuts (p. 50), and Couscous with Red Peppers and Orange (p. 65).

The Second Time Around: Use the leftovers in dishes with an Indian or Mediterranean accent.

Roast Chicken with Fennel and Mushroom Dressing

Serves at least 4

I put fennel in everything—salads, soups, sautés, and most definitely roasts. Cooked, it has a sweet flavor that brightens up a dish, like an onion only with a little more complexity. In this roast chicken, fennel pairs with mushrooms, croutons, and thyme to form a simple dressing which cooks under the butterflied bird.

FOR 1 BIRD	FOR 2 BIRDS	
		Kosher salt and freshly ground black pepper
1	2	3½- to 4-pound chicken(s), spatchcocked (p. 23), rinsed and patted dry with paper towels
2 tablespoons	¼ cup	unsalted butter, softened to room temperature
1½ tablespoons	3 tablespoons	chopped fresh thyme
1 tablespoon	2 tablespoons	balsamic vinegar
10 ounces	10 ounces	white button mushrooms, left whole, or large mushrooms, quartered
½ pound	½ pound	good crusty bread (like a baguette or a country bread), cut into 1-inch cubes
1	1	fennel bulb, trimmed of fronds and cut into ½-inch pieces
8	8	oil-packed sun-dried tomatoes, cut in half
4	4	cloves garlic, smashed

1. Sprinkle 2½ teaspoons salt and ½ teaspoon black pepper all over each chicken, including the cavity. Place a rack in a pan, put the chicken on top, and let sit for up to 24 hours, uncovered, in the refrigerator. (If you've brined the chicken, skip this step. Just sprinkle the bird with ½ teaspoon salt and ½ teaspoon black pepper and proceed with the rest of the recipe.)

2. Preheat the oven to 425°F. Set an oven rack to the middle position. In a small bowl, mix the butter with half the thyme and all of the vinegar. Using a brush, spread the butter between the skin and the breast meat, taking care not to rip the skin, then brush the remaining butter all over the bird, including the cavity.

continued

3. In a large bowl, toss the mushrooms, bread, fennel, sun-dried tomatoes, and garlic with the remaining thyme, 1 teaspoon salt, and ½ teaspoon pepper. Scatter this mixture over the bottom of the roasting pan. Set the chicken on top, skin side up. Roast the chicken until it's nicely browned all over and an instant-read thermometer inserted into the thickest part of the thigh registers 165° to 170°F, about 40 minutes.

4. Transfer the chicken to a cutting board and let rest for 10 minutes. Meanwhile, return the pan to the oven for 10 minutes to brown and crisp the top of the dressing. Carve the chicken, drizzle with any juices accumulated on the cutting board, and serve with the dressing.

Perk It Up: Balsamic-Sun-Dried Tomato Vinaigrette (p. 61) matches well with this chicken; drizzle it over right before serving.

On the Side: Roasted Beets with Shallots and Thyme (p. 50) or Snap Peas and Carrots with Lemon (p. 73).

The Second Time Around: The chicken and fennel are great in casseroles and hearty stews.

Roast Chicken with Southwestern Rub and Cornbread and Jalapeño Stuffing

Serves at least 4

If you have some cornbread in the bread bin, this is the recipe for you. Making cornbread isn't hard, but I would advise going with store-bought if you don't have any on hand—it helps to get a running start on dinner. For a little twist, toss some diced chorizo or browned sausage into the stuffing.

FOR 1 BIRD	FOR 2 BIRDS	
		Kosher salt and freshly ground black pepper
2 teaspoons	4 teaspoons	chili powder
1 teaspoon	2 teaspoons	ground cumin
1 teaspoon	2 teaspoons	ground chipotle powder
1 teaspoon	1 teaspoon	light brown sugar
1 teaspoon	1 teaspoon	garlic powder
1	2	3½- to 4-pound chicken(s), spatchcocked (p. 23), rinsed, and patted dry with paper towels
¾ pound	¾ pound	cornbread or corn muffins, broken into large crumbs
2	2	jalapeños, cored, seeded, and finely diced
4	4	scallions (white and green parts), trimmed and thinly sliced
¼ pound	¼ pound	extra-sharp Cheddar cheese, finely shredded
¼ cup	¼ cup	chopped fresh cilantro

1. In a small bowl, mix together 2½ teaspoons salt and ½ teaspoon pepper for each bird, the chili powder, cumin, chipotle powder, brown sugar and garlic powder, and then sprinkle this rub all over the chicken, including the cavity. Place a rack in a pan, put the chicken on top, and let sit for up to 24 hours, uncovered, in the refrigerator. (If you've brined the chicken, reduce the salt in the rub to ½ teaspoon and proceed with the rest of the recipe.)

2. Preheat the oven to 425°F. Set an oven rack to the middle position. Toss the cornbread with the jalapeños and scallions in a large bowl, sprinkle generously with salt and pepper (about ½ teaspoon each), and toss well. Scatter the mixture in a roasting pan and top with the chicken, skin side up. Roast the chicken until it's nicely browned all over and an instant-read thermometer inserted into the thickest part of the thigh registers 165° to 170°F, about 40 minutes.

3. Let rest for 5 to 10 minutes, then carve the chicken and serve with a large spoonful of the dressing, and a sprinkling of the Cheddar and cilantro.

Perk It Up: Build on the flavors in this roast chicken with a pat of Smoky Chipotle Butter (p. 61).

On the Side: Snap Peas and Carrots with Lemon (p. 73) or Mashed Potatoes with Cheddar, Chiles, and Scallions (p. 85).

The Second Time Around: These flavors work well in other Tex-Mex preparations like quesadillas, burritos, and tacos.

ROASTED VEGETABLES

If you haven't roasted any vegetables in the same pan with the bird, here are a couple of recipes. I like to keep the temperature in these recipes at 425°F so the vegetables can cook in the same oven with the chicken. If you have a relatively small oven like mine, though, you may want to roast the vegetables before the bird so as not to overcrowd the oven. Just give the vegetables a quick five-minute flash back in the hot oven before serving.

Spiced Sweet Potato Fries

Serves 4 as a side dish

1 teaspoon chili powder
1 teaspoon paprika
1 teaspoon garlic powder
1 teaspoon kosher salt
1 teaspoon light brown sugar
½ teaspoon ground cumin
2 pounds sweet potatoes, sliced into
    1-inch-wide wedges
2 tablespoons olive oil

Preheat the oven to 425°F. In a small bowl, toss together the chili powder, paprika, garlic powder, salt, brown sugar, and cumin. In a large bowl, toss the potatoes with the oil, then with the spice mix until evenly coated. Transfer the potatoes to a large baking sheet and roast, flipping occasionally, until tender, browned, and crisped in places, about 25 minutes. Serve immediately.

Roasted Beets with Shallots and Thyme

Serves 4 as a side dish

1 bunch beets (about 1½ pounds), trimmed,
    rinsed well, patted dry, and cut into
    ¼- to ½-inch-thick rounds
2 shallots, sliced ¼ inch thick
2 tablespoons olive oil
2 teaspoons chopped fresh thyme
1 teaspoon kosher salt
½ teaspoon freshly ground black pepper

Preheat the oven to 425°F. In a large bowl, toss all the ingredients together until evenly coated with oil. Transfer to a large baking dish and roast, flipping occasionally, until tender and browned, 25 to 35 minutes. Serve immediately.

Roasted Acorn Squash with Maple Butter and Walnuts

Serves 4 as a side dish

2 acorn squash, cut in half
¼ cup unsalted butter, softened
1 tablespoon light brown sugar
¾ teaspoon kosher salt
¼ teaspoon freshly ground black pepper
Large pinch of ground cinnamon
Pinch of ground allspice
Pinch of ground nutmeg
2 tablespoons maple syrup
¼ cup chopped walnuts, toasted on a
    baking sheet at 375°F until lightly browned
1 teaspoon chopped fresh thyme

Preheat the oven to 425°F. Set the squash in a large roasting dish. In a small bowl, mash together 3 tablespoons of the butter with the brown sugar, salt, pepper, and the spices. Using a brush or your fingers, spread the flavored butter all over the squash and transfer to the oven. Roast until browned and completely tender, 45 to 50 minutes. Check by poking with a paring knife—the squash should offer no resistance. Mix the maple syrup with the remaining 1 tablespoon butter and brush all over the squash. Serve with a sprinkling of the walnuts and thyme.

Prosciutto-Wrapped Asparagus with Mozzarella and Sun-Dried Tomatoes

Serves 4 as a side dish

1½ pounds thick asparagus, fibrous ends snapped off and bottom half peeled
2 tablespoons olive oil
1 teaspoon kosher salt
½ teaspoon freshly ground black pepper
8 very thin slices prosciutto
6 ounces fresh mozzarella cheese, cut into thin rounds
8 oil-packed sun-dried tomatoes, thinly sliced

1. Preheat the oven to 425°F. In a large bowl, toss the asparagus with the oil, salt, and pepper. Transfer to a large baking sheet and cook, tossing occasionally, until tender and browned in places, 15 to 20 minutes.

2. Meanwhile, set the prosciutto onto a large serving platter and top each with a couple slices of the mozzarella and the sun-dried tomatoes. Set 3 or 4 of the asparagus spears across each slice of prosciutto and roll into bundles. Serve immediately or at room temperature.

Garlicky Sear-Roasted Cauliflower

Serves 4 as a side dish

1 tablespoons unsalted butter
1 tablespoon olive oil
3 cloves garlic, smashed
1 small head cauliflower, broken into small florets
Kosher salt and freshly ground black pepper
½ cup Garlic-Thyme breadcrumbs (p. 205)

1. Preheat the oven to 425°F. Set a heavy, 12-inch ovenproof skillet (I like using cast iron) over medium heat. Add the butter, oil and garlic and cook, swirling the pan, until the garlic sizzles and the butter starts to brown. Add the cauliflower,

sprinkle generously with salt and pepper (about ½ teaspoon each) and cook, stirring occasionally, until the florets start to brown, about 6 minutes.

2. Sprinkle the breadcrumbs all over the cauliflower and transfer the skillet to the oven. Roast until the florets are tender and the crumbs are browned, 15 to 20 minutes. Serve immediately.

Roasted Fennel and Pears

Serves 4 as a side dish

2 pounds fennel (about 2 large), trimmed, quartered, cored, and cut into ½-inch pieces
2 Bartlett pears, cut in half, cored, and cut into ½-inch pieces
2 tablespoons olive oil
1 teaspoon chopped fresh thyme
Kosher salt and freshly ground black pepper
2 tablespoons chopped fresh tarragon
16 shaved strips of Parmesan cheese (use a vegetable peeler to do this)

Preheat the oven to 425°F. In a large bowl, toss together the fennel, pears, oil, and thyme. Sprinkle generously with salt and pepper, about 1 teaspoon and ½ teaspoon respectively. Transfer to a large roasting dish and roast, flipping occasionally, until tender and browned in places, about 30 minutes. Serve immediately with a sprinkling of the tarragon and the shavings of Parmesan.

Chinese Salt and Pepper Roast Chicken

Serves at least 4

One of my favorite Chinese dishes is salt and pepper shrimp. The shrimp are fried whole, then seasoned with salt and pepper, tossed with scallions and jalapenos, and served over crisp iceberg lettuce. The hot shrimp heat up the jalapeños and scallions, activating their oils and forming an intensely flavorful mixture. I've taken to applying this technique to roast chicken. A properly cooked bird has a browned and crisp coating (just like fried food), which comes to life when tossed with the scallion-jalapeño mix.

FOR 1 BIRD	FOR 2 BIRDS	
		Kosher salt and freshly ground black pepper
1	2	3½- to 4-pound chicken(s), rinsed and patted dry with paper towels
2	4	jalapeños, cored, seeded, and finely diced
1 bunch	2 bunches	scallions (white and green parts), trimmed and thinly sliced
1	1	head iceberg lettuce, outer leaves removed, cored, and thinly sliced

1. Sprinkle 2½ teaspoons salt and 1 teaspoon black pepper all over each chicken, including the cavity. Place a rack in a pan, put the chicken on top, and let sit for up to 24 hours, uncovered, in the refrigerator. (If you've brined the chicken, skip this step. Just sprinkle the bird with ½ teaspoon salt and 1 teaspoon black pepper and proceed with the rest of the recipe.)

2. Preheat the oven to 425°F. Set an oven rack to the middle position. Set the chicken breast side up on a rack in a large roasting pan and roast until the breasts are nicely browned all over, about 35 minutes. Gently flip the chicken (I like using tongs to clutch the inside of the cavity and the side of the bird) and cook until an instant-read thermometer inserted into the thickest part of the thigh registers 165°F to 170°F—this should take another 15 to 20 minutes.

3. Transfer to a cutting board and let rest for 5 minutes breast side up. Carve the chicken, transfer to a large bowl, and toss with the jalapeños and scallions. Scatter the lettuce on a large serving platter, arrange the chicken over it, top with any jalapeños or scallions left in the bowl, and serve immediately.

On the Side: Steamed white rice and Stir-Fried Broccoli (p. 72).

The Second Time Around: This roast chicken does well in leftovers dishes with an Asian flair, such as fried rice, Asian salads, or Asian noodles.

Grill-Roasted Thai Chicken with Lemongrass

Serves at least 4

Lemongrass is one of those simple ingredients that makes Thai (and Vietnamese) food taste so exotic. The sharp, lemony flavor of this Asian herb (it shares some of the same essential oils as lemon) works nicely in stir-fries, sautés, or rubs like this one. Lemongrass is increasingly available at supermarkets, though you're sure to find it at your nearest Asian grocer. To use, peel and discard the herb's husky, long, thin strands to get at the tender, inner core.

FOR 1 BIRD	FOR 2 BIRDS	
2 tablespoons	¼ cup	soy sauce
2 tablespoons	¼ cup	minced garlic
2 tablespoons	¼ cup	finely chopped lemongrass
2 teaspoons	4 teaspoons	kosher salt
1 teaspoon	2 teaspoons	freshly ground black pepper
½ teaspoon	1 teaspoon	ground coriander
1	2	3½- to 4-pound chicken(s), spatchcocked (p. 23), rinsed, and patted dry with paper towels
¼ cup	½ cup	finely chopped fresh cilantro
1	2	lime(s), cut into wedges, for serving

1. In a small bowl, stir together the soy sauce, garlic, lemongrass, salt, pepper, and coriander. Set this mixture in a zip-top bag along with the chicken, close the bag, massage the two together, and then let sit for at least 1 and up to 24 hours in the refrigerator. (If you've brined the chicken, reduce the amount of salt in the soy sauce mix to ½ teaspoon and proceed with the rest of the recipe.)

2. Prepare a charcoal fire or heat up the gas grill (heat all burners to medium-low). For a charcoal fire, pile a couple of layers of briquettes on one side and a sparse single layer of charcoal on the other side of the grill so that you end up with a medium hot zone and a moderate to cool zone. Your fire should be ready when the briquettes are mostly gray (or, if you're using hardwood, when they are red hot).

3. Set the chicken on the grill (on the hotter part of the charcoal grill) skin side down, cover on the gas grill, and cook until the skin starts to brown (without blackening), 10 to 15 minutes. Flip the chicken and reduce the heat to low on the gas grill or transfer to the cooler side of the fire on the charcoal grill. Cover (with the vents open on the charcoal grill) and cook,

continued

checking occasionally to ensure the chicken is not burning, until it's nicely browned all over and an instant-read thermometer inserted into the thickest part of the thigh registers 165° to 170°F—this should take another 25 to 30 minutes.

4. Transfer to a cutting board and let rest for 5 to 10 minutes breast side up. Then carve the chicken and serve with a sprinkling of the cilantro and a wedge of lime for squeezing.

On the Side: Steamed jasmine rice and Stir-Fried Broccoli (p. 72).

The Second Time Around: This grilled bird goes well in salads, sandwiches, and wraps with Asian flavors.

Moroccan Spiced Chicken Roasted over a Bed of Couscous and Apricots

Serves at least 4

I love one-pot meals. They allow all of the ingredients in a dish to mix and meld, intensifying and unifying their flavors. They also make a cook's life easier by setting all of the staples of a meal—meat, starch, and vegetable—into a single dish. Note that in this recipe the couscous towards the sides of the pan will become crisp and browned, like the top of a lasagna, only crunchier.

FOR 1 BIRD	FOR 2 BIRDS	
		Kosher salt
2 teaspoons	4 teaspoons	ground cumin
1 teaspoon	2 teaspoons	ground coriander
1 teaspoon	2 teaspoons	freshly ground black pepper
1 teaspoon	1 teaspoon	light brown sugar
¼ teaspoon	½ teaspoon	ground cinnamon
¼ teaspoon	½ teaspoon	cayenne pepper
2½ cups	2½ cups	water

I	2	3½- to 4-pound chicken(s), spatchcocked (p. 23), rinsed, and patted dry with paper towels
2 cups	2 cups	couscous
½ cup	½ cup	diced apricots
¼ cup	¼ cup	sliced almonds, toasted on a baking sheet at 425°F until light brown
4	4	scallions (white and green parts), trimmed and thinly sliced
I	I	navel orange, peel left on, cut into very thin rounds

1. In a small bowl, mix together 2½ teaspoons salt for each bird with the cumin, coriander, black pepper, brown sugar, cinnamon and cayenne pepper, and then sprinkle it all over the chicken, including the cavity. Place a rack in a pan, put the chicken on top, and let sit for up to 24 hours, uncovered, in the refrigerator. (If you've brined the chicken, reduce the salt in the rub to ½ teaspoon and proceed with the rest of the recipe.)

2. Preheat the oven to 425°F. Set an oven rack to the middle position. To prepare the couscous, bring the water to a boil. Add the couscous and 1 teaspoon salt, cover, remove from the heat, and let sit for 5 minutes. Fluff the couscous with a fork, toss with the apricots, almonds, and scallions, and transfer to a large roasting pan. Top with the sliced orange and set the chicken on top, skin side up.

3. Roast the chicken until it's nicely browned all over and an instant-read thermometer inserted into the thickest part of the thigh registers 165°F to 170°F, about 40 minutes.

4. Transfer the chicken to a cutting board to rest for 5 to 10 minutes. Carve the chicken and serve with the couscous and a couple of slices of the orange.

Perk It Up: Drizzle with Orange-Rosemary Pan Sauce (p. 32) to intensify the citrus flavors. (You won't have any juices from the roasting pan, as they'll have been absorbed by the couscous.)

On the Side: Orange-Glazed Carrots (p. 73).

The Second Time Around: The spice of this roast chicken pairs well with leftovers with a Mediterranean slant.

Greek Roast Chicken with Lemon, Black Olives, and Potatoes

Serves at least 4

This bird has all the ingredients you would expect in a Greek dish—lemon, black olives, oregano, and feta—all of which add a wonderful brightness and vibrancy. The potatoes are roasted along with the chicken and form a sort of warm salad with the feta, lemon, and olives.

FOR 1 BIRD	FOR 2 BIRDS	
1	2	3½- to 4-pound chicken(s), rinsed and patted dry with paper towels
		Kosher salt and freshly ground black pepper
2 tablespoons	¼ cup	dried oregano
3 tablespoons	¼ cup	olive oil
1 pound	1 pound	red potatoes, cut into 1½-inch pieces
¾ cup	¾ cup	pitted kalamata olives, drained
1	1	lemon, zested and juiced
¼ pound	¼ pound	feta cheese, crumbled

1. Sprinkle each bird all over, including the cavity, with 2½ teaspoons salt, 1 teaspoon pepper, and half the oregano. Let sit for up to 24 hours, uncovered, in the refrigerator on a wire or roasting rack in a pan. (If you've brined the chicken, reduce the amount of salt in the spice mix to ½ teaspoon and proceed with the rest of the recipe.)

2. Preheat the oven to 425°F. Set an oven rack to the middle position. Set the chicken breast side up on a rack in a large roasting pan. Brush each bird with 1 tablespoon of the oil. In a large bowl, toss the potatoes with the remaining olive oil and oregano, 1 teaspoon salt, and ½ teaspoon pepper. Scatter around the perimeter of the pan, underneath the chicken.

3. Roast the chicken until the breasts are nicely browned all over, about 35 minutes. Gently flip the chicken (I like using tongs to clutch the inside of the cavity and the side of the bird) and cook until an instant-read thermometer inserted into the thickest part of the thigh registers 165°F to 170°F—this should take another 15 to 20 minutes.

4. Transfer to a large cutting board and let rest for 5 to 10 minutes breast side up. Meanwhile, return the pan to the oven for 10 minutes to finish browning the potatoes.

5. Carve the chicken. Toss the potatoes with the olives, lemon zest, feta, and any juices accumulated on the bottom of the carving board. Serve the chicken and warm potato salad with a drizzle of the lemon juice.

On the Side: Spinach with Raisins and Pine Nuts (p. 43).

The Second Time Around: This roast chicken is mild enough to go in most any leftover dish. The leftover potatoes are great in soups, braises, or stews.

Grill-Roasted Chicken with Tex-Mex Spice Crust and Grilled Corn Salsa

Serves at least 4

I like to make this chicken on a midsummer's night when it's warm enough to sit outside and laze around the dinner table. The pairings are lively. A vibrant spice rub full of ground chiles coats the bird and a grilled corn salsa accompanies it at the dinner table. These assertive flavors almost beg for a beer or something cool and strong to wash them down. While I like grilling corn whole in its husk when I'm serving it on its own (the husk protects the corn during grilling), for salsas and sauces, I prefer to shuck and grill it directly on the grill grates for an intense smoky flavor.

FOR 1 BIRD	FOR 2 BIRDS	
1 tablespoon	2 tablespoons	kosher salt
1 tablespoon	2 tablespoons	chili powder
1 teaspoon	2 teaspoons	ground chipotle powder
1 teaspoon	2 teaspoons	dried oregano
1 teaspoon	2 teaspoons	garlic powder
1 teaspoon	2 teaspoons	ground cumin
1 teaspoon	2 teaspoons	light brown sugar
1	2	3½- to 4-pound chicken(s), spatchcocked (p. 23), rinsed and patted dry with paper towels
2 ears	2 ears	corn, shucked
1	1	large red onion, sliced ½ inch thick
2 tablespoons	2 tablespoons	olive oil
		Freshly ground black pepper
1	1	large ripe tomato, diced
1	1	jalapeño, cored, seeded, and finely diced
¼ cup	¼ cup	chopped fresh cilantro
1 teaspoon	1 teaspoon	sherry vinegar or balsamic vinegar

1. In a small bowl, for each bird mix together 2½ teaspoons salt, the chili powder, chipotle powder, oregano, garlic powder, cumin and brown sugar. Set this mixture in a zip-top bag along with the chicken, close the bag, massage the two together, and let sit for at least 1 and up to 24 hours in the refrigerator. (If you've brined the chicken, reduce the amount of salt in the spice mix to ½ teaspoon and proceed with the rest of the recipe.)

Before you start grilling, make sure to firmly scrape the grill grates with a wire brush. Then lightly oil the grates with an old dishtowel or a wad of paper towels to avoid sticking.

2. Prepare a charcoal fire or heat up the gas grill (heat all burners to medium-low). For a charcoal fire, pile a couple of layers of briquettes on one side and a sparse single layer of charcoal on the other side of the grill so that you end up with a moderate zone and a cool zone. Your fire should be ready when the briquettes are mostly gray (or, if you're using hardwood, when they are red hot).

3. Drizzle the corn and onion with the olive oil and sprinkle with salt and pepper, then set them on the cooler part of the grill. Cover and cook the corn, flipping every couple of minutes, until browned all over, about 10 minutes. Remove to a large cutting board. Grill the onions, flipping every couple of minutes, until well browned and just tender to the tooth, about 25 minutes (it's okay if they char a bit). Remove to the board to cool.

4. Meanwhile, set the chicken on the grill (on the hotter part of the charcoal grill) skin side down, covered on the gas grill, and cook until the skin starts to brown (checking occasionally to avoid burning), 10 to 15 minutes. Gently flip the chicken (I like using tongs and a large metal spatula in tandem) and reduce the heat to low on the gas grill or transfer the chicken to the cooler side of the fire on a charcoal grill. Cover (with the vents open on the charcoal grill) and cook, checking occasionally to ensure that the chicken is not burning, until it's nicely browned all over and an instant-read thermometer inserted into the thickest part of the thigh registers 165°F to 170°F—this should take another 25 to 30 minutes. Transfer to a cutting board and let rest for 10 minutes.

5. Using a chef's knife and working over a large bowl, cut the kernels from the cobs. Coarsely chop the onion and add to the bowl, along with the tomato, jalapeño, cilantro, and vinegar. Toss well. Season with salt and pepper to taste.

6. Carve the chicken and serve immediately with the salsa.

Perk It Up: For an extra kick, serve this with a pat of Smoky Chipotle Butter (p. 61) or a drizzle of Lime and Jalapeño Vinaigrette (p. 60).

On the Side: Grilled red peppers and onions or sliced ripe tomatoes.

The Second Time Around: These flavors work nicely in quesadillas, burritos, tacos and the like. Sprinkle over any leftover salsa.

VINAIGRETTES, QUICK SAUCES, AND FLAVORED BUTTERS

Though my versions of pan sauces are pretty simple, sometimes I favor the spontaneity of these no-cook sauces and accompaniments. All are full of bright flavors that can dress up any roasted bird. They're also easy to throw together either before or while you're cooking the chicken.

Vinaigrettes and flavored butters are great items to have on hand. While vinaigrettes play a prominent role in the second-time-around recipes in this book, they're also great served with a freshly roasted bird, their tang perking up dry breast meat and giving a roast bird some sauciness.

Flavored butters run along the same lines, and then there are quick sauces like Carolina BBQ, which relies on vinegar for its punch.

Lime and Jalapeño Vinaigrette

Enough for 1 bird

2 tablespoons fresh lime juice
1 teaspoon Dijon mustard
1 teaspoon light brown sugar
¼ cup grapeseed or vegetable oil
1 Jalapeño, cored, seeded, and finely diced
2 tablespoons chopped fresh cilantro
1 small clove garlic, minced
   and mashed to a paste
¾ teaspoon kosher salt
½ teaspoon freshly ground black pepper

In a large bowl, whisk together the lime juice, mustard, and brown sugar. Slowly drizzle in the oil, whisking rapidly, then add it in a steadier stream as the mixture thickens and emulsifies. Fold in the jalapeño, cilantro, garlic, salt, and pepper. This will keep, tightly covered, in the refrigerator for up to 2 days. Whisk well before serving.

Black Olive and Sherry Vinaigrette

Enough for 1 bird

1½ tablespoons sherry vinegar
1½ teaspoons Dijon mustard
¼ cup extra-virgin olive oil
1 shallot, finely diced
¼ cup finely chopped kalamata olives
1 teaspoon chopped fresh thyme
½ teaspoon kosher salt
½ teaspoon freshly ground black pepper

In a large bowl, whisk together the vinegar and mustard. Slowly drizzle in the oil, whisking rapidly, then add it in a steadier stream as the mixture thickens and emulsifies. Fold in the shallot, olives, thyme, salt, and pepper. This will keep, tightly covered, in the refrigerator for up to 2 days. Whisk well before serving.

Balsamic-Sun-Dried Tomato Vinaigrette

Enough for 1 bird

1½ tablespoons balsamic vinegar
1 teaspoon Dijon mustard
¼ cup extra virgin olive oil
4 oil-packed sun-dried tomatoes, finely diced
1 teaspoon chopped fresh rosemary
¾ teaspoon kosher salt
½ teaspoon freshly ground black pepper

In a large bowl, whisk together the vinegar and mustard. Slowly drizzle in the oil, whisking rapidly, then add it in a steadier stream as the mixture thickens and emulsifies. Fold in the sun-dried tomatoes, rosemary, salt, and pepper. This will keep, tightly covered, in the refrigerator for up to 1 week. Whisk well before serving.

Smoky Chipotle Butter

Enough for 1 bird

½ cup unsalted butter, softened
1 canned chipotle chile
2 tablespoons adobo sauce from the canned chipotles
¼ cup chopped fresh cilantro
2 tablespoons fresh lime juice
½ teaspoon kosher salt
½ teaspoon freshly ground black pepper

1. Place all the ingredients in a food processor and pulse until the mixture is uniform but still chunky, about 12 pulses.

2. Form into a log shape in wax paper or plastic wrap (tightening the ends as if it were a sausage) and refrigerate for up to 1 week, or freeze for up to 1 month.

Carolina BBQ Sauce

Enough for 1 bird

½ cup cider vinegar
1 tablespoon light brown sugar
1 tablespoon ketchup
1 tablespoon Original Frank's® Hot Sauce
½ teaspoon crushed red pepper flakes

In a large bowl, whisk together all the ingredients. Serve immediately or refrigerate for up to 1 week.

Shallot-Herb Butter

Enough for 1 bird

½ cup unsalted butter, softened
½ cup finely chopped fresh parsley
1 tablespoon chopped fresh thyme
2 teaspoons finely chopped fresh rosemary
2 tablespoons finely diced shallots
1 lemon, zest only, finely grated
1 tablespoon fresh lemon juice
½ teaspoon kosher salt
½ teaspoon freshly ground black pepper

1. Place all the ingredients in a food processor and gently pulse until the mixture is uniform but still chunky, about 10 pulses.

2. Form into a log shape in wax paper or plastic wrap (tightening the ends as if it were a sausage) and refrigerate for up to 1 week, or freeze for up to 1 month.

Grill-Roasted Tandoori Chicken

Serves at least 4

Intensely aromatic, moist, and smoky, Indian tandoori chicken is a wonderful mix of spice and heat. True tandoori chicken is prepared in a tandoor, or deep, clay oven. While it's hard to replicate the intense cooking conditions of a tandoor oven, a hot grill gives the chicken a nice, smoky edge. Yogurt serves as the base for the marinade, along with curry, garlic, and ginger. For best results, marinate this chicken at least 8 hours before cooking.

FOR 1 BIRD	FOR 2 BIRDS	
½ cup	1 cup	plain yogurt
2 tablespoons	¼ cup	peeled and minced fresh ginger
2 tablespoons	¼ cup	minced garlic
1 tablespoon	2 tablespoons	curry powder
1 tablespoon	2 tablespoons	sweet paprika
1 tablespoon	2 tablespoons	kosher salt
1 teaspoon	2 teaspoons	freshly ground black pepper
1	2	3½- to 4-pound chicken(s), spatchcocked (p. 23), rinsed and patted dry with paper towels
¼ cup	½ cup	chopped fresh cilantro
1	2	lime(s), cut into wedges, for serving

1. Stir together the yogurt, ginger, garlic, curry powder, paprika, salt, and pepper in a medium-size bowl until well mixed. Set it in a zip-top bag along with the chicken, close the bag, massage the two together, and let sit for at least 4 and up to 24 hours in the refrigerator. (If you've brined the chicken, reduce the amount of salt in the mixture to ½ teaspoon and proceed with the rest of the recipe.)

2. Prepare a charcoal fire or heat up the gas grill (heat all burners to medium-low). For a charcoal fire, pile a couple of layers of briquettes on one side and a sparse single layer of charcoal on the other side of the grill so that you end up with a moderate zone and a cool zone. Your fire should be ready when the briquettes are mostly gray (or, if you're using hardwood, when they are red hot).

3. Set the chicken on the grill (on the hotter part of the charcoal grill) skin side down, cover on the gas grill, and cook until the skin starts to brown (checking occasionally

to avoid burning), 10 to 15 minutes. Gently flip the chicken (I like using tongs and a large metal spatula in tandem), then reduce the heat to low on the gas grill or transfer the chicken to the cooler side of the fire on the charcoal grill. Cover (with the vents open on the charcoal grill) and cook, checking occasionally to ensure that the chicken is not burning, until it's nicely browned all over and an instant-read thermometer inserted into the thickest part of the thigh registers 165°F to 170°F—this should take another 25 to 30 minutes.

4. Let rest for 5 to 10 minutes, then carve the chicken and serve with a sprinkling of the cilantro and a wedge of lime for squeezing.

On the Side: Couscous with Red Peppers and Orange (p. 65) or Rice Pilaf with Mushrooms (p. 64).

The Second Time Around: This assertive roast chicken does well in leftovers with similar flavors, like curries or quick stir-fries.

STARCHY SIDES

While it's nice to serve plain steamed rice, couscous, or a baked potato with a roast chicken, it doesn't take much to dress them up. Instead of the baked potato, grate some Russets, form into cakes, and sear in a nonstick skillet. Or sauté some onions and mushrooms with rice for a rice pilaf. And that couscous can be warmed up with sliced oranges, diced peppers, and a pinch of spice.

Potato and Scallion Cakes

Serves 4

2 pounds russet potatoes, peeled
3 scallions, thinly sliced
Kosher salt and freshly ground black pepper
2 tablespoons olive oil
Large pinch of sweet paprika

1. Grate the potatoes on the large holes of a box grater. Squeezing the grated potatoes between your hands over the sink, wring out as much of the moisture as you can. In a large bowl, toss with the scallions and 1 teaspoon each of salt and pepper.

2. Heat the oil in a large nonstick skillet (preferably 12-inches wide) over medium-high heat until shimmering hot, about 1½ minutes. Form the mixture into 4 cakes and set in the pan evenly spaced. Cook without touching them until browned nicely underneath, about 4 minutes. Reduce the heat to medium, flip the cakes, press down with a spatula to flatten them slightly, and cook until nicely browned and cooked through, about 5 minutes. Set on a plate lined with paper towels, sprinkle with the paprika, salt and pepper to taste, and serve immediately.

Rice Pilaf with Mushrooms

Serves 4

1 ounce dried shiitake mushrooms
1½ cups boiling water
¼ cup unsalted butter
1 large Spanish onion, finely diced
Kosher salt
2 cups long-grain rice
2½ cups low-salt chicken broth
2 teaspoons chopped fresh thyme

1. Soak the mushrooms in the boiling water until tender, about 10 minutes, then discard their stems and cut into ¼-inch dice. Strain the mushroom soaking liquid through a coffee filter or a paper towel and set aside.

2. Melt 2 tablespoons of the butter in a large saucepan over medium heat. Add the onion, sprinkle generously with salt (about ½ teaspoon), and cook, stirring occasionally, until translucent and soft, about 8 minutes. Add the mushrooms and cook, stirring, for 1 minute. Add the rice and cook, stirring, for 1 minute to coat with some of the butter. Stir in the broth, mushroom soaking liquid, thyme, and ½ teaspoon salt and bring to a boil. Cook until almost all of the liquid cooks off, then reduce the heat to low, cover, and cook for 20 minutes. Remove from the heat and let sit for 5 minutes. Fluff with a fork, stir in the remaining 2 tablespoons butter, and serve.

Couscous with Red Peppers and Orange

Serves 4

2 tablespoons olive oil
1 small yellow onion, finely diced
½ red bell pepper, cored, seeded, and finely diced
Kosher salt
1 teaspoon ground cumin
Pinch of cayenne pepper
Pinch of ground cinnamon
2½ cups low-salt chicken broth
2 cups couscous
1 navel orange, peeled and cut into ½-inch dice
¼ cup chopped almonds, toasted on a baking sheet at 375°F until browned and fragrant
¼ cup chopped fresh cilantro

Heat the oil in a large saucepan over medium heat until shimmering hot, about 2 minutes. Add the onion and bell pepper, sprinkle generously with salt (about ¾ teaspoon), and cook, stirring occasionally, until soft and browned in places, about 6 minutes. Add the cumin, cayenne, and cinnamon and cook, stirring, for 30 seconds. Add the broth and bring to a boil. Add the couscous and ½ teaspoon salt, cover, remove from the heat, and let sit for 5 minutes. Fluff the couscous with a fork, taste for salt, toss with the orange, almonds, and cilantro, and serve immediately.

Creamy Polenta

Serves 4 to 6

4 cups low-salt chicken broth
1 cup polenta or coarse-ground cornmeal
½ teaspoon kosher salt, plus more to taste
¼ cup shredded fontina cheese
¼ cup freshly grated Parmesan cheese
¼ cup mascarpone or ricotta cheese
Freshly ground black pepper

Bring the broth to a boil in a large saucepan. Whisk in the polenta and salt. Reduce the heat to a gentle simmer and cook, stirring often, until thickened and cooked through with a creamy texture, about 20 minutes. Stir in the cheeses and season generously with salt and pepper to taste. Serve immediately.

Anago's Garlicky Grill-Roasted Split Chickens with Lemon and Herbs

Serves at least 4

The first restaurant I ever cooked in was Anago, an upscale American bistro in downtown Boston. The cook there, Bob Calderone, taught me everything I ever needed to know about food. Beyond being an extremely talented chef, Bob balances excellence and easy-going tranquility (a rarity in the food world)—no pot-throwing tantrums in Bob's kitchen.

This dish was one of the staples on Bob's menu and one of the finer roast birds I've ever tried. In the late afternoon, an hour or so before dinner, Bob would start up a large wood fire on the grill, then set a couple of dozen birds on a rack about four feet above the fire, far enough away that the flames jumping off the thick logs just gently crisped and smoked the birds.

While it may be hard to reproduce Bob's grill set-up, the flavorings are pretty simple. Cover a bird or two with a paste of salt, garlic, and plenty of herbs, let sit overnight to allow the flavors to mix and meld, then grill over a moderate flame until the chicken is just done. Simple and wonderful.

FOR 1 BIRD	FOR 2 BIRDS	
1	2	3½- to 4-pound chicken(s), spatchcocked (p. 23), rinsed and patted dry with paper towels
2½ teaspoons	5 teaspoons	kosher salt
1 teaspoon	2 teaspoons	freshly ground black pepper
3	6	cloves garlic, coarsely chopped
2 teaspoons	4 teaspoons	chopped fresh thyme
2 teaspoons	2 teaspoons	chopped fresh rosemary
2 teaspoons	4 teaspoons	chopped fresh marjoram
1	1	lemon, cut into wedges, for serving

1. Rub the chicken all over with the salt and pepper. In a medium bowl, toss together the garlic, thyme, and rosemary, then pat all over the chicken. Set it in a zip-top bag (you might want to use a couple to keep the smell contained—the garlic is powerful stuff), and let sit for at least 4 and up to 24 hours in the refrigerator. (If you've brined the chicken, reduce the amount of salt in the herb rub to ½ teaspoon and proceed with the rest of the recipe.)

2. Prepare a charcoal fire or heat up the gas grill (heat all burners to medium-low). For a charcoal fire, pile a couple of layers of briquettes on one side and a sparse single layer of charcoal on the other side of the grill so that you end up with a moderate zone and a cool zone. Your fire should be ready when the briquettes are mostly gray (or, if you're using hardwood, when they are red hot).

3. Set the chicken on the grill (on the hotter part of the charcoal grill) skin-side down, cover on the gas grill, and cook until the skin starts to brown (checking occasionally to avoid burning), 10 to 15 minutes. Gently flip the chicken (I like using tongs and a large metal spatula in tandem), then reduce the heat to low on the gas grill or transfer the chicken to the cooler side of the fire on the charcoal grill. Cover (with the vents open on the charcoal grill) and cook, checking occasionally to ensure that the chicken is not burning, until it's nicely browned all over and an instant-read thermometer inserted into the thickest part of the thigh registers 165°F to 170°F—this should take another 25 to 30 minutes.

4. Let rest for 5 to 10 minutes, then carve the chicken and serve immediately with a squeeze of lemon.

Perk It Up: Cinnamon and Cider Brine (p. 9) soaks pleasant spice and sweetness into the bird before cooking.

On the Side: Mashed Potatoes with Lemon and Black Pepper (p. 85) and Green Beans with Balsamic Vinegar and Almonds (p. 73) or Braised Garlicky Collard Greens (p. 43).

The Second Time Around: This mild, grilled bird will go nicely in any salad, sandwiches, or stew where its garlic and herb flavoring will add some depth.

Italian Grilled Chicken Under a Brick with Smoky Balsamic Tomatoes

Serves at least 4

This is my take on the Italian classic *pollo al mattone*, or chicken under a brick. The brick weighs down the bird, giving it impressive grill marks and helping it cook quickly and evenly. Chances are you won't have a brick lying around. In that case, just use a heavy, flame-proof skillet (I pull out my cast-iron pan). If you do have a brick, wrap it in foil first.

FOR 1 BIRD	FOR 2 BIRDS	
1	2	3½- to 4-pound chicken(s), spatchcocked (p. 23), rinsed and patted dry with paper towels
3	5	Cloves garlic, minced
2 tablespoons	¼ cup	chopped fresh oregano, plus more for sprinkling
1 tablespoon	2 tablespoons	chopped fresh thyme
1	2	lemon(s), just the zest, finely grated
		Kosher salt and freshly ground black pepper
8	8	plum tomatoes, cut in half and seeded
1 tablespoon	1 tablespoon	balsamic vinegar

1. Sprinkle each chicken with half the garlic, oregano, and thyme, and all of the lemon zest, 2½ teaspoons salt, and 1 teaspoon pepper. Let sit for at least 1 hour and up to 24 hours in the refrigerator in a zip-top plastic bag for the best results. (If you've brined the chicken, reduce the amount of salt to ½ teaspoon and proceed with the rest of the recipe.)

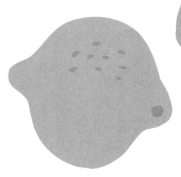

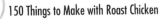

2. In a large bowl, toss the tomatoes with the vinegar, the remaining garlic, oregano, and thyme and 1 teaspoon each salt and pepper. Let sit for at least 15 minutes and up to 1 hour at room temperature.

3. Prepare a charcoal fire or heat up the gas grill (heat all burners to medium-low). For a charcoal fire, pile a couple of layers of briquettes on one side and a sparse single layer of charcoal on the other side of the grill so that you end up with a moderate zone and a cool zone. Your fire should be ready when the briquettes are mostly gray (or, if you're using hardwood, when they are red hot). Set the tomatoes cut side down on the grill (the cooler part of the charcoal grill) and cook, flipping occasionally, until shriveled, completely tender, and charred in places, about 25 minutes. Transfer to a large plate and sprinkle with salt.

4. Meanwhile, set the chicken skin side down on the grill (on the hotter part of the charcoal grill). Set a foil-covered brick or a heavy skillet across the top of the bird. Cover if using a gas grill and cook until the skin starts to brown (checking occasionally to avoid burning), 10 to 15 minutes. Gently flip the chicken (I like using tongs and a large metal spatula to accomplish this), then reduce the heat to low on the gas grill or transfer the chicken to the cooler side of the fire on the charcoal grill. Cover (with the vents open on the charcoal grill) and cook, checking occasionally to ensure it's not burning, until nicely browned all over and an instant-read thermometer inserted into the thickest part of the thigh registers 165°F to 170°F—this should take another 25 to 30 minutes.

5. Let rest for 10 minutes, then carve and serve with the grilled tomatoes.

On the Side: Mashed Potatoes with Lemon and Black Pepper (p. 85).

The Second Time Around: The smokiness of this grilled bird will go nicely in any dish where its garlic and herb flavoring can add some depth, particularly a pasta where you can add any leftover tomatoes.

Grilled Chicken Teriyaki with Scallions

Serves at least 4

A couple of years ago I visited a buddy of mine who was cooking in Japan at one of Osaka's most acclaimed *kaiseki* restaurants. *Kaiseki* is an elegant and elaborate form of dining based on the Japanese tea ceremonies. As excited as I was to eat at my friend's restaurant, I loved our subsequent visits to the street vendors even more. Teriyaki—thin, grilled strips of chicken or beef—was my favorite. The glazed chicken, marinated in a sharp mix of soy, ginger, sake, and sugar, was neither too salty nor too sweet. Both tastes were balanced with a pleasant smokiness, which I think I've achieved here in my version. As with the other glazes in this book, take care to avoid burning. Maintaining a steady, low fire and staying vigilant are the keys to success.

FOR 1 BIRD	FOR 2 BIRDS	
2 tablespoons	¼ cup	minced garlic
2 tablespoons	¼ cup	peeled and minced fresh ginger
¾ cup	1½ cups	soy sauce
1 tablespoon	2 tablespoons	toasted sesame oil
1	2	3½- to 4-pound chicken(s), spatch-cocked (p. 23), rinsed and patted dry with paper towels
3 tablespoons	6 tablespoons	canola or peanut oil
¼ cup	½ cup	firmly packed light brown sugar
¼ cup	½ cup	honey
3 tablespoons	6 tablespoons	rice vinegar
¼ teaspoon	½ teaspoon	crushed red pepper flakes
1½ tablespoons	3 tablespoons	cornstarch
¼ cup	¼ cup	water
½ bunch	½ bunch	scallions, trimmed
		Kosher salt

1. In a small bowl, mix together half the garlic, ginger, and soy sauce, and all of the sesame oil. Set it in a zip-top bag along with the chicken, close the bag, massage the two together, and let sit for at least 1 and up to 24 hours in the refrigerator. (If you've brined the chicken, skip this step and proceed with the rest of the recipe.)

2. Make the teriyaki sauce: In a small saucepan over medium-high heat, heat the remaining garlic and ginger with 2 tablespoons of the canola oil until they sizzle steadily and just start to brown, about 2 minutes. Stir in the remaining soy sauce, the brown sugar, honey, vinegar, and red pepper flakes and bring to a boil. In a small bowl, stir the cornstarch with the water until well combined, then whisk into the sauce and bring to a boil so the sauce thickens. Remove from the heat and let cool. (This will keep in the refrigerator up to 1 week.)

3. Prepare a charcoal fire or heat up the gas grill (heat all burners to medium-low). For a charcoal fire, pile a couple of layers of briquettes on one side and a sparse single layer of charcoal on the other side of the grill so that you end up with a moderate zone and a cool zone. Your fire should be ready when the briquettes are mostly gray (or, if you're using hardwood, when they are red hot). Set the chicken on the grill (on the hotter part of the charcoal grill) skin side down, cover (if using a gas grill) and cook until the skin starts to brown (checking occasionally to avoid burning), about 10 minutes. Flip the chicken and reduce the heat to low on the gas grill or transfer the chicken to the cooler side of the fire on the charcoal grill.

4. Divide the teriyaki sauce between two small bowls. Use one of the bowls to brush the glaze all over the top of the bird. Cover with the vents open on the charcoal grill and cook, checking occasionally to ensure that it's not burning, until nicely browned all over and an instant-read thermometer inserted into the thickest part of the thigh registers 165°F to 170°F—this should take another 25 to 30 minutes.

5. Meanwhile, toss the scallions with the remaining canola oil and sprinkle lightly with salt. Set on the cooler part of the grill and cook, flipping every couple of minutes, until browned and tender, 10 to 15 minutes. (If you don't have enough space on the grill, you can grill them while the chicken rests off the grill.)

6. Transfer the chicken to a carving board, brush all over with the remaining teriyaki glaze and let rest for 5 to 10 minutes. Then carve and serve immediately with the scallions.

Perk It Up: To soak the flavors of the glaze all the way into the bird, try brining with Soy-Ginger Brine (p. 9) and skipping the marinade (step 1).

On the Side: Steamed basmati rice and Stir-Fried Broccoli (p. 72).

The Second Time Around: Not surprisingly, this grilled bird works well in Asian dishes like fried rice or lo mein.

STOVETOP VEGETABLES SIDES

As much as I like roasting vegetables, when I'm in a hurry, I'll often cook vegetables on the stovetop while the bird is in the oven. Most of these preparations are quick, leaning toward the stir-fry or sauté end of the spectrum and following a simple formula: I brown the vegetables with aromatics like garlic, onions, and shallots. Then I add some sort of flavorful liquid and cook the vegetables until they've reached the proper level of tenderness. For broccoli, this means crisp-tender, while more hearty vegetables like carrots or Brussels sprouts are best cooked until fully tender.

Brussels Sprouts with Bacon, Apple, and Sage

Serves 4

¼ pound bacon (about 4 slices), cut into thin strips
1 tablespoon olive oil
1 pound Brussels sprouts, trimmed and cut in half (or quartered, if large)
½ Granny Smith apple, peeled, cored, and diced
Kosher salt and freshly ground black pepper
¼ cup apple juice
1 tablespoon cider vinegar
¼ cup freshly grated Parmesan cheese
1 tablespoon chopped fresh sage

1. Cook the bacon with the oil in a large, heavy skillet over medium heat until it browns and renders much of its fat, about 6 minutes (reduce the heat if it begins to burn). Transfer to a large plate lined with paper towels and set aside.

2. Add the Brussels sprouts and apple to the skillet, sprinkle generously with salt and pepper (about ½ teaspoon each) and cook, stirring, until both begin to brown, about 3 minutes. Add the apple juice and vinegar, reduce the heat to a gentle simmer, cover with the lid slightly askew, and cook until the sprouts are tender but toothy, about 6 minutes. Season with salt and pepper to taste, sprinkle with the Parmesan, sage, and crisp bacon, and serve immediately.

Stir-Fried Broccoli

Serves 4

2 tablespoons canola or peanut oil
1 pound broccoli, cut into 1-inch florets
1 red bell pepper, cored, seeded, and cut into thin strips
3 cloves garlic, smashed
½ teaspoon kosher salt
2 tablespoons soy sauce
1½ tablespoons rice vinegar
1 teaspoon light brown sugar
1 teaspoon toasted sesame oil
3 tablespoons water

1. Heat the oil in a heavy 12-inch skillet over medium-high heat until shimmering hot, about 1½ minutes. Add the broccoli, bell pepper, and garlic, sprinkle with the salt and cook, stirring often, until the vegetables are browned in places, 3 to 4 minutes.

2. Whisk the remaining ingredients together in a large bowl. Add to the vegetables, stir well, reduce the heat to medium-low, and cover with the lid slightly askew. Cook the vegetables until just crisp-tender, about 3 minutes. Serve immediately.

Orange-Glazed Carrots

Serves 4

3 tablespoons unsalted butter
1½ pounds carrots, sliced 1 inch thick on the diagonal
Kosher salt and freshly ground black pepper
1 cup water
Juice and finely grated zest of 2 navel oranges
2 tablespoons light brown sugar
½ teaspoon ground cinnamon
Large pinch of ground allspice
3 tablespoons chopped fresh parsley

Melt 2 tablespoons of the butter in a large sauté pan over medium-high heat. Add the carrots, sprinkle with salt and pepper (about ½ teaspoon each) and cook, tossing, until they start to brown, about 5 minutes. Add the water, orange juice, brown sugar, cinnamon, and allspice. Bring to a boil, then reduce to a steady simmer, cover with the lid slightly askew, and cook until the carrots are just tender, about 15 minutes. Remove the lid, increase the heat to medium-high and cook, stirring, until most of the liquid reduces and the carrots become glazy, about 5 minutes. Stir in the remaining 1 tablespoon of butter and the orange zest and serve sprinkled with parsley.

Snap Peas and Carrots with Lemon

Serves 4

2 tablespoons olive oil
½ pound carrots, peeled and cut into ¼-inch-thick rounds
1 medium-size yellow onion, cut in half and sliced into very thin half moons
¾ pound snap peas, trimmed
Kosher salt and freshly ground black pepper
¼ cup low-salt chicken broth
2 tablespoons unsalted butter
Grated zest of 1 lemon
3 tablespoons chopped fresh parsley

Heat the oil in a large skillet over medium-high heat until shimmering hot, about 1½ minutes. Add the carrots, onion, and snap peas, sprinkle with ½ teaspoon each salt and pepper, and cook, stirring, until the onion is browned in places and the carrots and peas are crisp-tender, about 5 minutes. Add the broth, reduce the heat to a gentle simmer, cover with the lid askew, and cook until the vegetables are tender but toothy, about 5 minutes. Stir in the butter and lemon zest, season with salt and pepper to taste, and serve with a sprinkling of the parsley.

Green Beans with Balsamic Vinegar and Almonds

Serves 4

2 tablespoons olive oil
3 cloves garlic, smashed
1 pound green beans, trimmed
¾ teaspoon kosher salt, plus more to taste
1 tablespoon balsamic vinegar
1 tablespoon honey
¼ cup water
2 tablespoons unsalted butter, cut into 4 or 5 pieces
3 ounces slivered almonds (about ⅓ cup), toasted on a baking sheet at 375°F until browned and fragrant
1 teaspoon chopped fresh thyme
Freshly ground black pepper

Heat the oil and the garlic in a large sauté pan over medium heat, stirring a few times, until the garlic browns and becomes fragrant, about 3 minutes. Add the green beans, sprinkle with the salt and cook, stirring often, until they start to brown and shrivel a bit, 3 to 4 minutes. In a small cup, stir together the vinegar, honey, and water. Add to the beans and toss well, then reduce the heat to low, cover, and cook until the beans are tender, about 5 minutes. Swirl in the butter, almonds, and thyme. Season with salt and pepper to taste and serve immediately.

Grill-Roasted Jamaican Jerk Chicken

Serves at least 4

Jerk chicken is one of those iconic regional dishes, like Southern ribs or New England fried clams, that must be treated respectfully—that is, with a nod to tradition. My version includes all the standard flavorings—a mix of allspice, nutmeg, clove, and cinnamon bolstered by the heat of a jalapeno and the aromatic punch of fresh ginger and garlic.

FOR 1 BIRD	FOR 2 BIRDS	
2	4	shallots, finely diced
1	2	jalapeño(s), cored, seeded, and finely diced
4	8	cloves garlic, minced
1 tablespoon	2 tablespoons	peeled and minced fresh ginger
1 tablespoon	2 tablespoons	kosher salt
1 teaspoon	2 teaspoons	freshly ground black pepper
½ teaspoon	1 teaspoon	ground cinnamon
½ teaspoon	1 teaspoon	ground allspice
¼ teaspoon	½ teaspoon	ground nutmeg
¼ teaspoon	½ teaspoon	ground cloves
1 tablespoon	2 tablespoons	olive oil
1	2	3½- to 4-pound chicken(s), spatchcocked (p. 23), rinsed and patted dry with paper towels
1	2	lime(s), cut into wedges, for serving

1. Place all the ingredients except the chicken and lime in a food processor or mortar and pestle and pulse or pound until you have a thick paste. Rub this evenly all over the chicken, then seal in a zip-top plastic bag (you might want to use a couple to contain the smell) and refrigerate for at least 8 and up to 24 hours. (If you've brined the chicken, reduce the amount of salt to ½ teaspoon and proceed with the rest of the recipe.)

2. Prepare a charcoal fire or heat up the gas grill (heat all burners to medium-low). For a charcoal fire, pile a couple of layers of briquettes on one side and a sparse single layer of charcoal on the other side of the grill so that you end up with a moderate zone and a cool zone. Your fire should be ready when the briquettes are mostly gray (or, if you're using hardwood, when they are red hot).

3. Set the chicken on the grill (on the hotter part of the charcoal grill) skin side down, cover if using a gas grill and cook until the skin starts to brown (checking occasionally to avoid burning), 10 to 15 minutes. Gently flip the chicken (I like using tongs and a large metal spatula to accomplish this), then reduce the heat to low on the gas grill or transfer the chicken to the cooler side of the fire on the charcoal grill. Cover, with the vents open on the charcoal grill, and cook, checking occasionally to ensure that it's not burning, until nicely browned all over and an instant-read thermometer inserted into the thickest part of the thigh registers 165°F to 170°F—this should take another 25 to 30 minutes.

4. Let rest for 5 to 10 minutes, then carve the chicken and serve immediately with a squeeze of lime.

On the Side: While you're grilling, throw on some red bell peppers, sliced red onions, and zucchini brushed with oil, then serve everything with steamed white rice.

The Second Time Around: Because of its strong flavoring, use this chicken in dishes where it will complement but not overpower the rest of the ingredients. I like it in curries, salads, and sandwiches.

Southern Spiced Chicken with Chipotle-Honey BBQ Sauce

Serves at least 4

While I don't have the experience or know-how of the Southern pitmasters, I have become obsessed with barbeque sauces. Here are two of my favorites. One is a traditional slow-cook-and-simmer sauce, while the other is a no-cook sauce with a surprising depth of flavor. Go with whichever one suits your schedule and mood.

FOR 1 BIRD	FOR 2 BIRDS	
2½ teaspoons	5 teaspoons	kosher salt
2 teaspoons	4 teaspoons	chili powder
1 teaspoon	2 teaspoons	garlic powder
1 teaspoon	2 teaspoons	freshly ground black pepper
1 teaspoon	1 teaspoon	light brown sugar
¼ teaspoon	½ teaspoon	onion powder
pinch	large pinch	cayenne pepper
1	2	3½- to 4-pound chicken(s), spatchcocked (p. 23), rinsed and patted dry with paper towels
		Barbecue sauce of your choice

1. In a small bowl, mix together the salt and all the spices, then rub evenly all over the chicken, including the cavity. Let sit for at least 30 minutes or seal in a zip-top plastic bag and refrigerate up to 24 hours. (If you've brined the chicken, reduce the salt in the spice rub to ½ teaspoon and proceed with the rest of the recipe.)

2. Prepare a charcoal fire or heat up the gas grill (heat all burners to medium-low). For a charcoal fire, pile a couple of layers of briquettes on one side and a sparse single layer of charcoal on the other side of the grill so that you end up with a moderate zone and a cool zone. Your fire should be ready when the briquettes are mostly gray (or, if you're using hardwood, when they are red hot).

3. Set the chicken on the grill (on the hotter part of the charcoal grill) skin side down, cover (if using a gas grill) and cook until the skin starts to brown (checking occasionally to avoid burning), 10 to 15 minutes. Gently flip the chicken (I like using tongs and a large metal spatula to accomplish this), then reduce the heat to low on the gas grill or transfer the chicken to the cooler side of the fire on the charcoal grill. Cover with the vents open on a charcoal grill and cook, checking occasionally to ensure that it's not burning, until nicely browned all over and an instant-read thermometer inserted into the thickest part of the thigh registers 165°F to 170°F—this should take another 25 to 30 minutes. Let rest for 5 to 10 minutes, then carve the chicken and drizzle with either sauce.

On the Side: Braised Garlicky Collard Greens (p. 43) and Your Basic Mashed Potatoes (p. 84).

The Second Time Around: This chicken with the barbecue sauce makes one great sandwich.

Slow-Cooked Chipotle-Honey BBQ Sauce

Makes about 4 cups

2 tablespoons vegetable oil
1 medium onion, finely diced
Kosher salt
2 teaspoons chili powder
2 teaspoons paprika
One 28-ounce can tomato purée
¼ cup tomato paste
¼ cup cider vinegar
¼ cup honey
3 tablespoons light brown sugar
3 tablespoons Worcestershire sauce
2 canned chipotle chiles, plus 2 tablespoons of the adobo sauce
2 tablespoons Dijon mustard
Freshly ground black pepper

In a medium saucepan over medium heat, heat the oil, then add the onion. Season lightly with salt and cook, stirring, until translucent, about 4 minutes. Add the chili powder and paprika and cook, stirring, for 30 seconds. Stir in the rest of the ingredients, reduce the heat to medium-low, and simmer until thickened slightly, about 30 minutes. Remove from the heat, season generously with salt and pepper to taste, and let cool to room temperature. Purée using an immersion blender or by batches in a regular blender. (This will keep, tightly covered, in the refrigerator up to 1 week or in the freezer up to 1 month.)

Quick Chipotle-Honey BBQ Sauce

Makes about 1 cup

½ cup honey
¼ cup cider vinegar
3 tablespoons tomato paste
1 canned chipotle chile, minced, plus 2 tablespoons of the adobo sauce
1 teaspoon Dijon mustard
Kosher salt and freshly ground black pepper

Stir together the honey, vinegar, tomato paste, chipotle and adobo sauce, and mustard in a small bowl until well combined. Season with salt and pepper to taste. (This will keep, tightly covered, in the refrigerator for up to 1 week.)

 A World of Roast Chicken 77

Sear-Roasted Chicken with Tomatoes and Rosemary

Serves at least 4

This is a high-heat version of chicken cacciatore. A sprinkling of tomatoes, herbs, and wine mixes with the chicken juices during roasting to form a light sauce that's great drizzled on the finished bird. There are many ways you can build on this basic recipe if you like. Stir some caramelized onions or sautéed peppers into the tomato broth to give it some sweetness. Or enrich it with a sprinkle of crumbled crisp bacon or pancetta, or cooked cannellini beans.

FOR 1 BIRD	FOR 2 BIRDS	
		Kosher salt and freshly ground black pepper
1	2	3½- to 4-pound chicken(s), spatchcocked (p. 23), rinsed, and patted dry with paper towels
1 tablespoon	2 tablespoons	olive oil
1 tablespoon	2 tablespoons	unsalted butter, softened
1½ pounds	3 pounds	plum tomatoes, cut into 1-inch pieces
4	8	cloves garlic, smashed
1 tablespoon	2 tablespoons	chopped fresh rosemary
½ teaspoon	1 teaspoon	crushed red pepper flakes
½ cup	1 cup	dry white wine

1. Sprinkle 2½ teaspoons salt and ½ teaspoon black pepper all over each chicken and let sit for up to 24 hours, uncovered, in the refrigerator. (If you've brined the chicken, skip this step. Just sprinkle the bird with ½ teaspoon salt and ½ teaspoon black pepper and proceed with the rest of the recipe.)

2. Preheat the oven to 425°F. Set an oven rack to the middle position. Set a large, heavy skillet over medium-high heat for 1½ minutes (if you're cooking two birds, you'll need two skillets). Turn your oven vent on high; this is going to smoke a bit. Add the oil and the butter and cook until the foam is almost gone and the butter starts to brown, about 1 minute.

Add the chicken, skin side down, and cook until nicely browned, about 5 minutes. Remove from the heat and flip the chicken.

3. In a medium bowl, toss the tomatoes with the garlic, rosemary, red pepper flakes, and 1 teaspoon each salt and black pepper for each bird. Scatter this around the pan, pour in the wine, and transfer to the oven. Cook until an instant-read thermometer inserted into the thickest part of the thigh registers 165°F to 170°F, 25 to 30 minutes.

4. Transfer the chicken to a cutting board and let rest 5 to 10 minutes. Set the pan over medium-high heat and cook until the liquid is reduced by about half, about 3 minutes. Add salt and pepper to taste. Carve the bird and serve with a spoonful of the tomato sauce.

On the Side: Simple Sautéed Spinach (p. 43) or Roasted Fennel and Pears (p. 51).

The Second Time Around: This Italian-inspired roast bird works well in other Mediterranean preparations. If you have any of the tomato jus left over, stir it into a pasta sauce or a stew.

Sear-Roasted Chicken with Bacon and Herbed Potatoes

Serves at least 4

No matter what I'm cooking, when in doubt, I'll add a handful of herbs and some crisped bacon. In this dish, sear the chicken first, then sprinkle some bacon, potatoes, and herbs around the perimeter of the skillet. Transfer the skillet to the oven, where the chicken will finish cooking while the potatoes, herbs, and bacon do their thing.

FOR 1 BIRD	FOR 2 BIRDS	
		Kosher salt and freshly ground black pepper
1	2	3½- to 4-pound chicken(s), spatchcocked (p. 23), rinsed, and patted dry with paper towels
1 tablespoon	2 tablespoons	olive oil
1 tablespoon	2 tablespoons	unsalted butter
1 pound	2 pounds	small Yukon Gold potatoes, cut into 1-inch pieces
1	2	large red onion, cut in half and thinly sliced into half moons
3 ounces	6 ounces	bacon, cut into thin strips
2 teaspoons	4 teaspoons	chopped fresh thyme
2 teaspoon	4 teaspoons	chopped fresh rosemary
¼ cup	½ cup	chopped fresh parsley (optional)

1. Sprinkle 2½ teaspoons salt and ½ teaspoon black pepper all over each chicken and let sit for up to 24 hours, uncovered, in the refrigerator. (If you've brined the chicken, skip this step. Just sprinkle the bird with ½ teaspoon salt and ½ teaspoon black pepper and proceed with the rest of the recipe.)

2. Preheat the oven to 425°F. Set an oven rack to the middle position. Set a large, heavy skillet over medium-high heat for 1½ minutes (if you're cooking two birds, you'll need two skillets). Turn your oven vent on high; this is going to smoke. Add the oil and the butter and cook until the foam from the butter is almost gone and the butter starts to brown, about 1 minute. Add the chicken, skin side down, and cook until nicely browned, about 5 minutes. Remove from the heat, flip the chicken, and spoon off all but about 1 tablespoon of the fat.

3. In a large bowl, toss the potatoes, onion, bacon, thyme, and rosemary together, then scatter all around and under the chicken. Transfer the pan to the oven and cook until an instant-read thermometer inserted into the thickest part of the thigh registers 165°F to 170°F, 25 to 30 minutes.

4. Transfer the chicken to a cutting board and let rest for 10 minutes. Meanwhile, return the skillet to the oven to finish browning the potatoes and onions, another 10 minutes, stirring occasionally. Carve the bird and serve with the potatoes, sprinkled with the parsley, if using.

On the Side: Simple Sautéed Spinach (p. 43) and Roasted Beets with Shallots and Thyme (p. 50).

The Second Time Around: This chicken is mild enough to be used in almost any dish. Any leftover potatoes would make a delicious addition to a soup or stew.

Sear-Roasted Chicken with Lots of Garlic

Serves at least 4

This dish is a riff on the bistro classic famed for its 40 cloves of garlic. I'm not much for counting, so I simply shoot for a lot of garlic. While in the traditional version, the chicken is braised with the garlic in a Dutch oven or casserole, I like sear-roasting the bird in this preparation. The skin crisps while the rest of the chicken soaks up the garlicky flavor.

FOR 1 BIRD	FOR 2 BIRDS	
		Kosher salt and freshly ground black pepper
1	2	3½- to 4-pound chicken(s), spatchcocked (p. 23), rinsed, and patted dry with paper towels
1 tablespoon	2 tablespoons	olive oil
1 tablespoons	2 tablespoons	unsalted butter
2 heads	4 heads	garlic, broken into individual cloves, smashed, and peeled
2 teaspoons	4 teaspoons	chopped fresh thyme
2 teaspoons	4 teaspoons	chopped fresh rosemary
¾ cup	1½ cups	low-salt chicken broth

1. Sprinkle 2½ teaspoons salt and ½ teaspoon black pepper all over each chicken and let sit for up to 24 hours, uncovered, in the refrigerator. (If you've brined the chicken, skip this step. Just sprinkle the bird with ½ teaspoon salt and ½ teaspoon black pepper and proceed with the rest of the recipe.)

2. Preheat the oven to 425°F. Set an oven rack to the middle position. Set a large, heavy skillet over medium-high heat for 1½ minutes (if you're cooking two birds, you'll need two skillets). Turn your oven vent on high; this is going to smoke a bit. Add the oil and the butter and cook until the foam is almost gone and the butter starts to brown, about 1 minute. Add the chicken, skin side down, and cook until nicely browned, about 5 minutes.

3. Remove the pan from the heat, flip the chicken, and scatter the garlic, thyme, and rosemary around the sides and under the bird. Set in the oven and cook until an instant-read thermometer inserted into the thickest part of the thigh registers 165°F to 170°F, 25 to 30 minutes.

4. Transfer the chicken to a carving board and let rest 5 to 10 minutes. Spoon off and discard most of the fat from the skillet and set it over medium-high heat. Add the broth and cook, stirring to scrape up any browned bits on the bottom of the pan, until it reduces by about half, about 5 minutes. Carve the bird and serve with the garlic cloves and a spoonful of the pan sauce.

Perk It Up: Build on this simple bird with a pat of Shallot-Herb Butter (p. 61) or a drizzle of Thyme-Mustard Vinaigrette (p. 98).

On the Side: Mashed Potatoes with Black Olives and Sun-Dried Tomatoes (p. 84) and Brussels Sprouts with Bacon, Apple, and Sage (p. 72)

The Second Time Around: Despite the abundance of garlic cloves, this chicken is mildly flavored and is a nice choice for most any dish. Purée any leftover garlic cloves into a paste and use as a spread on sandwiches or in a soup for added richness.

THE BEST MASHED POTATOES

I *like* mashed potatoes, though it seems like most everyone else on the planet *loves* mashed potatoes. Mashed potatoes do go well with roast chicken and, by adding a few bright flavors to the fluffy spuds, you can take them in a totally different direction to match the meal.

Good mashed potatoes are not hard to make. The trick is in getting them soft and creamy without resorting to gobs of butter or cream. Below I've included a basic method for mashed potatoes as well as a number of variations.

Your Basic Mashed Potatoes

Serves 4 to 6

> 2 pounds russet potatoes, peeled
>   and cut into 1½-inch pieces
> 3 cloves garlic, smashed
> Kosher salt
> ⅔ cup whole milk, more if needed
> ¼ cup unsalted butter
> Freshly ground black pepper

1. Set the potatoes and garlic in a medium pot, cover with at least 2 inches of water, and add 1 tablespoon salt. Bring to a boil, reduce the heat to a simmer, cover, and cook with the lid slightly askew until the potatoes are completely softened, about 15 minutes (test by poking with a wooden skewer or a paring knife). Drain well and return the potatoes to the pot.

2. Meanwhile, heat the milk and butter over medium-low heat until the butter is melted. Add the milk mixture to the drained potatoes and mash thoroughly with a masher or a whisk until smooth. Add 1 or 2 tablespoons of milk if the potatoes are dry. Season with salt and pepper to taste and serve, or use in one of the mashed potato recipes that follow.

Mashed Potatoes with Black Olives and Sun-Dried Tomatoes

Serves 4 to 6

> ½ cup pitted black olives, drained and chopped
> 8 oil-packed sun-dried tomatoes, thinly sliced
> ½ cup freshly grated Parmesan cheese
> ¼ cup chopped fresh parsley or thinly sliced
>   scallions, plus more for sprinkling
> 1 recipe Your Basic Mashed Potatoes

Mash all of the ingredients into the potatoes and serve with a sprinkling of the parsley.

Mashed Potatoes with Olive Oil, Rosemary, and Thyme

Serves 4 to 6

> 3 tablespoons extra-virgin olive oil
> 2 teaspoons finely chopped fresh rosemary
> 2 teaspoons chopped fresh thyme
> 1 recipe Your Basic Mashed Potatoes

Mash all of the ingredients into the potatoes and serve.

Mashed Potatoes with Cheddar, Chiles, and Scallions

Serves 4 to 6

- 1 cup shredded sharp Cheddar cheese (about 1/4 pound)
- 4 scallions (white and green parts), trimmed and thinly sliced
- 1 canned chipotle chile, minced, plus 2 tablespoons of the adobo sauce
- 1/4 teaspoon chili powder
- 1 recipe Your Basic Mashed Potatoes
- 1/2 cup sour cream

Mash half of the Cheddar, three quarters of the scallions, the chipotle chile, the adobo sauce, and the chili powder into the mashed potatoes. Serve with the sour cream and a sprinkling of the remaining Cheddar and scallions.

Mashed Potatoes with Lemon and Black Pepper

Serves 4 to 6

- 1 recipe Your Basic Mashed Potatoes
- 1 cup shredded Pecorino Romano
- 2 tablespoons chopped fresh oregano
- Freshly grated zest of 1 lemon
- 1 tablespoon lemon juice, more to taste
- 1 teaspoon freshly ground black pepper

Mash all of the ingredients into the potatoes and serve with a sprinkling of the herbs.

Leek and Parmesan Mashed Potatoes

Serves 4 to 6

- 2 tablespoons unsalted butter,
- 1 pound leeks (white and light green parts), cut into 1/2-inch dice, soaked in water to cover, drained, and patted dry
- Kosher salt
- 2 teaspoons chopped fresh rosemary
- Freshly grated zest of 1 lemon
- 1/2 cup freshly grated Parmesan cheese
- 1 recipe Your Basic Mashed Potatoes
- Freshly ground black pepper

Melt the butter in a large saucepan over medium heat. Add the leeks, sprinkle generously with salt (about 1 teaspoon), and cook, stirring often until the leeks soften completely and start to brown, about 8 minutes. Mash the leeks, rosemary, lemon zest, and Parmesan into the potatoes. Season with salt and pepper to taste.

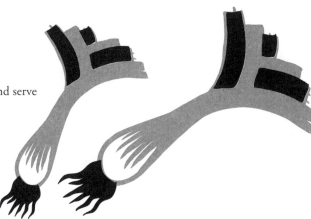

 A World of Roast Chicken 85

Sear-Roasted Chicken with Spring Onions and Asparagus

Serves at least 4

I love making this chicken in the spring and early summer when I can find fresh asparagus and onions at the local farmer's market. Spring onions are similar to their year-round counterparts, only fresher and sweeter. Do use thick asparagus if you can find them—they're just as sweet as the thinner spears and have a pleasant meaty texture that holds up nicely to roasting.

FOR 1 BIRD	FOR 2 BIRDS	
		Kosher salt and freshly ground black pepper
1	2	3½- to 4-pound chicken(s), spatchcocked (p. 23), rinsed, and patted dry with paper towels
1 tablespoon	2 tablespoons	olive oil
1 tablespoon	2 tablespoons	unsalted butter, softened
¾ pound	1½ pounds	asparagus (preferably thick), fibrous ends snapped off, cut into 2–inch pieces
½ pound	1 pound	spring onions or small red onions, thinly sliced
3	6	cloves garlic, smashed
1 tablespoon	2 tablespoons	chopped fresh thyme

1. Sprinkle 2½ teaspoons salt and ½ teaspoon black pepper all over each chicken and let sit for up to 24 hours, uncovered, in the refrigerator. (If you've brined the chicken, skip this step. Just sprinkle the bird with ½ teaspoon salt and ½ teaspoon black pepper and proceed with the rest of the recipe.)

2. Preheat the oven to 425°F. Set an oven rack to the middle position. Set a large, heavy skillet over medium-high heat for 1½ minutes (if you're cooking two birds, you'll need two skillets). Turn your oven vent on high; this is going to smoke a bit. Add the oil and the butter and cook until the foam is almost gone and the butter starts to brown, about 1 minute. Add the chicken, skin side down, and cook until nicely browned, about 5 minutes.

3. Flip the chicken, scatter the asparagus, onions, garlic, and thyme under the bird and around the pan, and transfer to the oven. Cook until the chicken is browned all over and an instant-read thermometer inserted into the thickest part of the thigh registers 165°F to 170°F, 25 to 30 minutes.

4. Transfer the chicken to a carving board and let rest 5 to 10 minutes. Set the vegetables on a serving platter and tent with foil. Skim off the fat from the pan juices. Carve the bird and serve with the vegetables and some of the pan juices.

Perk It Up: A drizzle of Balsamic Sun-Dried Tomato Vinaigrette (p. 61) or Black Olive and Sherry Vinaigrette (p. 60) goes nicely with the vegetables in this dish.

On the Side: Leek and Parmesan Mashed Potatoes (p. 85) or Mashed Potatoes with Lemon and Black Pepper (p. 85)

The Second Time Around: This mildly flavored chicken and any leftover vegetables work nicely in soups, stews, braises, and pastas.

 A World of Roast Chicken   87

Chapter 3
Super Salads

Salads and leftover chicken were meant

for each other. A tangy vinaigrette perks up the flavor of cold chicken and revives any dryness in its texture. Crisp greens and vegetables add crunch, color, and interest (of course, they're good for you, too). And, this happy pairing can form a meal. I'm the first to admit that I'm not a salad-for-dinner-kinda guy, but the chicken adds substance and if you serve the salad with some good bread or warm pita, you've got a fine lunch for friends or a light but balanced dinner for the family.

The salads in this chapter break down into two basic categories. The first consists of "salad" salads—classics like Cobb or Caesar—in which a base of leafy greens is sprinkled with colorful toppings, some sort of vinaigrette, and, of course, chicken. The second grouping covers what we traditionally know as chicken salads, or salads where chicken is the focus, not just one of the toppings.

The formula for the green salads is quite simple. Whisk together a vinaigrette—in most cases you can make it a couple days ahead—assemble the greens, prepare any toppings, and set them in a large serving bowl. Once you're ready to serve the salad, toss it with half of the vinaigrette, then drizzle with the remaining vinaigrette as you set it on plates.

The chicken salads are even simpler. Befitting their casual, summery nature, they're easy to throw together, refrigerate, and then set out for a crowd. I've included a few traditional mayonnaise-based chicken salads, as well as others whose ingredients and flavor pairings display a more worldly outlook.

With these recipes, you don't have to get too fussy about what specific leftover roast chicken you use (though I do give you suggestions), as most of the vinaigrettes are assertive enough to point the chicken in the proper flavor direction. One thing I have noticed is that leftover grill-roasted chicken works particularly well in salads. The intense smokiness of grilled chicken stands up nicely to the vinaigrettes and imparts another layer of complexity. Fortunately, grilling season is also salad season, so, fire up the grill and cook a couple of chickens, then toss the leftovers into vibrant salads over the next couple of nights.

Lemony Chicken Caesar Salad with Thyme Croutons

Serves 4 to 6

I almost always order a Caesar salad anytime I see it on a menu. It's a culinary litmus test—a good indicator of a kitchen's prowess. I also like to make it at home. This version is lighter than most as the dressing contains no raw egg, which helps avoid health hazards. As for anchovies, I fall somewhere in the middle on that debate. Here, I leave them out for the sake of simplicity. If you're an anchovy fan, go crazy: chop up a couple, and add them to the vinaigrette if you like.

LEMONY CAESAR VINAIGRETTE:

2 tablespoons mascarpone or ricotta cheese
1 teaspoon red wine vinegar
½ teaspoon Worcestershire
2 teaspoons Dijon mustard
1 small clove garlic, minced and mashed
   to a paste (see sidebar on the facing page)
¾ cup olive oil
Juice of 1 lemon
⅓ cup freshly grated Parmesan cheese
Kosher salt and freshly ground black pepper

SALAD:

2 romaine hearts (about ¾ pound), bottoms
   trimmed, cut crosswise into 2-inch-wide strips
⅓ cup freshly grated Parmesan cheese
2 cups Thyme Croutons (recipe follows)
2 cups thinly sliced leftover chicken
Freshly ground black pepper

> ## CHIX PICKS
>
> The smokiness of grill-roasted chicken livens up the simple flavors in this salad. Try Anago's Garlicky Grill-Roasted Split Chickens with Lemon and Herbs (p. 66) or Italian Grilled Chicken Under a Brick with Smoky Balsamic Tomatoes (p. 68).

1. Make the vinaigrette. In a mini-chop or blender, purée the mascarpone, vinegar, Worcestershire, mustard, and garlic. At first, slowly drizzle in the oil, while pureeing, then add in a steadier stream as the mixture thickens and emulsifies. Add half the lemon juice, then the Parmesan. Season generously with salt and pepper to taste (about 1 teaspoon of each) and more lemon juice if you like. Set aside or cover tightly and refrigerate for up to 2 days.

2. Prepare the salad. Add the romaine and half the Parmesan to a large bowl and top with the croutons. Toss the Romaine with half the vinaigrette and taste for salt and pepper. Set the dressed greens onto plates and top each with some of the chicken. Drizzle with the remaining vinaigrette and Parmesan. Sprinkle with pepper and serve immediately.

Thyme Croutons

Makes 2 cups

- ½ pound crusty baguette or country bread, cut into 1-inch pieces
- 2 teaspoons chopped fresh thyme
- 2 tablespoons olive oil
- Kosher salt

Preheat the oven to 450°F. In a medium bowl, toss the bread cubes with the thyme and olive oil and season generously with salt (about ½ teaspoon). Transfer to a large baking sheet and cook, in a single layer, tossing every 5 minutes, until browned and crisp, about 15 minutes. Set aside to cool. Will keep, tightly covered, for 3 to 4 days.

HOW TO MINCE GARLIC FOR A SALAD

For me, there's minced garlic and then there's *minced* garlic. Plain old minced garlic meant for sautés or sauces does not need to be perfectly chopped. Cooking, especially over moderate heat, tends to mellow garlic's flavor, smoothing out any imperfections in the size of the pieces. However, when preparing garlic for dishes in which it will remain raw, such as vinaigrettes or salsas, the cloves need to be minced as fine as possible. Poorly chopped garlic can make for uneven flavoring and unpleasant eating (picture biting into a sizable piece of raw garlic while you're eating your salad).

A mortar and pestle is great for mashing garlic into a fine paste, but it's a little clunky to pull one out for a quick weeknight meal. Instead, I find that you can use a chef's knife to mince garlic just as well. To do so, mince a couple cloves of garlic, sprinkle with about ½ teaspoon salt, and press the side of the chef's knife over the garlic, scraping the flat side of the blade back and forth over it until the garlic becomes a thick paste. After about 3 or 4 scrapes, you should be there. Whisk this garlic paste into your preparation, but remember to use it sparingly, as it's strong stuff.

Southwestern Chicken Salad with Spinach and Chipotle-Balsamic Vinaigrette

Serves 4 to 6

Though they may come from opposite ends of the culinary universe, chipotles and balsamic vinegar make a fine pairing. The sweetness of the vinegar cuts the smoky heat of the peppers, creating a pleasantly spicy vinaigrette. For a little more depth, sprinkle the salad with crisp bacon, canned black beans or fresh corn.

CHIPOTLE-BALSAMIC VINAIGRETTE:

1 canned chipotle in adobo sauce, minced, plus 2 tablespoons of sauce

3 oil-packed sun-dried tomatoes, chopped

2 tablespoons balsamic vinegar

2 teaspoons light brown sugar

2 teaspoons Dijon mustard

½ cup extra-virgin olive oil

Kosher salt and freshly ground black pepper

SALAD:

10 ounces baby spinach

Kosher salt and freshly ground black pepper

2½ cups thinly sliced leftover chicken

1 small red onion, thinly sliced

1 ripe avocado, pitted and diced

3 cups Fried Tortilla Strips (p. 111) or tortilla chips, broken into large pieces

¼ cup lightly packed fresh cilantro leaves

CHIX PICKS

Go with a grill-roasted bird with Tex-Mex or Southwestern flavors. Try a roast chicken with the Southwestern Chile Spice Rub (p. 11) or Grill-Roasted Chicken with Tex-Mex Spice Crust and Grilled Corn Salsa (p. 58)—you can sprinkle the leftover salsa over the salad.

1. Make the vinaigrette. In a large bowl, whisk together the chipotle and sauce, tomatoes, vinegar, brown sugar, and mustard. At first, slowly drizzle in the oil, whisking rapidly, then add in a steadier stream as the mixture thickens and emulsifies. Season generously with salt and pepper to taste (about 1 teaspoon and ½ teaspoon, respectively).

2. Set the spinach in a large bowl. Toss with half the vinaigrette and season with salt and pepper to taste. Set the dressed greens on 4 plates and top with chicken, onion, avocado, and tortilla strips. Drizzle with the remaining vinaigrette, sprinkle with the cilantro, and serve.

Chicken Salad with Blue Cheese, Apple, and Frisée

Serves 4

Frisée has thin green leaves that look like they've been stretched and teased for a trip to the mall in the 1980's. You might also recognize this lettuce as the light green curls in a mesclun salad mix. Here, frisée gives this simple salad a dressy feel, perfect for a casual lunch or light supper with friends. Golden Delicious apples are great for entertaining as you can cut them ahead and they won't turn brown. Assemble all of the salad's ingredients up to a couple of hours before serving, then dress it just before serving.

1½ tablespoons balsamic vinegar
½ teaspoon Dijon mustard
Kosher salt and freshly ground black pepper
⅓ cup extra-virgin olive oil
2 heads frisée, cored and trimmed of dark outer leaves
1 Golden Delicious apple, peeled, cored, and cut into ¼-inch-thick slices
¼ pound blue cheese, crumbled
½ cup chopped walnuts, toasted on a baking sheet at 375°F until lightly browned and fragrant
¼ cup lightly packed fresh tarragon leaves
2 cups sliced leftover chicken

CHIX PICKS

Any mildly flavored roast chicken or grill-roasted chicken will do. Try a roast chicken with Rosemary-Balsamic Glaze (p. 13) or with Lemon-Herb Rub (p. 13).

1. Make the vinaigrette. In a medium bowl, whisk the vinegar and mustard together with ¼ teaspoon salt and a few generous grinds black pepper. Slowly drizzle in the olive oil, whisking so it thickens and forms an emulsion.

2. In a large bowl, gently toss together the frisée, sliced apple, blue cheese, walnuts, and tarragon. Toss this with half the vinaigrette and season with salt and pepper to taste. Top with the chicken, drizzle with the remaining vinaigrette, and serve.

Classic Cobb Salad

Serves 4

As good as this salad is, it has quite a few components, so I generally only make it when I already have at least three or four of the items on hand. It's my leftover version of bingo: Blue cheese? Check. Greens? Check. Leftover chicken? Check. Bingo! I will boil an egg or two, grab some bacon from the freezer, pick up an avocado, and I'm on my way.

VINAIGRETTE:
¼ cup red wine vinegar

2 teaspoons Dijon mustard

⅔ cup extra-virgin olive oil

Kosher salt and freshly ground black pepper

3 tablespoons thinly sliced fresh chives

SALAD:
6 ounces baby spinach

½ pound red leaf lettuce, heavy stems removed, cut into 2-inch pieces

2 cups diced leftover chicken

2 ripe avocados, pitted and diced

6 ounces bacon (about 6 slices), cooked until crisp and coarsely chopped

2 hard-boiled eggs, peeled and coarsely chopped

¼ pound blue cheese, crumbled (about ½ cup)

1 large ripe red tomato, diced

1 large ripe yellow tomato (substitute another red tomato if you can't find yellow), diced

> ## CHIX PICKS
>
> Try a roast chicken with full flavors to match the rich ingredients in this salad, like one slathered with Smoky Chipotle Butter (p. 61) or drizzled with Lime and Jalapeno Vinaigrette (p. 60).

1. Make the vinaigrette. In a medium bowl, whisk together the vinegar and mustard. At first slowly drizzle in the oil, whisking rapidly, then add in a steadier stream as the mixture thickens and emulsifies. Season generously with salt and pepper to taste (about 1 teaspoon of each). Stir in the chives and set aside or refrigerate, tightly covered, for up to 2 days.

2. Scatter the greens on a large serving platter. Top with the chicken, avocado, bacon, eggs, blue cheese, and tomatoes, assembling each topping in a row. Drizzle the salad with half the dressing. Set out the remaining vinaigrette and allow guests to help themselves.

The Chicken and the Egg Spinach Salad

Serves 4

I love eggs for dinner. Maybe it's because I love breakfast so much. Here, the eggs are poached, set atop a bed of baby spinach along with some sliced chicken, then drizzled with a warm bacon dressing (the crisp strips further the breakfast theme). Note, this dressing won't form a perfect emulsion, but that's okay. Simply give it another good whisk just before dressing the salad.

Kosher salt
1 tablespoon distilled white vinegar
4 large eggs
1/4 pound bacon (about 4 thick strips)
2 shallots, finely diced
1 tablespoon Dijon mustard
1/3 cup red wine vinegar
2 teaspoons chopped fresh thyme
1/2 cup extra-virgin olive oil
Freshly ground black pepper
10 ounces baby spinach
2 cups thinly sliced leftover chicken

CHIX PICKS

Try Jerrod's Roast Chicken with Vermont Maple Glaze, Sweet Potatoes, and Sage (p. 35) or Roast Chicken with Rosemary-Mustard Crust and Browned Onions (p. 30)—you can toss any leftover onions from the latter into the salad.

1. Poach the eggs. Fill a large skillet with about 1 1/2 inches of water and bring to a boil. Reduce the heat to medium-low and stir in a couple tablespoons of salt and the white vinegar. Gently crack the eggs into the water and cook until the yolks just begin to set, about 3 minutes. Using a slotted spoon, transfer them to a bowl filled with cold water for about 1 minute, then transfer to a large plate.

2. Meanwhile, in a medium-size, heavy skillet, cook the bacon over medium heat, flipping occasionally, until it browns and renders much of its fat, about 5 minutes. Remove the bacon, drain on paper towels, and crumble once it's cool.

3. Add the shallots to the bacon fat in the skillet and cook, stirring, until translucent and softened, about 2 minutes. Remove the pan from the heat and whisk in the mustard, red wine vinegar, and thyme. Still whisking, slowly drizzle in the olive oil. Season with salt and pepper to taste. Transfer to a large measuring cup.

4. When you're ready to serve, set the spinach in a large bowl. Whisk the dressing well and drizzle half of it over the spinach. Toss well and season with salt and pepper to taste. Divide the spinach among 4 plates, top with the chicken, bacon, and a poached egg, then drizzle with the remaining vinaigrette. Serve immediately.

Arugula, Heirloom Tomato, and Herbed Chicken Salad

Serves 4

This is a farmer's market salad, best made at the height of summer when you have your pick of ripe local tomatoes. Feel free to embellish it with whatever looks good, whether it be summer corn, new potatoes, or sweet onions.

Despite its simplicity, the presentation for this salad is quite impressive. For a little twist, use heirloom tomatoes of different colors, alternating them on the plate. To make curls with Parmesan cheese, use a good-sized block of cheese and a sturdy vegetable peeler (preferably Y-shaped). Use some force to shave off the curls.

2 cups very thinly sliced leftover chicken
3 tablespoons balsamic vinegar
½ cup extra-virgin olive oil
Kosher salt and freshly ground black pepper
½ pound baby arugula, soaked and spun dry
2 large, ripe heirloom tomatoes, thinly sliced
16 Parmesan curls (preferably Parmigiano Reggiano)

1. In a small bowl, toss the chicken with 1 tablespoon of the vinegar and 2 tablespoons of the oil. Sprinkle with salt and pepper to taste.

2. Set the arugula in a large serving bowl and toss with the remaining 2 tablespoons vinegar and 6 tablespoons oil. Season with salt and pepper to taste (about 1 teaspoon and ½ teaspoon, respectively).

3. Fan the tomatoes in circular patterns on 4 plates. Sprinkle generously with salt and pepper (about 1 teaspoon and ½ teaspoon). Top with the chicken and a healthy mound of arugula. Garnish with the Parmesan curls and serve immediately.

CHIX PICKS

Any roast chicken infused with plenty of herbs will go nicely in this salad, like Bistro Roast Chicken with Lemon and Thyme (p. 34) or Sear-Roasted Chicken with Spring Onions and Asparagus (p. 86). If you have any Balsamic-Sun-Dried Tomato Vinaigrette (p. 61) on hand, it would be perfect drizzled over this instead of the oil and vinegar.

Sesame Chicken Salad with Snap Peas and Orange-Soy Dressing

Serves 4

My fiancé, Marguerite, loves snap peas, so I'm constantly looking for ways to work them into dinner. Here, they add crunch to a salad of chicken, cucumbers, and carrots. The salad actually gets better after sitting a bit as the snap peas soak up the sweet flavors of the dressing.

ORANGE-SOY DRESSING:
2 teaspoons Dijon mustard
1/3 cup fresh orange juice
1/2 cup grapeseed or canola oil
2 tablespoons soy sauce
1 tablespoon rice vinegar

SALAD:
2 tablespoons hoisin sauce
1 tablespoon rice vinegar
1 teaspoon toasted sesame oil
2 1/2 cups thinly sliced leftover chicken
10 ounces sugar snap peas, trimmed and cut into 1-inch pieces
1/2 English cucumber, thinly sliced
1 cup shredded carrot
1 1/2 tablespoons sesame seeds, toasted in a dry skillet over medium heat until light brown and fragrant

CHIX PICKS

Try using a roast chicken with Asian flavors like Grilled Chicken Teriyaki with Scallions (p. 70) or Grill-Roasted Thai Chicken with Lemongrass (p. 53).

1. Prepare the dressing. Whisk together the mustard and orange juice in a small bowl. Slowly drizzle in the oil, whisking rapidly, then add in a steadier stream as the mixture thickens and emulsifies. Whisk in the soy sauce and vinegar and set aside for immediate use, or refrigerate, tightly covered, for up to 2 days.

2. In a medium bowl, whisk together the hoisin, vinegar, and sesame oil. Toss with the chicken. Add the snap peas, cucumber, and carrot and toss well. Toss this mixture with half the dressing. Sprinkle with the sesame seeds and serve with the remaining vinaigrette on the side.

Chicken with Haricots Verts, Cherry Tomatoes, and Thyme-Mustard Vinaigrette

Serves 4

This salad incorporates many of the classic ingredients in a niçoise salad, though sliced chicken takes the place of tuna as its centerpiece. I've left the potatoes optional. They're great in the salad, but if you don't have any leftover potatoes on hand simply go without and serve with a couple of slices of good, crusty bread.

THYME-MUSTARD VINAIGRETTE:
3 tablespoons red wine vinegar
1 tablespoon Dijon mustard
½ cup extra-virgin olive oil
1 shallot, finely diced
2 teaspoons finely chopped fresh thyme
Kosher salt and freshly ground black pepper

SALAD:
¾ pound Sweet 100 or other ripe cherry
    or grape tomatoes, cut in half
Kosher salt and freshly ground black pepper
3 cups sliced leftover chicken
2½ cups diced cooked potatoes, preferably
    boiled red potatoes (optional)
10 ounces green beans, trimmed, cut in half,
    blanched in boiling water until tender, about
    2 minutes, plunged into cold water, and drained
1 cup pitted kalamata or gaeta olives, drained and cut in half

> ## CHIX PICKS
>
> Any mildly flavored roast chicken with plenty of herbs will do. Try Greek-Roast Chicken with Lemon, Black Olives, and Potatoes (p. 56) or Roast Chicken with Caramelized Shallots and Fingerling Potatoes (p. 38)—you can use any leftover shallots in the vinaigrette and the potatoes in the salad. If you have any Black Olive and Sherry Vinaigrette (p. 60) left over, substitute that for the Thyme-Mustard Vinaigrette.

1. Make the vinaigrette. In a medium-size bowl, whisk together the vinegar and mustard. At first slowly drizzle in the oil, whisking rapidly, then add in a steadier stream as the mixture thickens and emulsifies. Fold in the shallot and thyme and season generously with salt and pepper to taste (about 1 teaspoon and ½ teaspoon, respectively). You can refrigerate this, tightly covered, for up to 2 days.

2. In a large bowl, sprinkle the tomatoes generously with salt and pepper (about 1 teaspoon each). Toss well. Add the chicken, potatoes (if using), green beans, and olives and toss again. Drizzle the salad with half of the vinaigrette and toss well. Sprinkle with a few generous grinds black pepper. Serve with the remaining vinaigrette on the side. (Note: If you're not using the potatoes, you may not need any additional vinaigrette.)

Warm Asian Slaw with Hoisin Chicken

Serves 6

I love slaws, especially after they've just been tossed—the cabbage still has all of its crunch and a clean flavor. Warming a slaw adds another level of freshness, as the heat just wilts the cabbage and melds it with the different flavors in the dish. Here, warm ginger and scallions infuse the cabbage and the slaw is topped with chicken that has been dressed with hoisin sauce (the Chinese equivalent of barbecue sauce), soy sauce, and rice vinegar. Make sure you use a premium brand of hoisin sauce (I prefer Koon Chun®, and Lee Kum Kee® is quite good, too).

1 small head green cabbage, cored and thinly sliced
1 cup shredded carrots
Kosher salt
¼ cup hoisin sauce
1 tablespoon soy sauce
¼ cup rice vinegar
2½ cups thinly sliced leftover chicken
¼ cup canola or peanut oil
1 tablespoon peeled and minced fresh ginger
6 scallions (white and green parts), trimmed and thinly sliced
2 teaspoons toasted sesame oil
2 teaspoons sesame seeds, toasted in a dry skillet over medium heat until lightly browned and fragrant

> ## CHIX PICKS
>
> Try a grill-roasted chicken with Asian flavors like Grill-Roasted Thai Chicken with Lemongrass (p. 53) or one brushed with Asian Barbecue Glaze (p. 14).

1. In a large bowl, toss the cabbage and carrots with 1 teaspoon salt and let sit for 10 minutes. In a medium bowl, whisk together the hoisin, soy sauce, and 1 tablespoon of the vinegar, then add the chicken and toss to coat with the mixture.

2. Heat the canola oil in a large skillet over medium-high heat until it's shimmering hot, about 2 minutes. Add the ginger and the whites of the scallions, reduce the heat to medium-low and cook, stirring, until the scallions have softened and are lightly browned, about 2 minutes. Transfer the oil, scallions, and ginger to the bowl with the cabbage and add the sesame oil and remaining 3 tablespoons vinegar. Toss well and taste for salt and vinegar. Top the slaw with the chicken and sprinkle with the scallion greens and sesame seeds. Serve immediately.

Grilled Chicken and Vegetable Salad

Serves 4

This dish is more method than recipe: good ingredients cooked simply so the flavors shine through. I like making this salad when I've got both leftover chicken and vegetables on hand. In case you don't have any leftover grilled vegetables, I've listed directions for grilling them. Feel free to add any other vegetables you've got in the garden—such as eggplant, peppers, or asparagus.

1 large red onion, cut into ½-inch-thick slices
2 medium zucchini, cut into ½-inch-thick slices
1 red bell pepper, cored and cut into 4 pieces
3 ears corn, shucked
6 tablespoons extra-virgin olive oil
2 teaspoons chopped fresh thyme
Kosher salt and freshly ground black pepper
2 cups diced leftover chicken
3 scallions (white and green parts), trimmed and thinly sliced
¼ cup chopped fresh parsley
2 tablespoons sherry vinegar or balsamic vinegar

CHIX PICKS

Try a mildly flavored grill-roasted (or roast) chicken like Anago's Garlicky Grill-Roasted Split Chickens with Lemon and Herbs (p. 66) or Italian Grilled Chicken Under a Brick with Smoky Balsamic Tomatoes (p. 68). You could grill the veggies while grill-roasting the chicken.

1. Prepare a charcoal fire or heat up the gas grill (heat all burners to medium-high). For a charcoal fire, pile a couple of layers of briquettes on one side and a single layer of charcoal on the other side of the grill so that you end up with a hot zone and a moderate to cool zone. Your fire should be ready when the briquettes are mostly gray (or, if you're using hardwood, when they are red hot).

2. Drizzle the onion, zucchini, pepper, and corn with 2 tablespoons of the oil, sprinkle with the thyme, and season generously with salt and pepper (about 1 teaspoon of each). Grill the vegetables, over the hot zone if using a charcoal fire, until browned, about 3 minutes. Flip and cook the peppers and zucchini until browned on the other side and just tender, about 4 minutes. Transfer both to a large plate.

3. Reduce the heat on the gas grill to medium-low or transfer the onions and corn to a cooler part of the charcoal fire. Cook, flipping occasionally, until just tender (they will still have a little crunch), about 6 minutes. Transfer to the plate and let cool to room temperature.

4. Chop the vegetables and cut the corn kernels from the cob. Combine with the chicken, scallions, and parsley in a large bowl, drizzle with the vinegar and remaining ¼ cup olive oil, and toss. Season with salt and pepper to taste and serve.

Black Bean Salad with Grilled Chicken and Corn

Serves 6

Cold bean salads are great summer food. Set them out on a crowded buffet table as an accompaniment to grilled burgers or steaks or serve as a main course tossed with grilled chicken and vegetables. The primary flavors in this salad—cilantro, lime, tomatoes, and onions—are summery, with cool and crisp textures jazzing up canned black beans. I like eating this with tortilla chips, using them as an edible fork. Dress this salad up with some crisp bacon or shredded Cheddar cheese if you like.

One 29-ounce or two 15-ounce cans
   black beans, rinsed well and drained
2 cups diced leftover chicken
Kernels cut from 2 ears grilled corn
   (see previous recipe for
   grilling instructions)
1 small red onion, finely diced
1 large ripe tomato,
   cut into ½-inch dice
1 canned chipotle chile in adobo
   sauce, minced
Juice of 2 limes
¼ cup extra-virgin olive oil
Kosher salt and freshly ground
   black pepper
1 ripe avocado, pitted and cut
   into ½-inch dice
¼ cup chopped fresh cilantro

CHIX PICKS

Try using a grill-roasted chicken with strong, spicy notes like Grill-Roasted Chicken with Tex-Mex Spice Crust and Grilled Corn Salsa (p. 58, fold in any leftover salsa) or Grill-Roasted Jamaican Jerk Chicken (p. 74).

In a large bowl, toss the beans with the chicken, corn, red onion, tomato, chipotle, half the lime juice, and the olive oil. Season generously with salt and pepper to taste and add more lime juice if you like. Top with the avocado and cilantro and serve.

White Bean Salad with Chicken, Tomatoes, and Lemon-Rosemary Oil

Serves 6 to 8

Croutons give this white bean salad crunch while the lemon-rosemary oil adds brightness. Though I like cooking beans from scratch, for quick weeknight cooking it's hard to beat the convenience of canned beans.

1 lemon, scrubbed
$^1\!/_2$ cup extra-virgin olive oil
2 cloves garlic, smashed
1 sprig plus 2 teaspoons chopped fresh rosemary
2 cups diced leftover chicken
One 29-ounce can or two 15-ounce cans cannellini beans, rinsed well and drained
2 large ripe tomatoes, cut into $^1\!/_2$-inch dice
2 cups Thyme Croutons (p. 91)
$^1\!/_4$ teaspoon Tabasco® sauce, or more to taste
Kosher salt and freshly ground black pepper
15 Parmesan curls (use a vegetable peeler to make them)

> ## CHIX PICKS
>
> A mildly flavored roast chicken with some herbs and lemon works best here. Try Bistro Roast Chicken with Lemon and Thyme (p. 34) or a bird patted with Lemon-Herb Rub (p. 13).

1. Prepare the lemon-rosemary oil. Using a peeler, shave six 1-inch-wide strips of the lemon zest, taking care only to remove the yellow and not the white pith. Juice the lemon and set aside. Heat the oil, lemon zest, garlic, and rosemary sprig in a medium saucepan over medium heat until it sizzles steadily and becomes fragrant, about 2 minutes. Let cool to room temperature, strain the oil, and transfer to a large bowl.

2. Add the chicken, beans, tomatoes, and chopped rosemary to the bowl and toss well. Add the flavored oil, Tabasco, 1 tablespoon of the lemon juice, and the croutons and toss well. Taste and season as desired with salt, pepper, or lemon juice, and/or Tabasco. (This can be made several hours in advance and refrigerated, tightly covered.)

3. To serve, pour the salad onto a large serving platter and sprinkle with the Parmesan curls. Serve immediately.

Summery Italian Chicken Salad with Fennel and Pears

Serves 4

Fennel (or anise) is one of those vegetables you should get to know if you don't already. Its flavor is similar to that of black licorice, only milder (much milder—I love fennel but I'm no fan of black licorice). This hearty vegetable is great in stews, adding an aromatic base. It also does well in salads, thinly sliced and paired with apples or pears, as in this recipe.

3 cups thinly sliced leftover chicken
2 Bartlett pears, cored and thinly sliced
1 large bulb fennel, quartered, cored, and very thinly sliced
1/4 cup lightly packed fresh tarragon leaves
2 tablespoons balsamic vinegar
1/3 cup extra-virgin olive oil
Kosher salt and freshly ground black pepper
16 toasted baguette crisps (or crostini) for serving

Place the chicken, pears, fennel, and tarragon in a large bowl and toss well with the vinegar and olive oil. Sprinkle with salt and pepper to taste and toss well. This can be refrigerated up to 8 hours, tightly covered, before serving with the crisps.

CHIX PICKS

Roast Chicken with Fennel and Mushroom Dressing (p. 47) would work well with this salad. The orange in a roast chicken slathered with Orange-Apricot Glaze (p. 14) also pairs nicely with the fennel and pear.

Brazilian Chicken, Mango, and Red Pepper Salad

Serves 6

One of the best things about working in a restaurant kitchen is being around people from all points on the globe. Often, the best meals don't ever leave the kitchen, but rather are made by the staff for the staff—bright, intensely seasoned dishes from each cook's native land.

This salad is a fine example of such a dish. I learned the recipe from cooking buddy Cremildo Silva. The flavors are true to Cremildo's native Brazil, with sweet mango paired with browned onions and red peppers. He likes to prepare it in the heat of summer as a cooling change of pace.

3 tablespoons canola oil
1 red bell pepper, cored, seeded, and very thinly sliced
1 large Spanish onion, very thinly sliced
Kosher salt and freshly ground black pepper
2 ripe mangos, peeled and thinly sliced off the pit
3 cups very thinly sliced leftover chicken
1/3 cup chopped fresh cilantro
Juice of 1 lime

> ## CHIX PICKS
>
> A roast bird with a sweet or spicy crust or glaze does particularly well with this dish. Try Grill-Roasted Tandoori Chicken (p. 62) or a bird drizzled with Orange-Rosemary Pan Sauce (p. 32).

1. Heat a large, heavy skillet over medium-high heat for 2 minutes. Add the oil and, once it's shimmering hot, add the bell pepper and onion. Sprinkle with 1 teaspoon salt and cook, stirring often, until the pepper and onion start to wilt and brown in places, about 4 minutes. Remove from the heat and let cool to room temperature.

2. In a large bowl, toss together the mangos, chicken, red pepper, onion, cilantro, and lime juice. Season with salt and pepper to taste and serve immediately.

Mom's Picnic Chicken Salad

Serves 6

Everyone has a favorite chicken salad they like to pack up and take on the road, whether it's for a picnic or potluck. The sour cream, lemon zest, and fresh herbs in my mother's version give the standard chicken salad a little twist.

¼ cup mayonnaise
¼ cup sour cream
Grated zest and juice of 1 lemon
¼ teaspoon Tabasco sauce
¼ cup chopped fresh parsley
2 tablespoons chopped fresh tarragon
Kosher salt and freshly ground black pepper
4 cups diced leftover chicken
1 small red onion, finely diced
2 ribs celery, diced

CHIX PICKS

Keep things simple with this pairing so you don't overpower the salad. Try Bistro Roast Chicken with Lemon and Thyme (p. 34) or Anago's Garlicky Grill-Roasted Split Chickens with Lemon and Herbs (p. 66).

1. In a small bowl, whisk together the mayonnaise, sour cream, lemon zest, 1 tablespoon of the lemon juice, the Tabasco, half of the parsley, and half of the tarragon. Season with salt and pepper to taste (about ½ teaspoon of each) and more lemon juice if need be.

2. Place the chicken, onion, and celery in a large bowl. Add the mayonnaise mixture and toss well. Sprinkle with the remaining parsley and tarragon. This can be made up to a day ahead and kept, tightly covered, in the refrigerator. Toss well before serving.

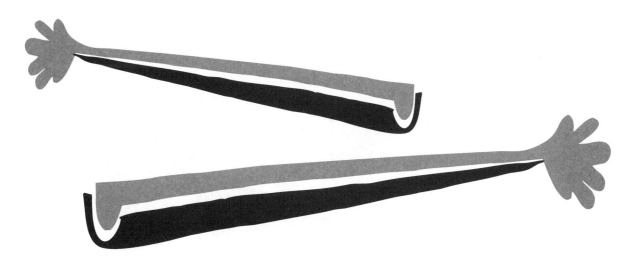

Curried Chicken Salad with Apple and Cilantro

Serves 4 to 6

I love how the addition of a few intense ingredients can give plain old chicken salad a new look. Apples and raisins offer crunch and sweetness while curry powder perks up the mayonnaise and yogurt in the dressing. You can make this salad a couple of hours ahead for a picnic or a party. Just toss it well before serving.

$^1/_3$ cup mayonnaise
3 tablespoons plain yogurt
1 teaspoon curry powder
Kosher salt and freshly ground black pepper
3$^1/_2$ cups diced leftover chicken
2 Golden Delicious apples, peeled, cored and cut into $^1/_2$-inch dice
1 cup Grilled Red Onions (p. 219) or 3 scallions, trimmed and thinly sliced
$^1/_4$ cup raisins
$^1/_4$ cup chopped fresh cilantro
Boston lettuce leaves for serving
1 lime, cut into wedges, for serving

1. In a small bowl, whisk together the mayonnaise, yogurt, and curry powder. Season with salt and pepper to taste.

2. In a large bowl, toss the chicken with the apples, onions or scallions, half of the raisins, and half of the cilantro. Toss with the dressing to coat evenly, sprinkle with the remaining raisins and cilantro, and serve with the lettuce leaves for wrapping and the lime wedges on the side. Or refrigerate, tightly covered, for up to a day before serving.

> ## CHIX PICKS
>
> Try a bird with Indian flavors like Grill-Roasted Tandoori Chicken (p. 62) or even E.G.'s Roast Chicken with Tarragon and Whole-Grain Mustard (p. 46).

BUILD YOUR OWN CHICKEN SALAD

Though I've included a couple of recipes for chicken salad in this chapter, I've come up with this basic method so you can sub in your favorite ingredients to create your own version. As anyone who's ever made chicken salad knows, it's more of a method than a rote recipe: dice up some cooked chicken and toss it with something creamy or rich (like mayonnaise or oil), something tangy (sour cream or vinegar), and whatever else you have on hand that will pair well with the particular flavorings—grilled vegetables, spices, fresh herbs, fruit, etc.

The recipe below offers a few simple guidelines for making all sorts of different chicken salads. I've left the ingredient quantities in ranges so you can make as much as you need depending on how many you're serving and how much leftover chicken you have. This means you will need to taste the salad as you go along to make sure it has enough dressing, vegetables, etc. (Always start with the low end of the range, as you can always add more.)

Serves 2 to 8

1. Chop up some chicken (2 to 5 cups)

2. Toss well with a dressing or vinaigrette (¼ to 1 cup)
   - yogurt
   - sour cream
   - mayonnaise
   - Thyme-Mustard Vinaigrette (p. 98)
   - Balsamic-Sun-Dried Tomato Vinaigrette (p. 61)
   - Black Olive and Sherry Vinaigrette (p. 60)
   - Lime and Jalapeno Vinaigrette (p. 60)

3. Throw in some veggies (2 to 4 cups)
   - grilled vegetables (corn, red peppers, onions, etc.)
   - chopped blanched broccoli or cauliflower florets
   - blanched asparagus cut into 2-inch lengths
   - celery or radishes,
   - Grilled Red Onions (p. 219), chopped

4. Add a little bit of sweet, savory, or crunch (2 tablespoons to 1 cup)
   - chopped or halved pitted olives
   - thinly sliced sun-dried tomatoes
   - capers
   - toasted walnuts or pecans
   - pesto
   - roasted red peppers, thinly sliced
   - raisins
   - chopped apple or pear
   - grapes, cut in half

5. Add your flavoring
   - 1 to 2 tablespoons chopped fresh thyme or rosemary
   - ¼ to ½ cup chopped fresh chives, basil, parsley, cilantro, dill, or tarragon
   - 1 to 2 teaspoons curry powder or chile powder

6. Season with salt and pepper to taste and serve.

Chapter 4

Soups, Stews, and Saucy Sauces

The day after Thanksgiving, cooks get

positively giddy about all the possible soups and stews they can make with the leftovers. I feel the same sort of rush when there's a leftover chicken in the refrigerator (I'll admit I may need to get out a little more). Though a chicken is considerably smaller than a turkey, it forms just as fine a base for soups, stews, or saucy sauces (sort of like a quick braise), all of which are the focus of this chapter.

I generally follow a basic formula with these sorts of leftover chicken dishes.

1. I often start by browning some bacon, ham, or other cured pork product, which gives the dish a salty edge and whose richness fills out any dryness in the chicken.

2. Then, I like to create a flavor base by sautéing aromatics like onions, garlic, leeks, and ginger.

3. I add some chicken broth, bring the mixture to a boil, and simmer for at least 10 or 15 minutes so all the different flavors mix and meld.

4. Then I stir in the chicken (preferably dark meat, which won't dry out) and simmer until it heats through and soaks up some of the broth or sauce.

5. Finally, I finish with a drop of cream or something rich (especially if there's no bacon in the mix) and a garnish of some fresh herbs.

Though most of the recipes in this chapter stick to this method, the dishes veer in different directions across the culinary map. They all fit within the confines of comfort food, though—meals that will warm you up on a chilly night.

Tortilla Soup with Shredded Chicken and Diced Avocado

Serves 4

I learned how to make this soup from my friend, Nena Rebollo. Though she lives in Llanes, a quaint fishing village in the north of Spain, Nena stays true to her Mexican roots, preparing the specialties of her youth, like this soup.

Tortilla soup is a simple chicken broth spiced with a heady dose of chiles. For the sake of convenience I use chili powder instead of whole chiles, sweating the spice along with some diced onions, to release its flavor.

2 tablespoons olive oil
1 small yellow onion, finely diced
2 cloves garlic, thinly sliced
Kosher salt
1½ tablespoons chili powder
¼ teaspoon ground chipotle powder
One 14.5-ounce can diced tomatoes
   and their juices
5 cups low-salt chicken broth
2 cups shredded leftover chicken
1 ripe avocado, pitted and diced
Juice of 1 lime
½ cup chopped fresh cilantro
Freshly ground black pepper
3 cups Fried Tortilla Strips (see recipe, facing page)
   or tortilla chips broken into large pieces

> ## CHIX PICKS
>
> Try using a roast chicken coated with a vibrant spice rub like Southwestern Chile Spice Rub (p. 11) or Sweet Southern Spice Rub (p. 12), which will complement the heat in this recipe.

1. Heat the oil in a large saucepan over medium heat for 1 minute. Add the onion and garlic, sprinkle with ½ teaspoon salt, and cook, stirring often, until the onion softens and becomes translucent, about 8 minutes. Add the chili powder and chipotle powder and cook, stirring, for 1 minute. Add the tomatoes and their juices and cook for a couple of minutes to heat through. Carefully transfer to a blender or food processor and purée it, then return it to the saucepan along with the broth and bring to a boil. Reduce the heat to a gentle simmer, stir in the chicken, and cook for 15 minutes to heat through.

2. Meanwhile, in a small bowl, gently toss the avocado with half the lime juice and half the cilantro, then season with salt and pepper to taste.

3. Stir the remaining lime juice and cilantro into the broth and season with salt and pepper to taste. Serve the soup with a large spoonful of the avocado mixture and a handful of the tortilla strips.

Fried Tortilla Strips

Makes about 3 cups

Vegetable oil for frying
4 small corn tortillas, cut into thin strips
Kosher salt

1. Fill a medium saucepan with oil so it's 2 inches deep. Attach a frying or candy thermometer to the side of the pot and heat the oil over medium heat until it hovers around 350°F, about 5 minutes.

2. Add half the strips and cook, stirring often, until browned and crisp, 1 to 2 minutes. Remove from the oil using a slotted spoon, drain on paper towels and sprinkle lightly with salt. Repeat with the remaining tortilla strips. Once the chips are cooled, store in an airtight container for up to 2 days.

MAKE A HOMEMADE BROTH WITH THE LEFTOVER BIRD

In keeping with this book's practical nature, I do endorse certain shortcuts throughout—good shortcuts, the kind that won't compromise a dish or your health. Canned chicken broth (especially the low-salt variety) is one of these shortcuts. But if you do have a little extra time for cooking, I would wholeheartedly encourage you to make a homemade broth with the leftover bird. It doesn't take much effort or work. Just toss a couple of chopped carrots, some onion, a bay leaf, and the leftover carcass (as well as the neck or wing tips if you have them) into a pot with a quart or two of water, bring to a boil, and then simmer for about 1 hour. Strain the broth and use as directed in the following recipes. Although this broth won't be quite as rich or flavorful as one made with raw bones and meat, it far outshines canned broth and saves you a couple of bucks as well.

Black Bean Soup with Shredded Chicken and Cilantro-Lime Cream

Serves 4

Canned black beans are one of those ingredients that can sub in handsomely for their fresh counterpart. Here they form the base for a puréed soup that's enriched with bacon and shredded chicken. I like serving it with a dollop of tangy cilantro-lime cream.

BLACK BEAN SOUP:

6 ounces bacon (about 6 thick slices), cut into thin strips

1 large Spanish onion, cut into 1/4-inch dice

1 red bell pepper, cored, seeded, and cut into 1/4-inch dice

Kosher salt

3 cloves garlic, minced

1 tablespoon chili powder

2 teaspoons ground cumin

1/2 teaspoon ground chipotle powder or 1/8 teaspoon cayenne pepper

3/4 cup beer (preferably a light lager)

One 29-ounce or two 15-ounce can(s) black beans, drained and rinsed well

4 cups low-salt chicken broth

2 tablespoons cider vinegar

2 cups shredded leftover chicken

Freshly ground black pepper

1 lime, cut into wedges for serving

CILANTRO-LIME CREAM:

1 cup sour cream

1/2 cup chopped fresh cilantro

Grated zest and juice of 1 lime, plus

Kosher salt and freshly ground black pepper

CHIX PICKS

A roast chicken with plenty of spice goes well with this soup. Try Roast Chicken with Southwestern Rub and Cornbread and Jalapeño Stuffing (p. 48) or Grill-Roasted Chicken with Tex-Mex Spice Crust and Grilled Corn Salsa (p. 58). If you have any of the salsa left from the latter, set atop this soup along with the cilantro-lime cream.

1. Cook the bacon in a large Dutch oven over medium heat, stirring occasionally, until it crisps and renders much of its fat, about 6 minutes. Transfer to a large plate lined with paper towels.

2. Add the onion and red pepper to the pot, sprinkle with salt (about ½ teaspoon) and cook, stirring occasionally, until the onion softens and becomes translucent, about 6 minutes. Stir in the garlic and cook for 1 minute. Add the chili powder, cumin, and chipotle powder and cook for 1 minute. Add the beer and cook, stirring, until it almost completely reduces, about 1 minute. Add the beans, broth, and vinegar and bring to a boil. Reduce the heat to a steady simmer, cover, and cook for 10 minutes.

3. Using an immersion blender, or by carefully working in batches with a regular blender, purée the broth and beans, then stir in the chicken and cook until heated through, about 10 minutes. Season with salt, black pepper, and more vinegar to taste.

4. Meanwhile make the cilantro-lime cream. In a medium bowl, whisk together the sour cream, cilantro, lime zest, and half the lime juice. Season with salt and pepper to taste, about ½ teaspoon of each. Add more lime juice if you like.

5. Serve the soup immediately with a sprinkling of bacon, a dollop of the cilantro-lime cream and the lime wedges for squeezing.

Smoky Chicken and Corn Chowder

Serves 4 to 6

I like to make this soup on a cool, late summer night when there is still plenty of fresh sweet corn at the local market. The coupling of grilled corn and crisped bacon adds smokiness to this basic corn chowder. You can embellish this broth with diced tomatoes or a handful of herbs from the garden.

¼ pound bacon (about 4 thick slices),
  cut into thin strips
1 medium-size yellow onion, finely diced
½ red bell pepper, cored, seeded,
  and cut into ¼-inch dice
Kosher salt
1 medium Yukon Gold potato,
  peeled and cut into ½-inch dice
4 cups low-salt chicken broth
3 cups cooked corn kernels (from 4 grilled
  ears—see Grilled Chicken and Vegetable
  Salad on p. 100) or frozen corn
2 cups diced leftover chicken
2 tablespoons heavy cream
Freshly ground black pepper
3 tablespoons thinly sliced fresh chives

CHIX PICKS

Balsamic-Glazed Rosemary Chicken with Bacon and Pearl Onions (p. 36) is a great fit, as you can add any leftover bacon or onions. Or a roast chicken with a spice rub like Sweet Southern Spice Rub (p. 12) livens up the richness of the creamy broth.

1. Cook the bacon in a large Dutch oven over medium heat, stirring occasionally, until it crisps and renders much of its fat, about 6 minutes. Transfer to a plate lined with paper towels.

2. Add the onion and bell pepper to the bacon fat, sprinkle generously with salt (about ½ teaspoon), and cook, stirring occasionally, until they soften and brown in places, about 6 minutes. Add the potato and broth, bring to a boil, then reduce the heat to a simmer, cover, and cook until the potato is completely tender when poked with a knife, about 15 minutes.

3. Stir in the corn, chicken, and cream and simmer for 10 minutes to heat through. Season generously with salt and pepper to taste and serve with a sprinkling of the crisped bacon and chives.

Asian Chicken Soup with Shiitakes and Udon Noodles

Serves 4

It doesn't take much to transform a simple chicken broth into a fine Asian soup. Dried shiitake mushrooms, ginger, and a mixture of soy sauce and rice vinegar infuse the broth. To flavor the broth evenly, I like to mince some of the ginger and thinly slice some, and include both. As for the noodles—either fresh or dried udon are fine—try to pick them up at the local Asian market where you'll find the best quality.

1 ounce dried shiitake mushrooms

2 cups boiling water

2 tablespoons peeled and minced fresh ginger, plus 1-inch knob, peeled and thinly sliced

2 tablespoons canola or peanut oil

4 scallions (white and green parts), trimmed and thinly sliced

4 cups low-salt chicken broth

2½ cups shredded leftover chicken

¼ pound baby spinach

2 tablespoons soy sauce

1 tablespoon rice vinegar

Kosher salt

½ pound fresh or dried udon noodles

> ## CHIX PICKS
>
> Go with a roast chicken with Asian flavorings like Grilled Chicken Teriyaki with Scallions (p. 70) or Grill-Roasted Thai Chicken with Lemongrass (p. 53).

1. Set the mushrooms in a medium bowl and add the boiling water. Weigh down the mushrooms with a small plate and soak until they're soft and plump, about 15 minutes.

2. Using a slotted spoon, transfer the mushrooms to a cutting board. Discard the stems and coarsely chop. Strain the mushroom liquid through a paper towel or coffee filter. Set aside the chopped mushrooms and mushroom soaking liquid.

3. Heat the minced ginger in the oil in a large saucepan over medium-high heat until it starts to sizzle, about 1½ minutes. Add the scallions and cook, stirring often, until translucent and softened, about 2 minutes. Add the mushrooms and cook, stirring, until they start to brown, about 3 minutes. Add the broth and mushroom soaking liquid and bring to a boil. Reduce the heat to a simmer, stir in the sliced ginger, chicken, spinach, soy sauce, and vinegar, and cook until the chicken heats through and the spinach wilts, about 10 minutes.

4. Meanwhile, bring a medium pot of water to a boil. Sprinkle generously with salt, about 1 tablespoon. Cook the noodles, stirring occasionally, until just tender to the tooth, about 4 minutes (dried noodles will take a few minutes longer). Drain and cool briefly under cold running water. Transfer the noodles to the soup and cook for a couple of minutes to heat through. Serve immediately.

Spicy Thai Chicken and Coconut Soup

Serves 4

This soup mixes notes of sweet (coconut milk), salty (fish sauce), and hot (Thai chiles) with aromatics like ginger and lemongrass. The effect is at once intense and warming. To work with lemongrass, pull away and discard the coarse outer leaves to reveal the tender inner stalk.

2 tablespoons canola oil
2 shallots, finely diced
2 tablespoons peeled and minced fresh ginger
2 tablespoons finely chopped fresh lemongrass
2 Thai bird or other small hot chiles, thinly sliced
1/2 teaspoon kosher salt
4 cups low-salt chicken broth
2 cups shredded leftover chicken
1/3 cup unsweetened coconut milk
1 tablespoon fish sauce
Juice of 2 limes
1/2 cup chopped fresh cilantro
Freshly ground black pepper

> ## CHIX PICKS
>
> For this soup, a roast chicken with intense Asian spice like Grill-Roasted Thai Chicken with Lemongrass (p. 53) would go perfectly or one coated with a spice rub like All-Purpose Poultry Spice Rub (p. 11).

1. Heat the oil in a large Dutch oven over medium heat for 1 minute. Add the shallots, ginger, lemongrass, and chiles and sprinkle with the salt. Cook, stirring occasionally, until the shallots are translucent, soft, and just starting to brown in places, about 4 minutes. Add the broth and bring to a boil. Reduce the heat to a gentle simmer and cook for 15 minutes.

2. Stir in the chicken, coconut milk, and fish sauce and cook for 10 minutes to heat the chicken through. Stir in the lime juice and half the cilantro and season with salt and pepper to taste. Serve immediately with a sprinkling of the remaining cilantro.

Split Pea Soup with Chicken, Lemon, and Mint

Serves 4 to 6

Most split pea soups have a heavy, sludge-like texture that's not very appetizing. This version is lighter, full of different flavors and textures. A sprinkling of bacon gives the soup some crunch, while lemon juice and mint lend brightness. You can also use ham (from a leftover ham or a hamsteak) if you like.

1/4 pound bacon (about 4 thick slices)
1 large yellow onion, cut into 1/4-inch dice
2 medium carrots, cut into 1/4-inch dice
2 stalks celery, cut into 1/4-inch dice
Kosher salt
1 1/2 cups green split peas, picked through, rinsed well, and drained
6 1/2 cups water
2 cups diced leftover chicken
3 tablespoons chopped fresh mint
1 tablespoon fresh lemon juice, or more to taste
Freshly ground black pepper

CHIX PICKS

Try a roast chicken with garlic and herbs like Roast Chicken with Rosemary-Garlic Croutons (p. 44)—use any leftover croutons as a garnish—or Sear-Roasted Chicken with Lots of Garlic (p. 82).

1. Brown the bacon in a large Dutch oven over medium heat until it crisps and renders much of its fat, about 6 minutes. Transfer to a plate lined with paper towels.

2. Add the onion, carrots, and celery to the pan, sprinkle generously with salt (about 1 teaspoon), and cook, stirring, until they soften and start to brown in places, about 7 minutes. Add the split peas and water and bring to a boil. Reduce the heat to a steady simmer, cover, and cook, stirring occasionally, until the peas are completely tender and the broth thickens somewhat, about 40 minutes.

3. Using an immersion blender, pulse the soup a couple of times to thicken its texture (or purée about 1 cup in a regular blender). Return the soup to low heat, stir in the chicken, and cook until it's warmed through, about 5 minutes. Stir in the mint and lemon juice and taste for salt, pepper, and more lemon juice. Crumble the crisped bacon, sprinkle it over the top of each serving, and serve immediately.

Greek Egg-Drop Soup with Chicken

Serves 4

Though the Greek preparation *avgolemono,* can be either a sauce or a soup, the main ingredients in the mixture remain the same—lemon juice, eggs, and chicken broth. In this soup, shredded leftover chicken, spinach, and rice fill out the mix. It's important to gently stir the eggs into the hot broth so they form thick ribbons—a teaspoon of cornstarch will help out.

5 cups low-salt chicken broth
1 teaspoon cornstarch
5 tablespoons fresh lemon juice (from about 1½ lemons)
3 large eggs, beaten
1½ cups shredded leftover chicken
1 cup cooked rice (leftover is fine), crumbled into individual grains
¼ pound baby spinach, coarsely chopped
Kosher salt and freshly ground black pepper

CHIX PICKS

Try a mild roast chicken in this soup like Roast Chicken with Rosemary-Garlic Croutons (p. 44) or Bistro Roast Chicken with Lemon and Thyme (p. 34).

1. Bring the broth to a simmer in a large saucepan over medium heat and remove from the heat.

2. In a medium bowl, whisk together the cornstarch and ¼ cup of the lemon juice, then stir in the eggs. Slowly drizzle the egg mixture into the broth while stirring.

3. Add the chicken, rice, and spinach, place over medium heat, and simmer, stirring, until heated through and the spinach has wilted, about 10 minutes. Season generously with salt and pepper to taste and serve immediately with a squirt of the remaining 1 tablespoon lemon juice.

Nana's Chicken Soup with Matzo Balls

Serves 4

My mother's mother ("Nana" to us kids) assumed the culinary duties for Passover. Each spring, we would make the trek up to Montreal where Nana always started the meal with this soup. Every Jewish cook has a recipe for matzo balls, though, not surprisingly, I happen to think that my nana's are the best. You can prepare the matzo balls and this soup up to 2 days before serving.

MATZO BALLS:

6 large eggs, beaten
1/3 cup canola oil
Kosher salt and freshly ground black pepper
1/3 cup water
2 cups matzo meal

SOUP:

2 tablespoons canola oil
1 small yellow onion, finely diced
2 medium carrots, cut into 1/2-inch dice
2 stalks celery, cut into 1/2-inch dice
Kosher salt and freshly ground black pepper
5 cups low-salt chicken broth
2 cups shredded leftover chicken

CHIX PICKS

Make sure not to overpower this simple broth with the leftover chicken. The garlic in Sear-Roasted Chicken with Lots of Garlic (p. 82) goes nicely with the mild flavors of this soup. Or try Roast Chicken with Rosemary-Mustard Crust and Browned Onions (p. 30).

1. In a large bowl, whisk together the eggs, oil, 1 tablespoon salt, 1/2 teaspoon pepper, and the water. Fold in the matzo meal and mix well. Cover with plastic wrap and refrigerate for 30 minutes to let firm up.

2. Fill a medium pot with water and a couple tablespoons of salt and bring to a boil. With wet hands or a 1/4-cup ice cream scoop, gently shape the matzo mixture into fifteen 2-inch balls. Gently drop them one at a time into the boiling water. Reduce the heat to medium-low, cover the pot, and simmer until the matzo balls are cooked through, about 30 minutes. Remove them from the water with a slotted spoon and set on a large sheet pan to cool.

3. Meanwhile, in another medium pot, over medium heat, add the oil, onion, carrot, and celery, sprinkle with 1/2 teaspoon each salt and pepper and cook, stirring occasionally until the vegetables almost completely soften, about 10 minutes. Add the broth and bring to a boil. Reduce the heat to a simmer and cook until the carrots are tender, about 30 minutes. Season with salt and pepper to taste.

4. Add the matzo balls and shredded chicken, cover, and simmer until the matzo balls are heated through, about 15 minutes. Serve immediately.

Chicken Soup with Orzo and Roasted Fall Vegetables

Serves 4 to 6

Once in a while, I like roasting vegetables for a soup. It's an extra step (as opposed to simply sautéing them in the same pot with the soup), but it gives them a wonderful caramelized finish, which makes for rich flavor. Feel free to stir in any leftover vegetables you have on hand, like green beans or roasted onions.

2 medium carrots, diced
1 small bulb fennel, diced
3 stalks celery, diced
2 tablespoons olive oil
Kosher salt and freshly ground black pepper
6 cups low-salt chicken broth
One 14.5-ounce can diced tomatoes
   and their juices
1 teaspoon chopped fresh rosemary
1 cup orzo
2 cups diced leftover chicken
½ cup freshly grated Parmesan cheese

1. Preheat the oven to 425°F.

2. On a large baking sheet, toss the carrots, fennel, and celery with the oil and sprinkle generously with salt and pepper. Roast, tossing every 10 minutes or so, until the vegetables begin to brown and soften, about 35 minutes.

3. Combine the broth, roasted vegetables, tomatoes and their juices, and rosemary in a large saucepan and bring to a boil. Reduce the heat to a simmer, add the orzo and cook, stirring occasionally, until the pasta is just tender, about 15 minutes.

4. Stir in the chicken and half the Parmesan and cook until heated through, about 10 minutes. Season liberally with salt and pepper to taste and serve immediately, sprinkled with the remaining Parmesan.

CHIX PICKS

A mildly flavored roast chicken goes nicely in this simple soup, like Roast Chicken with Fennel and Mushroom Dressing (p. 47) or a bird coated with Lemon-Herb Rub (p. 13).

Potato Soup with Leeks and Chicken

Serves 4 to 6

It always amazes me how few ingredients it takes to make a wonderful potato soup—indeed, with just potatoes, leeks, and broth, you're well on your way. Heavy cream and chicken enrich the mixture a bit, while Parmesan and a splash of vinegar add complexity. Just be sure to wash the leeks well to get out any grit and to cook the potatoes through so they purée smoothly.

2 tablespoons unsalted butter

1 pound leeks (white and light green parts), finely diced, soaked, and patted dry

Kosher salt and freshly ground black pepper

1 1/4 pounds russet potatoes, peeled and cut into 1-inch pieces

4 cups low-salt chicken broth

1/4 cup freshly grated Parmesan cheese

1 tablespoon sherry vinegar

1 teaspoon chopped fresh rosemary

2 cups diced leftover chicken

3 tablespoons heavy cream

CHIX PICKS

Try Sear-Roasted Chicken with Bacon and Herbed Potatoes (p. 80)—you can add any leftover potatoes to this dish. The spice in Chinese Salt and Pepper Roast Chicken (p. 52) also adds life to this hearty potato soup.

1. Melt the butter in a large saucepan over medium heat. Add the leeks, sprinkle with 1/2 teaspoon salt, and cook, stirring often, until softened and translucent, about 8 minutes. Add the potatoes and broth and bring to a boil. Add the Parmesan, vinegar, and rosemary, reduce the heat to a gentle simmer, cover, and cook until the potatoes are fork tender, 10 to 15 minutes.

2. Purée the soup using an immersion blender (or, working in batches, use a regular blender, then return the soup to the pan). Season generously with salt and pepper to taste. Stir in the chicken and cream and cook over medium-low heat until heated through, about 10 minutes. Add salt and pepper to taste and serve immediately.

Lentil Soup with Herbed Chicken and Root Vegetables

Serves 4

There are a couple of different varieties of lentils you can find at the local market. I would suggest trying the small, green French du Puy, which are more expensive than brown lentils, but hold their shape well and have a wonderfully delicate flavor.

3 ounces bacon (about 3 thick slices), cut into thin strips

I large Spanish onion, finely diced

2 medium carrots, cut into ¼-inch dice

I medium celery root, peeled and cut into ¼-inch dice

Kosher salt and freshly ground black pepper

⅔ cup dry white wine

6 cups low-salt chicken broth

½ pound lentils (about 2 cups), picked through, rinsed well, and drained

2 teaspoons chopped fresh thyme

2 cups diced leftover chicken

I tablespoon sherry vinegar or balsamic vinegar

CHIX PICKS

The sweetness of Balsamic-Glazed Rosemary Chicken with Bacon and Pearl Onions (p. 36) pairs nicely with this lentil soup—toss any leftover bacon or pearl onions into the soup. Or try Jerrod's Roast Chicken with Vermont Maple Glaze, Sweet Potatoes, and Sage (p. 35).

1. Brown the bacon in a large Dutch oven over medium heat until it crisps and renders much of its fat, about 6 minutes. Transfer to a plate lined with paper towels.

2. Add the onion, carrots, and celery root to the pot, sprinkle generously with salt (about 1 teaspoon) and cook, stirring, until softened and starting to brown in places, about 8 minutes. Add the wine and cook, stirring, until it almost completely reduces, about 2 minutes. Add the broth, lentils, and thyme and bring to a boil. Reduce the heat to a simmer, cover, and cook until the lentils are just tender, about 40 minutes.

3. Stir in the chicken and vinegar and cook until the lentils are completely softened and the chicken is heated through, about 10 minutes. Season generously with salt and pepper to taste. Serve immediately with a sprinkling of the crisped bacon.

Glazed Chicken with Orange–Apricot Glaze (page 14) and Brussels Sprouts with Bacon, Apple, and Sage (page 72)

Korean Bibimbap with Sesame Chicken and Stir-Fried Vegetables (page 174)

Brazilian Chicken, Mango, and Red Pepper Salad (page 104)

Stuffed Peppers with Chicken, Chorizo, and Rice (page 198)

Couscous with Chicken, Orange, and Roasted Butternut Squash (page 164)

Spicy Southwest Chicken Sandwich with
Avocado and Bacon (page 220)

Spiced Sweet Potato Fries (page 50)

Chicken with Haricot Verts,
Cherry Tomatoes, and Thyme-Mustard
Vinaigrette (page 98)

Green Beans with Balsamic Vinegar and Almonds (page 73)

Roast Chicken with Caramelized Shallots and Fingerling Potatoes (page 38)

Grill-Roasted Chicken with Tex-Mex Spice and Grilled
Corn Salsa (page 58)

Classic Cobb Salad (page 94)

Grilled Pizza with Buffalo Chicken and Blue Cheese (page 259)

Tortilla Soup with Shredded Chicken and Diced Avocado (page 110)

Chicken, Asparagus, and Caramelized Onion Quiche (page 270)

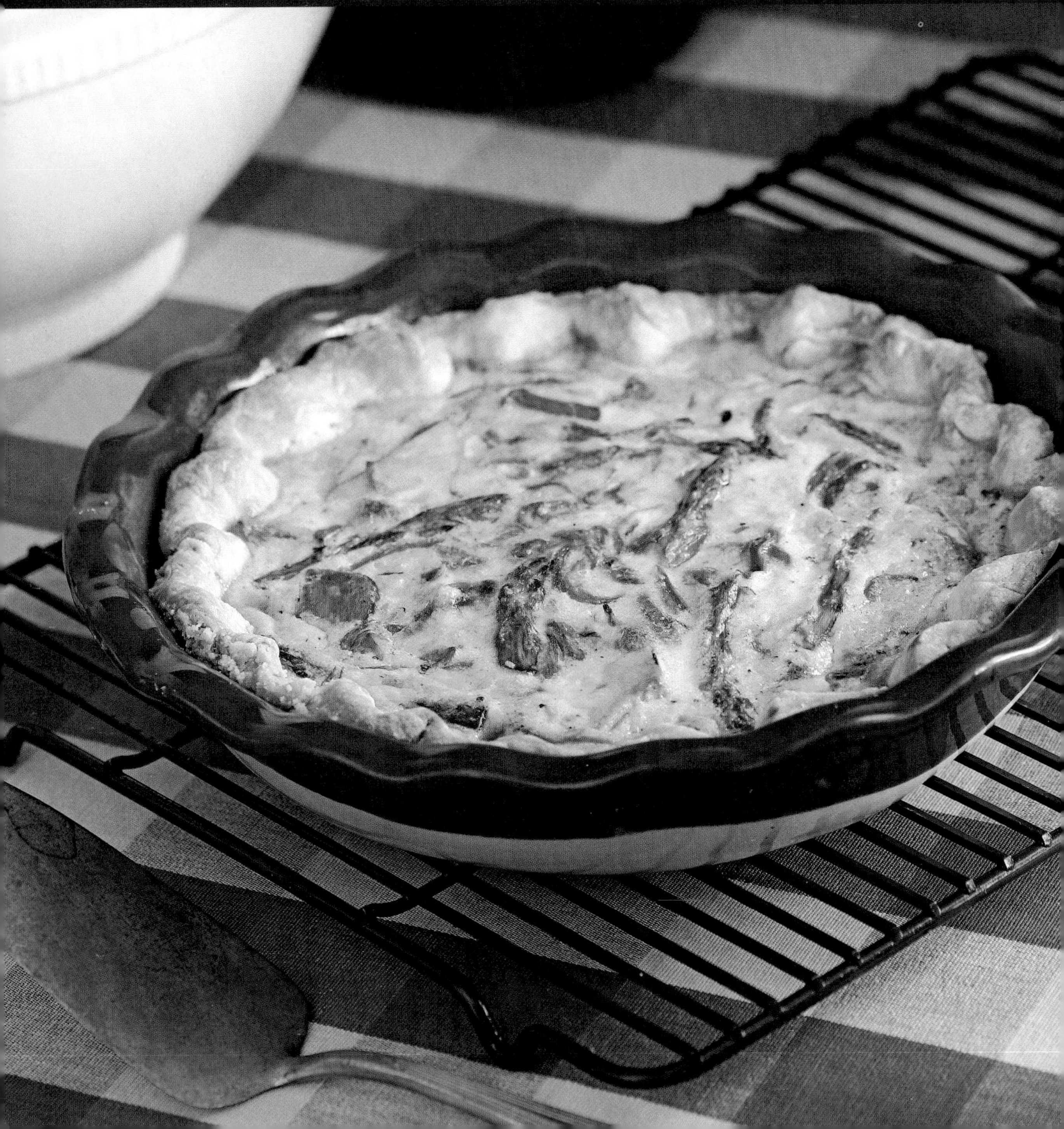

Chicken and Barley Soup with Thyme and Mushrooms

Serves 6

This is one of those soups where you can use water instead of chicken broth—there are enough vegetables to form a rich, aromatic broth. Using chicken broth, whether canned or homemade, only intensifies the flavor of the soup.

2 tablespoons olive oil
1 large yellow onion, finely diced
2 medium-size carrots, finely diced
2 stalks celery, finely diced
Kosher salt
10 ounces white mushrooms, thinly sliced
3½ ounces fresh shiitake mushrooms, stemmed and diced
½ cup dry white wine
1 cup pearled barley
6 cups low-salt chicken broth or water
One 14.5-ounce can diced tomatoes, drained
1 tablespoon chopped fresh thyme
Freshly ground black pepper
2½ cups diced leftover chicken

CHIX PICKS

A simple roast chicken with plenty of herbs complements this soup. Try Roast Chicken with Rosemary-Mustard Crust and Browned Onions (p. 30) or Jerrod's Roast Chicken with Vermont Maple Glaze, Sweet Potatoes, and Sage (p. 35).

1. Heat the oil in a large Dutch oven or casserole over medium heat for 1 minute. Add the onion, carrots, and celery, sprinkle with ½ teaspoon salt and cook, stirring often, until the vegetables soften and the onion becomes translucent, 8 to 10 minutes. Stir in the mushrooms, season with another ½ teaspoon salt, and cook stirring, until they brown in places and cook through, about 4 minutes. Add the wine and cook until it almost completely reduces, about 1 minute. Add the barley, broth, tomatoes, and 2 teaspoons of the thyme, sprinkle generously with salt and pepper, and bring to a boil. Reduce the heat to a gentle simmer, cover and cook, stirring occasionally, until the barley puffs and becomes tender, about 30 minutes.

2. Stir in the chicken and cook until heated through, about 10 minutes. Season generously with salt and pepper to taste. Serve immediately, sprinkled with the remaining 1 teaspoon thyme.

Curried Chicken, Cauliflower, and Potato Stew

Serves 4

It's hard to go wrong with the classic pairing of cauliflower, potato, and curry. I like stewing these three together until the potatoes and cauliflower soften and create a pleasant, thick broth, which is sweetened and enriched by the coconut milk. Serve with steamed basmati rice.

2 tablespoons olive oil

1 small yellow onion, finely diced

2 tablespoons peeled and minced fresh ginger

Kosher salt and freshly ground black pepper

2 teaspoons curry powder

2 teaspoons sweet paprika

1¼ pounds russet potatoes, peeled and cut into 1-inch pieces

1 pound cauliflower, cut into 1-inch pieces

1½ cups low-salt chicken broth

½ cup unsweetened coconut milk

2½ cups diced leftover chicken

1 cup frozen peas, thawed

½ cup chopped fresh cilantro

Juice of 1 lime

CHIX PICKS

A roast chicken coated with curry powder goes well with this stew. Try Grill-Roasted Tandoori Chicken (p. 62) or E.G.'s Roast Chicken with Tarragon and Whole-Grain Mustard (p. 46).

1. Heat the oil in a large Dutch oven or casserole over medium heat for 1 minute. Add the onion and ginger, sprinkle with salt and pepper (about 1 teaspoon of each), and cook, stirring often, until the onion is translucent and completely softened, 8 to 10 minutes. Add the curry powder and paprika and cook, stirring, for 1 minute to release the flavors in the spices. Add the potatoes, cauliflower, broth, and coconut milk, bring to a boil, then reduce the heat to a simmer. Cover with the lid partly askew and cook until the potatoes and cauliflower are tender, about 20 minutes.

2. Stir in the chicken, peas, and half the cilantro and cook until heated through, about 10 minutes. Stir in half the lime juice and season generously with salt, pepper, and lime juice to taste. Serve, topped with a sprinkling of the remaining cilantro.

Chicken Brunswick Stew

Serves 6

This Southern classic generally contains some mix of chicken, tomatoes, corn and lima beans. Though I like using fresh corn in the summer months, the rest of the year I will make due with the frozen variety. I also like throwing in some diced ham for a smoky, salty edge.

¼ cup olive oil
½ pound ham steak or leftover ham, cut into 1-inch dice
1 medium onion, finely diced
1 red bell pepper, cored, seeded and cut into ¾-inch pieces
2 cloves garlic, minced
One 14.5-ounce can diced tomatoes, drained
1½ cups low-salt chicken broth
2½ cups diced leftover chicken
3 cups fresh (from 4 ears) or frozen corn
1 cup frozen lima beans
2 teaspoons chopped fresh thyme
Kosher salt and freshly ground black pepper

CHIX PICKS

A simple roast bird complements the mild ingredients in this stew. Try Sear-Roasted Chicken with Tomatoes and Rosemary (p. 78)—you can add any leftover sauce to the stew. The herbs in Roast Chicken with Rosemary-Mustard Crust and Browned Onions (p. 30) also pair well with this stew.

1. Heat 2 tablespoons of the oil in a large sauté pan over medium heat until shimmering hot, about 2 minutes. Add the ham and cook, stirring, until browned, about 5 minutes. Transfer to a large plate.

2. Add the remaining 2 tablespoons oil and the onion and bell pepper and cook, stirring, until softened and starting to brown in places, 8 to 10 minutes. Add the garlic and cook, stirring, for 30 seconds. Add the tomatoes and broth and bring to a boil. Stir in the chicken, corn, and lima beans, reduce the heat to a simmer, cover with the lid slightly askew, and cook until heated through, about 10 minutes. Stir in the thyme and season generously with salt and pepper to taste. Serve immediately.

Summery Stew with Three Beans, Corn, and Chicken

Serves 4

This dish is an example of what happens when I go to the local farmer's market—
I buy everything and then throw it all in a pot! With good summer produce, you
can't go wrong loading vegetables into a large casserole and slowly stewing them
until they become tender and form an intense broth.

2 tablespoons olive oil

2 spring or small red onions, finely diced

Kosher salt

½ pound wax beans, trimmed and cut
into 1½-inch pieces

½ pound Romano or broad beans,
trimmed and cut into 1½-inch pieces

½ pound green beans, trimmed and cut
into 1½-inch pieces

3 cups low-salt chicken broth

¾ pound new or red potatoes,
cut into ½-inch pieces

1 large ripe tomato, diced, or one
14.5-ounce can diced tomatoes, drained

2 cups diced leftover chicken

Kernels cut from 2 ears of corn (about 1½ cups)

2 teaspoons chopped fresh thyme

Freshly ground black pepper

¼ cup freshly grated Parmesan cheese

CHIX PICKS

A mildly flavored roast chicken goes well
with this summery stew like Roast Chicken
with Caramelized Shallots and Fingerling
Potatoes (p. 38) or Roast Chicken with
Rosemary-Garlic Croutons (p. 44)—toss in
any leftover potatoes or garnish the stew with
any leftover croutons.

1. Heat the oil in a large Dutch oven over medium-high heat until shimmering hot, about
1½ minutes. Add the onions, sprinkle with 1 teaspoon salt, reduce the heat to medium, and
cook, stirring, until softened, about 6 minutes. Add the beans and cook, stirring, for a couple of minutes. Add the broth, potatoes, and tomato and bring to a boil. Reduce the heat to
a gentle simmer, cover and cook until the potatoes and beans are tender, about 20 minutes.

2. Stir in the chicken, corn, and thyme and cook until the chicken is heated through, about
10 minutes. Season generously with salt and pepper to taste. Serve immediately with a sprinkling of the Parmesan.

Ajiaco (Colombian Chicken, Corn, and Potato Stew)

Serves 4

This potato and corn stew is traditional in Cuban and Colombian cuisines. I was first introduced to it by a Colombian cook friend of mine, Hugo Munoz. Hugo likes to throw all sorts of potatoes into the broth along with corn and chicken and intense flavorings like jalapeños, lime juice, and capers. Though in most ajiacos the corn is served on the cob (cut into 2-inch pieces), in this version I slice the kernels off the cobs to accommodate the quick cooking needed for the leftover chicken.

2 tablespoons olive oil
1 medium-size yellow onion, finely diced
Kosher salt
3 cloves garlic, minced
2 jalapeños, cored, seeded and finely diced
1 large russet potato, peeled and cut into 1-inch chunks
1 medium-size Yukon Gold potato, cut into 1-inch chunks
3 cups low-salt chicken broth
2 cups fresh (from 3 ears) or frozen corn
2½ cups diced leftover chicken
Freshly ground black pepper
Juice of 1 lime
2 tablespoons capers, drained, rinsed, and chopped
½ cup chopped fresh cilantro
¾ cup sour cream

CHIX PICKS

A bird coated with Sweet Southern Spice Rub (p. 12) or Southwestern Chile Spice Rub (p. 11) complements the heat and tanginess of this chicken stew.

1. Heat the oil in a large Dutch oven over medium-high heat until shimmering hot, about 1½ minutes. Add the onion, sprinkle with 1 teaspoon salt, reduce the heat to medium, and cook, stirring, until softened and browned in places, about 6 minutes. Add the garlic and jalapeños and cook, stirring a few times, for 1 minute. Add the potatoes and broth and bring to a boil. Reduce the heat to a simmer, cover, and cook until the potatoes are fork tender, about 20 minutes.

2. Stir in the corn and chicken and cook until the corn softens a bit and the chicken heats through, about 10 minutes. Season generously with salt and pepper to taste.

3. Just before serving, stir in the lime juice, capers, and half the cilantro. Serve with a dollop of the sour cream and a sprinkling of the remaining cilantro.

Mane's West African Chicken and Peanut Stew

Serves 4

Quecuto Mane is the original grill cook at b.good and one of the finest cooks I've ever come across. Eternally upbeat and energetic, Quecoto is always eager to share the dishes of his native Guinea-Bissau, a small country near Senegal and Liberia on the western coast of Africa. Chicken and peanut stew is a traditional preparation in Quecuto's homeland. He sautés aromatics like shallots and ginger to start, then braises them with chicken, peanut butter, and tomato paste. If you like, you can fold in some corn or sweet potatoes, which are traditional components in this stew.

2 tablespoons canola or vegetable oil
1 large shallot, finely diced
1 jalapeño, cored, seeded, and minced
1 tablespoon peeled and minced fresh ginger
Kosher salt
1 teaspoon chili powder
1 cup low-salt chicken broth
½ cup chunky peanut butter
2 tablespoons tomato paste
1 tablespoon cider vinegar
3 cups diced leftover chicken
Freshly ground black pepper
3 scallions (white and green parts), trimmed and thinly sliced

CHIX PICKS

A roast chicken with some spice melds well with this stew. Try Grill-Roasted Tandoori Chicken (p. 62) or a grill-roasted bird coated with All-Purpose Poultry Spice Rub (p. 11).

Heat the oil in a large Dutch oven over medium heat until shimmering hot, about 2 minutes. Add the shallot, jalapeño, and ginger, sprinkle with 1 teaspoon salt, and cook, stirring, until they sizzle steadily and just begin to brown at the edges, about 1½ minutes. Add the chili powder and cook, stirring, for 1 minute. Stir in the broth, peanut butter, tomato paste, and vinegar and bring to a boil. Reduce the heat to a gentle simmer, stir in the chicken, and cook until heated through, about 10 minutes. Season with salt and pepper to taste and serve immediately with a sprinkling of the scallions.

Spicy New Mexican Green Chile Chicken Stew

Serves 4 to 6

Green chiles like poblanos and Anaheims form the foundation of New Mexican cuisine. In most preparations, these chiles are first roasted to concentrate their flavor, then folded into salsas, stews, and braises. You can use either type of chile in this recipe—whichever is available at the market or looks better. I prefer the sweetness of Anaheims but poblanos always seem to be in better shape in the produce case.

1 pound Anaheim or poblano chiles
3 tablespoons olive oil
Kosher salt
1 large Spanish onion, finely diced
3 cloves garlic, minced
3 cups low-salt chicken broth
1 pound russet potatoes, peeled and cut into ¾-inch dice
2½ cups diced leftover chicken
2 tablespoons cider vinegar
½ cup chopped fresh cilantro
Freshly ground black pepper

CHIX PICKS

Any roast chicken with plenty of spice will go nicely in this stew, like Grill-Roasted Jamaican Jerk Chicken (p. 74) or Grill-Roasted Chicken with Tex-Mex Spice Crust and Grilled Corn Salsa (p. 58)—use any leftover corn salsa as a garnish.

1. Heat the oven broiler to high and set an oven rack so it's about 6 inches from the heating element. Toss the chiles with 1 tablespoon of the oil and 1 teaspoon salt. Set on a large baking sheet lined with aluminum foil. Broil the chiles, flipping them every couple of minutes, until their skins are browned uniformly, 6 to 10 minutes (the strength of broilers can vary greatly). Transfer to a large bowl, cover with plastic wrap, and let sit for 15 minutes to steam off the skins.

2. Remove the plastic wrap and let cool for 10 minutes (or to room temperature if you like). Then core, seed, and skin the peppers. Coarsely chop and set aside.

3. Heat the remaining 2 tablespoons oil in a large Dutch oven over medium heat until shimmering hot, about 2 minutes. Add the onion, sprinkle with 1 teaspoon salt, and cook, stirring occasionally, until translucent, about 8 minutes. Add the garlic and chiles and cook for 2 minutes, stirring occasionally. Add the broth and potatoes and bring to a boil. Reduce the heat to a gentle simmer, cover, and cook until the potatoes are fork tender, about 20 minutes.

4. Stir in the chicken, vinegar, and half the cilantro and cook until heated through, about 10 minutes. Season with salt and pepper to taste. Serve immediately with a sprinkling of the remaining cilantro.

Murillo's Spanish Cocido

Serves 4 to 6

When I studied for a year in college in Salamanca, Spain, I was lucky enough to live with four Spanish law students in an old apartment in the center of town. My room-mates were young, messy bachelors. Nobody woke before noon or attended classes or did much of anything for that matter—they were quite a bit of fun. They were also good cooks, particularly my friend Juan Murillo. Permanently ruffled and smiling, Murillo taught me the tricks to making a proper Spanish *cocido*, the popular chickpea stew native to the central regions of that country.

Much of what makes a Spanish *cocido* so special is the cured pork—chorizo and jamon Serrano in particular—native to Spain. Back here in the States, I've had to learn how to rework the recipe using the ingredients available at hand. In this ver-sion, pancetta, an unsmoked Italian bacon, takes the place of jamon Serrano (you could use a slice of salt pork instead), while Portuguese-style chorizo (available in most markets) subs in for Spanish chorizo.

¼ pound pancetta, cut into ¼-inch pieces
¾ pound Spanish or Portuguese chorizo, cut into ¼-inch dice
1 large onion, finely diced
Kosher salt
3 cloves garlic, minced
2 teaspoons Spanish paprika (pimenton de la Vera) or sweet Hungarian paprika
¾ pound kale, stemmed, leaves chopped, washed and spun dry
1 large russet potato, peeled and cut into 1-inch chunks
One 15-ounce can chick peas (garbanzo beans), rinsed and drained
4 cups low-salt chicken broth
2 teaspoons tomato paste
3 cups diced leftover chicken
Freshly ground black pepper

CHIX PICKS

The paprika in All-Purpose Poultry Spice Rub (p. 11) or Sweet Southern Spice Rub (p. 12) complements the flavors in this Spanish stew.

1. Heat the pancetta and chorizo together in a large Dutch oven over medium heat, stirring often, until they crisp and brown and render much of their fat, about 8 minutes. Using a slotted spoon, transfer to a large plate lined with paper towels.

2. Add the onion to the pot, sprinkle generously with salt (about 1 teaspoon) and cook, stirring occasionally, until it softens and browns in places, about 6 minutes. Add the garlic and paprika and cook, stirring, for 1 minute. Add the kale, sprinkle with another ½ teaspoon salt and cook, stirring occasionally, until it colors a dark green and wilts somewhat, about 3 minutes. Add the potato, chickpeas, broth, browned pork, and tomato paste and bring to a boil. Reduce the heat to a simmer, cover, and cook until the potato is fork tender, about 20 minutes.

3. Stir in the chicken and cook for 10 minutes to heat through.

4. Season with salt and pepper to taste and serve immediately.

Chicken, Fennel, and Sausage Stew

Serves 4

I like using fennel as a base for stews. It has a pleasant anise flavor, which gives a dish an aromatic sweetness. In this stew, this flavor is further complemented by Italian sausage (which has fennel seeds). Serve, tossed with pasta (try a small shape like penne or rigatoni) or set on top of risotto.

2 tablespoons olive oil
1 pound sweet Italian sausage,
   cut into 1-inch pieces
1 large bulb fennel, trimmed and
   cut in 1/4-inch dice
Kosher salt
1 cup low-salt chicken broth
2 tablespoons balsamic vinegar
2 1/2 cups diced leftover chicken
1 tablespoon heavy cream
10 drops Tabasco or other hot sauce
2 teaspoons chopped fresh thyme
Freshly ground black pepper
1/4 cup freshly grated Parmesan cheese

CHIX PICKS

Roast Chicken with Fennel and Mushroom Dressing (p. 47) shares the same flavors as this stew or try Balsamic-Glazed Rosemary Chicken with Bacon and Pearl Onions (p. 36).

1. Heat the oil in a large Dutch oven over medium-high heat until shimmering hot, about 1 1/2 minutes. Add the sausage and cook, tossing occasionally, until well browned all over, about 5 minutes. Stir in the fennel, sprinkle lightly with salt and cook, stirring until it browns all over and starts to soften, about 5 minutes. Add the broth and vinegar and bring to a boil. Reduce the heat to a simmer, cover with the lid slightly askew, and cook until the sausage cooks through and the fennel is tender, about 15 minutes—slice into one of the thicker pieces of each to check.

2. Stir in the chicken, cream, Tabasco, and thyme and cook another 10 minutes to heat through. Season with salt and pepper to taste. Serve immediately with a sprinkling of the Parmesan.

Chicken Gumbo with Andouille Sausage, Shrimp, and Okra

Serves 6

It's the intense, nutty flavor of a roux that makes a gumbo. This mixture of flour and butter can take up to 45 minutes to properly brown over low heat, but I like to speed things up over a medium flame to get the same color in about 10 minutes.

2 tablespoons olive oil
¾ pound andouille or chorizo sausage, cut into ¾-inch-thick rounds
1 large Spanish onion, finely diced
2 ribs celery, finely diced
1 green bell pepper, cored, seeded, and finely diced
6 ounces okra, stemmed and thinly sliced into rounds
Kosher salt
2 tablespoons all-purpose flour
4 cups low-salt chicken broth
One 14.5-ounce can diced tomatoes and their juices
2 bay leaves
2½ cups diced leftover chicken
½ pound large shrimp, peeled and deveined
1 tablespoon gumbo file powder (optional)
Freshly ground black pepper
4 scallions (white and green parts), thinly sliced

> ## CHIX PICKS
>
> A spice-rubbed chicken pairs well with the big flavors in this gumbo. Try a roast chicken sprinkled with Southwestern Chile Spice Rub (p. 11) or Sweet Southern Spice Rub (p. 12).

1. Heat the oil in large skillet over medium-high heat until shimmering hot, about 1½ minutes. Add the sausage and cook, stirring, until it starts to brown and crisp, about 4 minutes. Transfer to a large plate lined with paper towels.

2. Add the onion, celery, bell pepper, and okra to the pan. Sprinkle generously with salt (about 1 teaspoon) and cook, stirring, until the vegetables soften and brown in places, about 6 minutes. Reduce the heat to medium-low, add the flour, and cook, stirring, until it colors a medium brown, about 10 minutes. Stir in the broth, tomatoes and their juices, and bay leaves, bring to a boil, then reduce the heat to a steady simmer. Stir in the sausage and chicken, cover, and cook until the vegetables are completely tender, about 20 minutes.

3. Stir in the shrimp and gumbo file powder (if using) and simmer until firm and cooked through, about 5 minutes. Season generously with salt and pepper to taste. Discard the bay leaves and serve immediately with a sprinkling of the scallions.

Spicy Chicken and Black Bean Chili

Serves 4

I'm a sucker for chili. Over the years, I've played around with all sorts of versions, including this one with leftover chicken. Puréeing some of the beans along with the canned tomatoes gives the chili a thick texture and a rich, slow-cooked feel.

One 28-ounce or two 15-ounce can(s)
black beans, drained and rinsed well
One 14.5-ounce can diced tomatoes
and their juices
1½ canned chipotle chiles, plus 2 tablespoons
of the adobo sauce
¼ pound bacon (about 4 thick slices),
cut into thin strips
1 large Spanish onion, finely diced
Kosher salt
1 tablespoon chili powder
¾ cup beer (I prefer a light lager)
2 cups shredded leftover chicken
½ cup chopped fresh cilantro
Freshly ground black pepper
1 ripe tomato, cored and cut into medium dice
1 ripe avocado, pitted and cut into medium dice
½ cup sour cream

CHIX PICKS

For this chili, try a bird with some spice and heat, like a roast chicken coated with Southwestern Chile Spice Rub (p. 11) or tossed with Lime and Jalapeno Vinaigrette (p. 60).

1. Combine 1 cup of the beans, the canned tomatoes and their juices, and the chipotles and their sauce in a food processor and process until smooth. Set aside.

2. Brown the bacon in a large Dutch oven over medium heat, stirring occasionally, until crisp, about 6 minutes. Transfer to a plate lined with paper towels.

3. Add the onion to the bacon fat, sprinkle generously with salt (about ½ teaspoon) and cook, stirring occasionally, until the onion softens and becomes translucent, about 6 minutes. Add the chili powder and stir for 20 seconds. Add the beer and cook, scraping the bottom of the pan with a wooden spoon to get up any browned bits, until it almost completely reduces, about 2 minutes. Add the remaining beans and the puréed bean mixture and bring to a simmer. Reduce the heat to medium-low, cover, and cook for 10 minutes. Stir in the chicken and cook until it heats through, about 5 minutes. Stir in half the cilantro and season with salt and pepper to taste.

4. Ladle into large bowls, sprinkle with the tomato, avocado, crisped bacon, and the remaining cilantro, and serve with a dollop of the sour cream.

Braised Sichuan Chicken with Broccoli and Tofu

Serves 4

When I'm not really sure what I want to make for dinner, this is the sort of meal I turn to. Tofu is easy to keep on hand in the refrigerator—it will hold for a week or two—and it's perfect tossed into most any stir-fry. In this one, the tofu is sautéed along with garlic, ginger, and hot peppers, then braised with a mix of soy sauce and oyster sauce; the chicken is tossed in just at the end of cooking.

3 cloves garlic, peeled and preferably smashed
One 2-inch piece fresh ginger, peeled and thinly sliced
1 Thai or Serrano chile, thinly sliced
2 tablespoons canola oil
3/4 pound firm tofu, cut into 1-inch dice
1 1/4 broccoli crowns, cut into 1 1/2-inch florets, blanched in boiling water for 2 minutes, cooled in cold water, and drained
2 teaspoons cornstarch
1/4 cup low-salt chicken broth
2 tablespoons soy sauce
1 tablespoon rice vinegar
1 tablespoon oyster sauce
2 teaspoons toasted sesame oil
2 1/2 cups diced leftover chicken
2 scallions (white and green parts), trimmed and thinly sliced
Steamed white rice, for serving

CHIX PICKS

A simple roast chicken with Asian flavorings pairs well with this braised chicken. Try Chinese Salt and Pepper Roast Chicken (p. 52) or a bird soaked in Soy-Ginger Brine (p. 9) before roasting.

1. Heat the garlic, ginger, and chile in the canola oil in a large sauté pan or wok over medium-high heat until they sizzle steadily for 1 minute. Add the tofu and cook, stirring, until it starts to brown, about 3 minutes. Add the broccoli and cook, gently tossing, until heated through, about 2 minutes.

2. In a small bowl, whisk together the cornstarch, broth, soy sauce, vinegar, oyster sauce, and sesame oil. Add this sauce and the chicken to the broccoli and bring to a boil so that the mixture thickens. Reduce the heat to low and cook for a couple of minutes so the flavors mix and meld.

3. Transfer to a serving platter, sprinkle with the scallions, and serve with the rice.

Chicken Braised with Mushrooms and Sun-Dried Tomatoes

Serves 4

When I began assembling the recipes for this book, this pairing was one of the first I tried and it didn't let me down. Mushrooms, sun-dried tomatoes, and chicken are an oft-used trinity in my kitchen—the tomatoes brighten up chicken with their tangy intensity while the mushrooms impart an earthy, almost beefy essence.

3 tablespoons olive oil
10 ounces white mushrooms, quartered
¼ pound shiitake mushrooms, stemmed and quartered
Kosher salt
2 cloves garlic, minced
¼ cup dry sherry
¾ cup low-salt chicken broth
1 tablespoon balsamic vinegar
6 oil-packed sun-dried tomatoes, thinly sliced
2 teaspoons chopped fresh rosemary
3 cups diced leftover chicken
2 teaspoons cornstarch
2 tablespoons water
½ cup freshly grated Parmesan cheese
Freshly ground black pepper

> ## CHIX PICKS
>
> A roast chicken brushed with Rosemary-Balsamic Glaze (p. 13) shares many of the same flavors as those in this dish. A bird drizzled with the Balsamic-Sun-Dried Tomato Vinaigrette (p. 61) also is a good fit.

1. Heat 2 tablespoons of the oil in a large sauté pan over medium-high heat until shimmering hot, about 1½ minutes. Add the mushrooms and sprinkle generously with salt, about 1 teaspoon. Cook, stirring occasionally, until browned and softened, about 5 minutes. Push the mushrooms to the side of the pan, add the remaining 1 tablespoon oil and the garlic, and cook, stirring, until it becomes fragrant and sizzles steadily for about 30 seconds. Stir together with the mushrooms. Add the sherry and cook, stirring, until it almost completely reduces, about 2 minutes. Add the broth, vinegar, tomatoes, and rosemary and bring to a boil. Add the chicken, reduce the heat to a gentle simmer, and cook until heated through, about 10 minutes.

2. In a small bowl, whisk the cornstarch and water. Add to the broth and cook, stirring, until the mixture thickens, about 1 minute. Stir in the Parmesan, season with salt and pepper to taste, and serve immediately.

Chicken Cacciatore

Serves 4

Hunter's style chicken is a traditional Italian dish that has become part of the standard repertoire of most American home cooks. With leftover chicken as its centerpiece, this cacciatore must be cooked quickly. Red peppers and mushrooms serve as the base for the tomato stew, while a splash of white wine offers body and some tang.

3 tablespoons olive oil

1 red bell pepper, cored, seeded, and cut into 1/4-inch dice

10 ounces mushrooms, thinly sliced

Kosher salt

2 cloves garlic, minced

1/2 cup dry white wine

One 28-ounce can diced tomatoes and their juices

3 cups leftover chicken cut into 2-inch pieces

2 teaspoons chopped fresh thyme

1/2 teaspoon crushed red pepper flakes

1/2 cup freshly grated Parmesan cheese

Freshly ground black pepper

> ## CHIX PICKS
>
> A simple roast chicken with plenty of herbs is a good match for this stew. Try Bistro Roast Chicken with Lemon and Thyme (p. 34) or Balsamic-Glazed Rosemary Chicken with Bacon and Pearl Onions (p. 36)—toss any bacon or onions from the latter in along with the chicken.

1. Heat 2 tablespoons of the oil in a large Dutch oven over medium heat until shimmering hot, about 2 minutes. Add the bell pepper and cook, stirring, until it starts to brown and soften, about 4 minutes. Raise the heat to medium-high, add the mushrooms, sprinkle with 1 teaspoon salt, and cook, stirring, until they soften and brown in places, about 3 minutes. Push the mushrooms to the side of the pan and add the remaining 1 tablespoon oil and the garlic. Cook, stirring, until it sizzles steadily for about 30 seconds. Add the wine and cook until it almost completely reduces, about 2 minutes. Add the tomatoes and their juices, bring to a boil, then reduce the heat to a steady simmer, cover, and cook for 5 minutes.

2. Stir in the chicken, thyme, and pepper flakes and cook for 10 minutes to heat through.

3. Stir in half the Parmesan and season with salt and black pepper to taste (about 3/4 teaspoon each). Serve immediately with a sprinkling of the remaining Parmesan.

Chapter 5
Pasta, Rice, and Grains

During the height of the low-carb craze,

it seemed like just about everything starch was to be avoided, if not banished from our diets altogether. Fortunately, things have settled down a bit and Americans seem to be embracing pasta and rice again. If anything, we now lean towards ones made with whole grains, which may be the most positive result of all that carb counting.

Whether you're partial to whole-wheat pasta or the white variety, I hope that the recipes in this chapter fit your tastes and mood. Leftover chicken simply goes too well with pastas, rice, and grains to be missed.

Pastas are a perfect partner for leftover chicken. While the pasta cooks, you can fold the chicken into a quick sauce—which will revive any dryness in the bird's texture—then toss both together and serve. Tetrazzini may be a familiar face paired with pasta, but there are many other directions you can follow. Allow the produce section of the market and your kitchen cupboard to offer inspiration.

I learned a good deal from a six-month apprenticeship with Giuliano Bugialli at his cooking school in the Chianti region of Tuscany—important techniques like how to make pasta and how to roll fresh gnocchi. The most significant lessons that *il professore* Bugialli taught me, though, were subtle ones: an appreciation for the Italian way of life and a deep respect for the country's distinctive regional cuisines. Bugialli is one of the fiercest guardians of traditional Italian cooking. If two villages in Tuscany make a specific pasta a little differently, you can be certain that Bugialli knows not only how they vary and the historical reasons why.

Despite this wonderful education from Bugialli, I must admit that many of the pastas in this chapter are not authentic Italian ones. But they do follow the basic Italian rules of cooking with what's fresh and what's on hand and seasoning things simply but generously so the flavors of the dish shine through.

While rice doesn't have the same cook-and-toss simplicity as pasta, it's not far behind in convenience. As opposed to pasta, where the major flavoring steps are done at the end of cooking, for many rice dishes the flavor base is formed at the beginning of cooking with aromatics like onions, garlic, and peppers. From there, these dishes veer off in different directions depending on the cuisine, including everything from vegetables to sausage.

Grain dishes might not yet have made it to the culinary mainstream of America, but they are easy to make and wonderfully flavorful. Grains such as barley or Italian farro can be steamed like rice or boiled and tossed with flavorful toppings just like pasta. And then there are grains like quinoa and wheatberries which can be made in large portions, making them perfect for a casual dinner with company or a summer block party.

Farfalle with Grilled Chicken, Feta, and Arugula

Serves 4

This pasta is a fine example of something I've never eaten in Italy but, I hope, respectfully honors that style of cooking. Sun-dried tomatoes, arugula, and feta are a wonderful combination and the leftover chicken gives the dish substance. I like to finish this with a drizzle of good olive oil, which adds richness and a peppery edge.

¼ cup extra-virgin olive oil
2 cloves garlic, minced
½ pound baby arugula, washed and spun dry
Kosher salt
2 cups diced leftover chicken
6 ounces feta cheese, crumbled
8 oil-packed sun-dried tomatoes, thinly sliced
2 teaspoons chopped fresh thyme
Freshly ground black pepper
¾ pound farfalle or penne rigate

1. Bring a large pot of water to a boil.

2. Meanwhile, heat 2 tablespoons of the oil and the garlic in a large skillet over medium-high heat and cook, stirring, until it sizzles steadily and starts to brown around the edges, about 1½ minutes. Add the arugula, sprinkle generously with salt (about ½ teaspoon), and cook, stirring a few times, until it just wilts, about 2 minutes. Stir in the chicken, feta, tomatoes, and thyme, toss well, and season with salt and pepper to taste. Remove from the heat and set aside.

3. Stir a couple of tablespoons of salt into the boiling water and cook the pasta until it's just tender to the tooth, about 11 minutes. Drain and add it to the skillet. Set over medium-high heat and cook, stirring frequently, for 2 minutes so the flavors mix and meld. Taste for salt and pepper and serve immediately with a drizzle of the remaining 2 tablespoons olive oil.

CHIX PICKS

Try any mildly flavored grill-roasted or roast chicken with this dish. The herb flavor in Anago's Garlicky Grill-Roasted Split Chickens with Lemon and Herbs (p. 66) or Italian Grilled Chicken Under a Brick with Smoky Balsamic Tomatoes (p. 68) will go wonderfully with this pasta—toss any leftover grilled tomatoes from the latter in along with the sun-dried ones.

HOW SALTY SHOULD PASTA WATER BE?

If you ever want to see just how important salt is, try cooking pasta in unsalted water. It will be practically flavorless and, no matter how much salt you add to it after cooking, it will still lack a little something.

In my pasta recipes, I tell you to stir a couple of tablespoons of salt into the water before adding the pasta. When in doubt, though, there's another rule of thumb you can follow with pasta water: It should taste about as salty as the ocean. That's pretty salty, but it ensures that the pasta will have a wonderful flavor and there will be no need to compensate by overseasoning the sauce.

Gemelli with Chicken, Asparagus, and Caramelized Onions

Serves 4

Caramelized onions are at the top of my list of go-to ingredients. I like to stir some into a pasta or braise or layer them on a pizza or sandwich. In most any dish, these onions add a wonderful sweetness and depth of flavor.

1/4 cup olive oil
1 pound fresh asparagus, bottoms trimmed, peeled if thick, and cut into 2-inch lengths
Kosher salt and freshly ground black pepper
1 large Spanish onion, thinly sliced
2 cups diced leftover chicken
1 cup low-salt chicken broth
2 teaspoons chopped fresh thyme
1 tablespoon sherry vinegar or balsamic vinegar
1/2 cup freshly grated Parmesan cheese
3/4 pound gemelli or penne

CHIX PICKS

Sear-Roasted Chicken with Spring Onions and Asparagus (p. 86) is a natural pairing for this dish—toss any leftover asparagus and onions into the pasta.

1. Heat 2 tablespoons of the oil in a large skillet over medium-high heat until shimmering hot, about 1 1/2 minutes. Add the asparagus and sprinkle generously with salt and pepper (about 1/2 teaspoon of each). Cook, stirring occasionally, until it browns and becomes just tender, about 4 minutes. Transfer to a large plate.

2. Add the remaining 2 tablespoons oil and the onion to the skillet, sprinkle generously with salt and cook, stirring, until it wilts and becomes translucent, about 5 minutes. Reduce the heat to medium-low and continue to cook, stirring occasionally, until the onion softens completely and turns a light caramel color, about another 20 minutes.

3. Return the asparagus to the pan and add the chicken, broth, and thyme. Bring to a boil, then reduce the heat to a simmer and cook for 5 minutes. Add the vinegar and 1/4 cup of the Parmesan. Season generously with salt and pepper to taste and reduce the heat to low.

4. Meanwhile, bring a large pot of water to a boil, then stir a couple of tablespoons of salt into the boiling water and cook the pasta until it's just tender to the tooth, about 12 minutes Drain and add the pasta to the skillet. Cook over medium-high heat, stirring, for 2 minutes so the flavors mix and meld. Serve immediately with a sprinkling of the remaining 1/4 cup Parmesan.

Spicy Penne with Chicken, Artichokes, and Tomatoes

Serves 4

When it comes to artichokes, I generally put my creative impulses on hold and instead opt for the traditional accompaniments. Artichokes have an assertive flavor that pairs well with black olives and tomatoes, the two ingredients that power this simple pasta dish. I do like to use canned artichokes (particularly artichoke bottoms) on a busy weeknight, but if you have the time or inclination, do cook the artichokes from scratch. The crushed red pepper flakes in this dish impart a wonderful spicy edge, but if you're heat-averse, you can halve the amount.

2 tablespoons olive oil
3 cloves garlic, smashed
1/2 teaspoon crushed red pepper flakes
One 14.5-ounce can diced tomatoes
  and their juices
2 cups diced leftover chicken
One 15-ounce can artichokes bottoms,
  rinsed and thinly sliced
1 cup kalamata or gaeta olives,
  drained and pitted
1/3 cup freshly grated Parmesan cheese
1 tablespoon chopped fresh thyme
Kosher salt and freshly ground black pepper
3/4 pound penne or gemelli

CHIX PICKS

To complement the artichokes, try Bistro Roast Chicken with Lemon and Thyme (p. 34) or a roast chicken with a Lemon-Herb Rub (p. 13).

1. Bring a large pot of water to a boil.

2. Meanwhile, heat the oil and garlic in a large skillet over medium heat until the garlic is browned all over and very fragrant, about 3 minutes. Add the red pepper flakes and tomatoes and their juices and bring to a boil. Reduce the heat to a simmer and cook for 5 minutes. Add the chicken, artichokes, olives, Parmesan, and 2 teaspoons of the thyme and cook, stirring, until heated through, about 2 minutes. Remove from the heat. Season with salt and pepper to taste.

3. Add a couple of tablespoons of salt to the boiling water and cook the pasta until it's just tender to the tooth, about 12 minutes. Drain, add the pasta to the skillet, and set over medium-high heat. Cook, stirring, for 2 minutes so the flavors mix and meld. Serve immediately with a sprinkling of the remaining 1 teaspoon thyme.

Rotini with Pesto, Chicken, and Green Beans

Serves 4

Pesto and greens beans are a classic Italian pairing. While there's nothing to match the old-world feel of a mortar and pestle, I fear that many cooks (myself included) at the end of a long day would pass out from exhaustion before finishing mashing the pesto. A food processor works well.

PESTO:

3½ cups packed fresh basil leaves (about 1 large bunch), washed and patted dry
¾ cup freshly grated Parmesan cheese
½ cup pine nuts, toasted on a baking sheet at 375°F until lightly browned
⅓ cup extra-virgin olive oil, more if needed
Kosher salt and freshly ground
    black pepper

PASTA:

10 ounces fresh green beans, trimmed
¾ pound rotini
2½ cups diced leftover chicken
6 oil-packed sun-dried tomatoes, thinly sliced
¼ cup freshly grated Parmesan cheese, for serving
3 tablespoons chopped fresh parsley

> ## CHIX PICKS
>
> Any mildly flavored roast chicken will do, but try a bird with plenty of garlic, like Sear-Roasted Chicken with Lots of Garlic (p. 82). The fresh herbs in Anago's Garlicky Grill-Roasted Split Chickens with Lemon and Herbs (p. 66) will complement the pesto in this pasta.

1. Bring a large pot of water to a boil.

2. Meanwhile, make the pesto. Place the basil, Parmesan, and pine nuts in a food processor. While processing, add the oil in a steady stream through the feed tube so the pesto becomes a loose, uniform mixture. Transfer to a small bowl, season with salt and pepper to taste, and set aside. This will keep, tightly covered, in the refrigerator up to 2 days.

3. Stir a couple of tablespoons of salt into the water and blanch the green beans just tender, about 3 minutes. Using a slotted spoon, transfer them to a bowl with cold water running over it and let sit until cold. Drain well.

4. In the same boiling water, cook the pasta until it's tender to the tooth, about 10 minutes. Drain and transfer to a large serving bowl along with the chicken, green beans, pesto, and tomatoes. Toss well and taste for salt and pepper. Serve immediately with a sprinkling of Parmesan and parsley.

Fettuccine with Chicken and Spinach in Porcini Cream Sauce

Serves 4

Known as cèpes in France and porcini in Italy, these thick wild mushrooms are foraged in the forests of Europe and parts of the United States. Even if you're lucky enough to find them locally, porcini are quite expensive. Dried porcinis are a better bet. They're relatively affordable and easy to keep on hand to pull out at a moment's notice. Here, they infuse a rich cream sauce along with shallots, vinegar, and fresh thyme.

¾ ounce dried porcini mushrooms, soaked in
   1½ cups boiling water until tender
2 tablespoons olive oil
2 shallots, finely diced
10 ounces fresh spinach, washed well and spun dry
Kosher salt
2 cups thinly sliced leftover chicken
2 tablespoons heavy cream
¾ cup freshly grated Parmesan cheese
1 tablespoon sherry vinegar or balsamic vinegar
2 teaspoons chopped fresh thyme
Freshly ground black pepper
¾ pound fettuccine or linguini

> ## CHIX PICKS
>
> The tanginess of the Balsamic-Glazed Rosemary Chicken with Bacon and Pearl Onions (p. 36) pairs nicely with the cream and mushrooms in this pasta sauce; add any leftover bacon or pearl onions to the sauce. If you've got leftover Wild Mushroom and Herb Jus (p. 33) from a roast chicken, toss it into this pasta.

1. Bring a large pot of water to a boil.

2. Meanwhile, remove the mushrooms from the soaking liquid and chop. Strain the liquid through a coffee filter. Set the mushrooms and liquid aside.

3. Heat the oil in a large skillet over medium heat. Add the shallots and cook, stirring, until soft and translucent, about 5 minutes. Add the mushrooms and cook, stirring, for 30 seconds. Raise the heat to medium-high, add the spinach, sprinkle generously with salt (about ½ teaspoon) and cook, tossing often with tongs, until just wilted, about 3 minutes. Add the mushroom soaking liquid, bring to a boil, reduce to a simmer, and cook for 2 minutes. Stir in the chicken, cream, half the Parmesan, the vinegar, and thyme. Bring to a boil, then reduce the heat to a simmer for 2 minutes. Season generously with salt and pepper to taste and remove from the heat.

4. Add a couple of tablespoons of salt to the boiling water and cook the pasta until it's just tender to the tooth, about 11 minutes. Drain and add to the skillet. Set over medium-high heat and cook, stirring often, for 2 minutes so the flavors mix and meld. Serve immediately with a sprinkling of the remaining Parmesan.

Bucatini with Chicken and Spicy Tomato and Black Olive Sauce

Serves 4

This is similar to a puttanesca, the classic Neapolitan pasta purportedly popular with the prostitutes of that southern Italian city because of its ease of preparation. As the legend would suggest, you can throw together this sauce in about the time it takes to boil water. It's also full of bold flavors: slowly browned cloves of garlic (see sidebar p. 147), red pepper flakes, capers, and olives pair with bucatini, long hollow strands of pasta that are a cross between spaghetti and penne. If bucatini is not available in your supermarket, substitute linguine or spaghetti.

4 cloves garlic, smashed
2 tablespoons olive oil
1/2 teaspoon crushed red pepper flakes
One 28-ounce can diced tomatoes
  and their juices
1/2 cup pitted gaeta or kalamata olives,
  drained and cut in half lengthwise
3 tablespoons capers, rinsed and chopped
2 cups diced leftover chicken
Kosher salt and freshly ground
  black pepper
3/4 pound bucatini or spaghetti
1/4 cup freshly grated Parmesan cheese

CHIX PICKS

Don't be shy about using a chicken with spice to stand up to the heat and brininess of this pasta. Try a roast or grill-roasted chicken coated with All-Purpose Poultry Spice Rub (p. 11) or go with Sear-Roasted Chicken with Tomatoes and Rosemary (p. 78), adding any leftover sauce to the pasta.

1. Bring a large pot of water to a boil.

2. Meanwhile, heat the garlic and olive oil together in a large skillet over medium heat until the cloves are lightly browned all over, about 3 minutes. Add the red pepper flakes and, after 20 seconds, the tomatoes and their juices, olives, and capers. Bring to a boil, cover, reduce the heat to a simmer and cook for 5 minutes. Stir in the chicken and season with salt and black pepper to taste. If you prefer, discard the garlic cloves. Reduce the heat to low.

3. Add a couple of tablespoons of salt to the boiling water and cook the pasta until it's just tender to the tooth, about 11 minutes. Drain and add to the skillet. Raise the heat to medium-high and cook, stirring, for 2 minutes so the flavors mix and meld. Serve immediately with a sprinkling of the Parmesan.

Spaghetti with Chicken, Capers, and Lemon

Serves 4

I make flavored oils often. They're easy to prepare, they store well, and they're great for dressing up a weeknight meal that needs some pizzazz. Gently heat fresh herbs or intensely flavored pantry items like smashed garlic cloves, capers, lemons, or chiles in plenty of oil until fragrant. Then strain the oil if you like (often I prefer leaving these ingredients in the oil so they continue to impart their flavor) and drizzle the flavored oil over steamed or stir-fried vegetables, onto grilled or roasted meats, or, as in this dish, use it as the base for a light pasta sauce.

1 lemon, scrubbed
1/4 cup olive oil
4 cloves garlic, smashed
2 cups diced leftover chicken
3 tablespoons capers, drained and rinsed
1/2 teaspoon crushed red pepper flakes
Kosher salt
3/4 pound spaghetti
1/4 cup chopped fresh parsley
Freshly ground black pepper

CHIX PICKS

Reinforce the lemony flavor in this dish with Greek Roast Chicken with Lemon, Black Olives, and Potatoes (p. 56) or Bistro Roast Chicken with Lemon and Thyme (p. 34).

1. Bring a large pot of water to a boil.

2. Meanwhile, using a vegetable peeler, shave six 1-inch-wide strips of the lemon's yellow rind (taking care to avoid the white pith below). Juice the lemon and set aside the juice.

3. Heat the oil and garlic together in a large skillet over medium heat, stirring a few times, until the garlic starts to sizzle steadily, about 2 minutes. Add the lemon strips and cook, stirring until the strips sizzle and become very fragrant, about 2 minutes. Add the chicken, capers, and red pepper flakes and cook, stirring, until the chicken heats through, about 2 minutes. Remove from the heat.

4. Add a couple tablespoons of salt to the boiling water and cook the pasta until it's just tender to the tooth, about 11 minutes. Reserve 1 cup of the cooking water, then drain the pasta and add it to the skillet along with ½ cup of the water. Raise the heat to medium-high and cook, stirring, for 2 minutes so the flavors mix and meld. Add more of the pasta water if the mixture starts to dry up. Stir in half the parsley and half the lemon juice. Season with salt and black pepper to taste (about 1 teaspoon of each); taste and add more lemon juice if you like. Serve immediately with a sprinkling of the remaining parsley.

SMASHED CLOVES OF FLAVOR

Garlic can take a wrong turn when it's chopped or minced. It's more susceptible to burning, which will leave its flavor sharp and acrid. For a milder hit of garlic, I'll often use whole smashed cloves. These large pieces of garlic gently infuse a dish without overpowering it. Form an aromatic base for a braise, sauté, or stew by throwing a couple cloves into the oil at the start of heating over a moderate flame until they begin to brown and infuse the oil. I like to leave the cloves in all the way through cooking and sometimes even in the finished dish (a nice rustic touch), though you can remove the cloves just before serving.

To smash the garlic, set the side of a chef's knife on top of an unpeeled clove and press down forcefully with the heel of your hand so the clove flattens and frays a bit and the skin releases from the garlic.

Linguine with Chicken, Cabbage, and Pancetta

Serves 4

Cabbage and cured pork are a classic pairing. The fat of bacon or pancetta stands up to the full flavor of the cabbage, giving it a rich, salty edge. For this dish, I like using Napa cabbage, which cooks quickly and has a mellow flavor. If you can't find it, substitute green or Savoy cabbage, though do take care to thinly slice and cook them until tender (which may take a little longer). Pancetta is the Italian version of bacon, only it's not smoked. Use bacon for this recipe if you can't find pancetta.

1 tablespoon olive oil
¼ pound pancetta or bacon,
   cut into thin strips
1 large head Napa cabbage, cored and cut
   into 2-inch-thick slices
2½ cups thinly sliced leftover chicken
Kosher salt and freshly ground black pepper
¾ pound linguine
½ cup freshly grated Parmesan cheese

CHIX PICKS

Bright citrus flavors cut through the heaviness of the bacon and cabbage. Try a roast chicken brushed with Orange-Apricot Glaze (p. 14) or sprinkled with Lemon-Herb Rub (p. 13).

1. Bring a large pot of water to a boil.

2. Meanwhile, heat the oil and pancetta in a large skillet over medium heat, flipping the pancetta occasionally, until it renders its fat and becomes crisp, about 5 minutes. Transfer to a plate lined with paper towels.

3. Add the cabbage and chicken to the pan, sprinkle generously with salt and pepper, and cook, stirring a few times, until the cabbage wilts and becomes just tender (it should still have a little crunch), about 3 minutes. Remove from the heat.

4. Add a couple of tablespoons of salt to the boiling water and cook the pasta until it's just tender to the tooth, about 11 minutes. Reserve 1 cup of the cooking water and drain the pasta. Add the pasta to the skillet along with ½ cup of the water. Raise the heat to medium-high and cook, stirring, for 2 minutes, so the flavors mix and meld. If the mixture begins to dry out, add a couple more tablespoons of the pasta water. Serve immediately, sprinkled with the Parmesan and bacon.

Baked Pasta with Chicken, Peas, and Farmer's Cheese

Serves 6

This dish was a staple in my house growing up. Like most kids, I only realized I missed it once I was away at school, broke and hungry. I've since learned to make this pasta myself and often turn to it when the cupboard is bare and I'm stressed for time.

Black pepper is a key element—the dish should have an assertive, peppery edge—so don't be shy with it. Farmer's cheese is similar to cottage cheese, only most of its liquid has been pressed out. It's mildly flavored and sweet and acquires a great creamy texture when tossed with hot pasta. If you can't find farmer's cheese, use ricotta, fresh, if possible.

2 tablespoons olive oil, more for greasing
Kosher salt
1 pound penne or ziti
2 1/2 cups diced leftover chicken
10 ounces farmer's or ricotta cheese
2 1/2 cups frozen petite peas
8 oil-packed sun-dried tomatoes,
   thinly sliced
1/4 cup chopped fresh mint
2 teaspoons chopped fresh thyme
Freshly ground black pepper
1/2 cup freshly grated Parmesan cheese
1 cup coarse fresh breadcrumbs (p. 151) or panko,
   toasted on a baking sheet at 375°F until lightly browned

CHIX PICKS

Any roast chicken with plenty of fresh herbs will go nicely with this dish. Try a bird sprinkled with Lemon-Herb Rub (p. 13) or basted with Rosemary-Balsamic Glaze (p. 13).

1. Preheat the oven to 450°F. Grease a 9 by 13-inch baking dish with oil.

2. Bring a large pot of water to a boil. Add a couple of tablespoons of salt to the boiling water and cook the pasta, stirring occasionally, until it's just tender to the tooth, about 11 minutes (it's alright if the pasta is still a little firm, as it will continue to cook in the oven).

3. Drain the pasta and return it to the pot. Add the chicken, farmer's cheese, peas, tomatoes, mint, and thyme and stir well. Season generously with salt and pepper to taste. Transfer the pasta to the prepared baking dish, sprinkle the top evenly with the Parmesan and bread-crumbs, and drizzle with the oil. Bake until the breadcrumbs are browned and the pasta is hot throughout, about 15 minutes. Let sit for 5 minutes, then serve.

Chicken and Spinach Lasagna with Mushrooms

Serves 6 to 8

This dish requires making a béchamel (or *balsamella* as it is known in Italy), a white sauce that starts with a butter-flour roux. While a béchamel has a rich, thick texture, it's not as heavy as cream. In this lasagna, I flavor the béchamel simply with salt and pepper, then fold in some Parmesan. The lasagna is alternately layered with the filling of sautéed spinach, mushrooms, and chicken and the béchamel.

4 tablespoons butter, plus more for greasing
3 tablespoons olive oil
7 ounces shiitake mushrooms, stemmed, caps thinly sliced
Kosher salt and freshly ground black pepper
2 cloves garlic, minced
1 pound fresh spinach, heavy stems removed, rinsed well, and spun dry
2½ cups thinly sliced leftover chicken
1½ teaspoons chopped fresh thyme
2½ cups whole milk
¼ cup all-purpose flour
½ cup freshly grated Parmesan cheese
1 pound lasagna noodles
½ pound Italian fontina cheese, shredded
½ cup coarse fresh breadcrumbs or panko (see sidebar, facing page)

> ## CHIX PICKS
>
> Balsamic-Glazed Rosemary Chicken with Bacon and Pearl Onions (p. 36) and Sear-Roasted Chicken with Spring Onions and Asparagus (p. 86) are both nice, as you can fold any leftover vegetables or bacon into the dish.

1. Preheat the oven to 425°F. Grease a 9 by 13-inch baking dish with butter.

2. Meanwhile, heat a large skillet over medium-high heat for 1 minute. Add half the oil and the shiitakes, sprinkle with salt and pepper and cook, stirring a few times, until browned in places, about 3 minutes. Transfer to a large plate. Add the remaining oil and the garlic and cook, stirring, until it sizzles steadily for about 30 seconds (be careful not to let it burn). Add the spinach, sprinkle generously with salt and cook, tossing often, until it's just wilted, about 3 minutes. Return the mushrooms and add the chicken and thyme to the pan and toss well. Remove from the heat.

3. Bring a large pot of water to a boil. Meanwhile, make the béchamel by heating the milk in a medium saucepan over low heat. At the same time, heat the butter in another medium saucepan over medium-low heat until it begins to foam. Add the flour and cook, stirring well, until light golden and fragrant, about 2 minutes. Whisk in the warm milk and heat, whisking often, until the mixture thickens (it should just come to a boil), about 10 minutes. Stir in the Parmesan, 1 teaspoon salt and 1 teaspoon black pepper, and let cool.

4. Add the pasta to the boiling water and cook until it's just tender to the tooth, about 11 minutes. Drain well. Set one layer of the pasta on the bottom of the prepared baking dish, overlapping the noodles so they overhang the edges of the dish. Top with half the spinach-and-chicken mixture. Add another layer of pasta, this one so it just covers the previous layer. Spoon half the béchamel over the pasta and spread with a spatula to evenly coat. Top with a layer of pasta. Spread the remaining spinach-and-chicken mixture over this. Top with a final layer of pasta and drizzle evenly with the remaining béchamel. Fold the overhanging pasta over towards the center. Sprinkle evenly with the fontina and top with the breadcrumbs. This can be assembled and refrigerated for up to a day ahead before baking.

5. Bake until the breadcrumbs are golden brown, the pasta is hot throughout, and the edges are bubbling, about 20 minutes. Let sit for 5 minutes, then serve.

HOMEMADE BREADCRUMBS

I like making my own breadcrumbs because they taste better and have a full, coarse texture that gives a nice crunch. And they're dead easy—in a food processor, pulse a few slices of stale bread until they form coarse, pea-sized pieces. You can toast the crumbs by tossing them with a little oil and some fresh herbs (such as thyme or rosemary), then heating them in a heavy skillet over low heat until they turn a golden brown. If you're adding these homemade crumbs to a baked pasta, though, toasting isn't necessary as the crumbs will brown when they bake with the pasta.

If you don't have any old bread for these breadcrumbs or if you're in a bit of a rush, you can always use Japanese panko instead. These crumbs, which the Japanese use for fried chicken or pork cutlets, have a coarse texture similar to homemade crumbs. You can find them in the Asian section of many large supermarkets.

Baked Penne with Chicken and Spicy Tomato-Cauliflower Sauce

Serves 6

This pasta is worth making even if your family is not full of cauliflower devotees. The white florets are sautéed on the stovetop, braised with canned tomatoes, then puréed with some cream into a thick pink sauce, leaving little clue as to the cauliflower's presence, save for its pleasant sweetness. The sauce is tossed with penne, then baked in a hot oven until the fontina cheese on top bubbles and browns and the sauce tightens up.

2 tablespoons olive oil,
  more for greasing
2 cloves garlic, halved
  and smashed
1 head cauliflower,
  cut into 1-inch florets
Kosher salt and freshly ground
  black pepper
One 28-ounce can diced
  tomatoes and their juices
1/2 teaspoon crushed red
  pepper flakes
2 tablespoons heavy cream
1/2 cup freshly grated Parmesan cheese
2 cups diced leftover chicken
2 teaspoons chopped fresh thyme
1 pound penne rigate
1/2 pound fontina cheese, shredded
1 cup Garlic-Thyme breadcrumbs (p. 205) or panko (p. 151)

CHIX PICKS

Any mildly flavored roast chicken will do. Try Roast Chicken with Fennel and Mushroom Dressing (p. 47) or Roast Chicken with Garlic-Rosemary Croutons (p. 44).

1. Preheat the oven to 450°F. Grease a 9 by 13-inch baking dish with olive oil.

2. Heat the garlic with the olive oil in a large skillet over medium-high heat until the cloves begin to brown and flavor the oil, about 2 minutes. Add the cauliflower, sprinkle generously with salt and pepper (about 1/2 teaspoon of each), and cook, stirring, until the florets start to brown, about 4 minutes. Add the tomatoes and their juices and red pepper flakes and bring to a boil. Reduce the heat to a simmer, cover with the lid slightly ajar, and cook until the cauliflower is tender, about 15 minutes.

CAN'T BEAT THE REAL THING

Like most people in this country, I grew up thinking of Parmesan as the cheese you shook out of the green can. It would be many years before I first tasted the real thing—Parmigiano Reggiano—and soon thereafter the green can was gone forever.

Parmigiano Reggiano is made exclusively in a small area in the north of Italy. Farmers in this region still follow traditional methods, making the cheese only during certain months of the year from a fresh batch of cow's milk each day. Parmigiano's lengthy aging process—at least fourteen months and often around two years—allows its flavors to develop, creating a wonderfully complex cheese that is at once sweet, sour, nutty, and rich.

The time-consuming nature of this process has a price. Parmigiano Reggiano is relatively expensive, but a little goes a long way. If you have any doubts about this, grate some imported Parmigiano and a domestic Parmesan. You'll find that a small sprinkling of Parmigiano outshines a healthy scattering of the domestic stuff. American Parmesan isn't aged nearly as long and thus lacks the same depth of flavor. For this reason, whenever I call for Parmesan, use Parmigiano if you can. And one last note: Make sure to grate Parmigiano just before serving it. Like black pepper, this cheese is most flavorful when it's just been grated.

3. Meanwhile, bring a large pot of water to a boil.

4. Add the cream and ¼ cup of the Parmesan to the sauce and, using an immersion blender, purée the sauce until smooth (or transfer the sauce to a regular blender in batches, carefully purée, and return to the skillet). Stir in the chicken and the thyme, season with salt and pepper to taste, and remove from the heat.

5. Add a couple of tablespoons of salt to the boiling water and cook the pasta until it's just tender to the tooth, about 11 minutes. (You'll want the pasta to be extra firm as it will continue to soften in the oven.) Drain the pasta and return it to the pot along with the sauce. Toss well and season with salt and pepper to taste.

6. Transfer the pasta and the sauce to the prepared baking dish. Sprinkle evenly with the fontina and the remaining ¼ cup Parmesan. Sprinkle the breadcrumbs evenly over the top of the pasta. Bake until the cheese and breadcrumbs brown and the sauce bubbles at the edges, 10 to 15 minutes. Let sit for 5 minutes, then serve.

Herbed Macaroni and Cheese with Chicken and Mushrooms

Serves 6 to 8

I'll admit this is not the dish for a sultry August evening. This is comfort food—frigid February, throw-on-the-pajamas-before-dinner-and-get-cozy kind of food. As opposed to the fussy layering system of a lasagna, here the béchamel is stirred together with the toppings, tossed with the pasta, then baked until browned and bubbly. The effect is wonderfully warming, the perfect dish for a winter night.

¼ cup (½ stick) unsalted butter,
   more for greasing
3 cups whole milk
¼ cup all-purpose flour
½ pound extra-sharp Cheddar cheese,
   shredded
½ cup freshly grated Parmesan cheese
Kosher salt and freshly ground black pepper
3 ounces bacon (about 3 slices),
   cut into thin strips
2 shallots, finely diced
½ pound mixed fresh mushrooms
   (like cremini, oyster, and shiitake),
   thinly sliced
2 cups diced leftover chicken
2 tablespoons balsamic vinegar
2 teaspoons chopped fresh thyme
1 pound pasta (preferably elbows)
½ cup thinly sliced fresh chives (about ½ bunch)
1 cup Garlic-Thyme breadcrumbs (p. 205) or panko

CHIX PICKS

Any mildly flavored roast chicken with plenty of herbs will go nicely with this pasta. Try Balsamic-Glazed Rosemary Chicken with Bacon and Pearl Onions (p. 36) or Roast Chicken with Caramelized Shallots and Fingerling Potatoes (p. 38). Any leftover onions or shallots would pair well with this dish.

1. Preheat the oven to 450°F. Grease a 9 by 13-inch baking dish with butter.

2. Make a béchamel by heating the milk in a medium saucepan over low heat. At the same time, heat the butter in another medium saucepan over medium-low heat until it begins to foam. Add the flour and cook, stirring well, until light golden and fragrant, about 2 minutes. Whisk in the warm milk and heat, whisking often, until the mixture thickens (it should just come to a boil), about 10 minutes. Stir in the Cheddar and ¼ cup of the Parmesan, season with salt and pepper to taste, and let cool.

3. Bring a large pot of water to a boil.

4. Meanwhile, cook the bacon in a large, heavy skillet over medium heat, stirring occasionally, until it browns and renders much of its fat, about 6 minutes. Transfer to a plate lined with paper towels. Add the shallots to the pan and cook, stirring, until translucent (but not browned), about 2 minutes. Add the mushrooms, sprinkle generously with salt and cook, stirring, until they soften and brown in places, about 4 minutes. Stir in the chicken, vinegar, and thyme and toss well.

5. Add a couple of tablespoons of salt to the water and cook the pasta until it's just tender to the tooth, about 11 minutes. (You'll want the pasta to be extra firm as it will continue to soften in the oven.) Drain the pasta and return it to the pot. Add the chicken-and-mushroom mixture, béchamel, and chives and toss well.

6. Transfer the pasta and the sauce mixture to the prepared baking dish. Sprinkle the remaining Parmesan and the breadcrumbs evenly over the pasta. Bake until the cheese and breadcrumbs brown, 10 to 15 minutes. Let sit for 5 minutes, then serve.

Warm Pasta Salad with Chicken, Broccoli, and Thyme

Serves 6 to 8

I love warm pasta salads. You can assemble all the ingredients ahead of time, cook up the pasta once your guests arrive, then toss and set out for all to eat at their leisure. The flavors of this pasta only improve after they've sat for a half hour or so.

Kosher salt

¾ pound broccoli crowns, cut into 1-inch florets

1 pound pasta shells

2½ cups thinly sliced leftover chicken

½ cup pitted kalamata or gaeta olives, drained

10 oil-packed sun-dried tomatoes, thinly sliced

½ cup freshly grated Parmesan cheese

4 scallions (white and green parts), trimmed and thinly sliced

1 teaspoon chopped fresh thyme

3 tablespoons extra-virgin olive oil

1 tablespoon sherry vinegar or balsamic vinegar

Freshly ground black pepper

CHIX PICKS

A roast chicken with some sweetness will go nicely with the tomatoes and vinegar in this recipe—try a bird brushed with Maple-Mustard Glaze (p. 14) or Orange-Apricot Glaze (p. 14).

1. Bring a large pot of water to a boil. Stir in a couple of tablespoons of salt and blanch the broccoli until it turns bright green and the stems are just tender, about 2 minutes. Using a slotted spoon, transfer the broccoli to a bowl with cold water running over it and let sit until cold. Drain well.

2. Meanwhile, cook the pasta in the same water until tender to the tooth, about 11 minutes. Drain well and transfer to a large serving bowl. Toss with the broccoli, chicken, olives, tomatoes, half the Parmesan and scallions, and the thyme. Drizzle in the olive oil and vinegar and season with salt and pepper to taste. Serve immediately with a sprinkling of the remaining Parmesan and scallions. The pasta will hold nicely at room temperature for an hour or so.

Pasta Salad with Cherry Tomatoes and Asparagus

Serves 4 to 6

Ricotta salata has a crumbly texture and a sweet, briny flavor similar to feta. Originally produced on the Italian island of Sicily, this cheese goes great with pastas, either freshly grated or, more often, crumbled. Here, the cheese is paired with halved cherry tomatoes and blanched asparagus for a quick pasta salad. If you can't find any ricotta salata at the local market, substitute with good feta.

1 pint ripe cherry or grape tomatoes (about $1/2$ pound), cut in half
2 teaspoons chopped fresh rosemary
Kosher salt and freshly ground black pepper
$3/4$ pound asparagus, bottoms snapped off, cut into $1 1/2$-inch pieces
1 pound gemelli or penne
2 cups diced leftover chicken
$1/2$ pound ricotta salata or feta cheese, crumbled
$1/4$ cup extra-virgin olive oil
$1 1/2$ tablespoons balsamic vinegar

1. In a large serving bowl, sprinkle the tomatoes with the rosemary, $1 1/2$ teaspoons salt, and a few generous grinds of black pepper.

2. Bring a large pot of water to a boil. Stir in a couple of tablespoons of salt and blanch the asparagus until bright green and tender, about 2 minutes. Using a slotted spoon, transfer to a bowl of ice cold water and let sit until cool. Drain well and add to the tomatoes.

3. Meanwhile, cook the pasta in the same water until it's just tender to the tooth, about 11 minutes. Drain well.

CHIX PICKS

Try using a grilled-roasted chicken, like Italian Grilled Chicken Under a Brick with Smoky Balsamic Tomatoes (p. 68)—add any leftover tomatoes to the pasta—or a grill-roasted chicken prepared with Thyme-Mustard Vinaigrette (p. 98). For a change of pace, substitute Black Olive and Sherry Vinaigrette (p. 70) for the oil and vinegar in this recipe.

4. Toss the pasta with the tomatoes, asparagus, chicken, and cheese. In a small bowl, whisk together the olive oil and vinegar. If serving hot, add this to the pasta, toss well, and serve. If serving later, add half the vinaigrette to the pasta, toss well, and refrigerate up to 8 hours. Before you serve, let the pasta come to room temperature, then toss with the remaining vinaigrette and serve.

Chicken Chow Mein

Serves 4

I love wok cooking. Without a powerful exhaust fan over my range at home, I often have to make do without the smoky, high heat central to this method. I've learned a few tricks for stir-frying to compensate for my modest home kitchen, though. The most important of these is to avoid crowding a pan. While there's always a temptation to cook in large quantities, especially when you're trying to feed a family, stir-frying in batches ensures that the food browns properly, cooks quickly, and ultimately has the deep flavor you're looking for.

When making noodles, as in this chow mein, I also often turn to a nonstick skillet, which crisps the noodles and prevents any sticking. Do toss in some diced pork or cooked shrimp if you have any on hand.

Kosher salt
½ pound Chinese egg noodles
¼ cup canola or peanut oil
1 clove garlic, minced
1 tablespoon peeled and minced fresh ginger
1 small yellow onion, thinly sliced
2 cups thinly sliced Napa cabbage
2 cups fresh bean sprouts
2 cups thinly sliced leftover chicken
2 tablespoons soy sauce
2 teaspoons toasted sesame oil

CHIX PICKS

Choose a bird with prominent sweet and/or Asian flavors, like a roast chicken brushed with Orange-Apricot Glaze (p. 14) or Grilled Chicken Teriyaki with Scallions (p. 70).

1. Bring a large pot of water to a boil. Add a couple of tablespoons of salt and cook the noodles, stirring a few times until just tender, about 3 minutes. Drain under cold running water until almost completely cooled to room temperature. Toss with 1 tablespoon of the canola oil and set on a baking sheet lined with paper towels to dry.

2. Heat 1½ tablespoons of the canola oil in a large nonstick skillet over medium-high heat until shimmering hot, about 1½ minutes. Add the noodles and cook, tossing often, until browned in places and heated through, about 3 minutes. Transfer to a large plate.

3. Add the remaining 1½ tablespoons canola oil to the skillet and, once it's hot, add the garlic and ginger. Cook, stirring, until they start to sizzle steadily (but don't burn), about 30 seconds. Add the onion and cook until browned and slightly softened, about 2 minutes. Add the cabbage and bean sprouts and cook, stirring, until they start to soften and wilt. Return the noodles to the pan along with the chicken and cook, stirring, until heated through, about 2 minutes. Add the soy sauce and sesame oil and cook, tossing, for 1 minute. Serve immediately.

Pad Thai with Chicken

Serves 2 to 3

Though pad thai may sound exotic, it's surprisingly easy to make. Even better, the ingredients for this noodle stir-fry are fairly accessible. The only two specialty items are dried rice noodles and fish sauce, both of which are increasingly available at many supermarkets or your local Asian market.

6 ounces dried Thai rice noodles

3 tablespoons canola oil or peanut oil

1/2 pound large shrimp, peeled, deveined, rinsed, and patted dry

Kosher salt

3 scallions (white and green parts), trimmed and thinly sliced

3 Thai bird chiles or 1 jalapeño, seeded and finely diced

1 tablespoon peeled and minced fresh ginger

2 large eggs, beaten

2 cups thinly sliced leftover chicken

2 cups fresh bean sprouts

1 1/2 tablespoons Thai fish sauce

1 tablespoon rice vinegar

1 tablespoon sugar

1/4 cup chopped dry-roasted peanuts

1 lime, cut into wedges, for serving

CHIX PICKS

Not surprisingly, Grill-Roasted Thai Chicken with Lemongrass (p. 53) is a good fit for this dish. Though intensely flavored, Grill-Roasted Tandoori Chicken (p. 62) is a fine match as well.

1. Fill a medium saucepan with lukewarm water. Add the rice noodles, and soak until just tender, about 15 minutes. Rinse well in a colander under cold running water, then drain well. Transfer to a baking sheet lined with paper towels.

2. Heat 1 1/2 tablespoons of the oil in a large nonstick skillet over medium-high heat until shimmering hot, about 1 1/2 minutes. Sprinkle the shrimp with 3/4 teaspoon salt and cook, stirring often, until opaque and firm to the touch, about 3 minutes. Transfer to a large plate.

3. Add the remaining 1 1/2 tablespoons oil to the skillet and, after a couple of seconds, the scallions, chile(s), and ginger and cook, stirring, until they start to brown, about 2 minutes. Add the eggs and cook, breaking them up with a wooden spoon, until just set, about 1 minute. Add the noodles, chicken, bean sprouts, and shrimp and cook, stirring, until the mixture heats through and starts to brown, about 3 minutes.

4. In a small bowl, stir together the fish sauce, vinegar, and sugar. Add to the skillet and cook, tossing, for 2 minutes. Serve immediately, sprinkled with the peanuts and with the lime wedges on the side.

Stir-Fried Chow-Foon Noodles with Chicken and Black Bean Sauce

Serves 4

This dish may not be for everyone as it entails a trip to an Asian specialty store for sheets of fresh rice noodles. For these noodles (often called chow foon on Chinese restaurant menus) alone, though, I often make trips to Boston's Chinatown. Quickly stir-fried, they have a soft but chewy texture that soaks up the flavors of the stir-fry. If you like, you can substitute Chinese egg noodles and make this a lo mein instead.

2 tablespoons spicy Chinese black bean sauce
1 tablespoon soy sauce
1 tablespoon rice vinegar
1 teaspoon toasted sesame oil
2 tablespoons water
2 tablespoons canola or peanut oil
1 tablespoon peeled and minced
   fresh ginger
6 scallions, trimmed and thinly sliced
10 ounces flat rice noodles, cut into
   ½-inch-wide noodles (if not already
   cut) and pulled apart
2 cups thinly sliced leftover chicken

CHIX PICKS

Try Asian flavors like a roast chicken prepared with Asian Barbecue Glaze (p. 14), or Chinese Salt and Pepper Roast Chicken (p. 52).

1. In a small bowl, stir together the black bean sauce, soy sauce, vinegar, sesame oil, and water and set aside.

2. Heat the canola oil in a large nonstick skillet over medium-high heat until shimmering hot, about 1½ minutes. Add the ginger and scallion whites and cook, stirring, until they start to brown (but don't burn), about 1 minute. Add the rice noodles and cook, tossing well, until browned in places and heated through, about 3 minutes. Add the chicken and the black bean sauce mixture and cook, stirring, until the chicken is heated through, about 2 minutes. Sprinkle with the scallion greens and serve immediately.

Chicken-Shiitake Ravioli in Soy-Ginger Broth

Serves 4

This dish is a cross between a soup and pasta. It can serve as a filling meal for two or as a dressy first course. The ravioli are made with wonton skins, which are a great substitute for fresh pasta

2 cloves garlic, minced
2 tablespoons canola or peanut oil
6 ounces shiitake mushrooms, stemmed, caps thinly sliced
Kosher salt and freshly ground black pepper
6 ounces baby spinach
1½ cups chopped leftover chicken
3 tablespoons soy sauce
1 teaspoon toasted sesame oil
32 wonton skins (preferably rounded)
2 large egg yolks, beaten
2 cups low-sodium chicken broth
2 tablespoons minced fresh ginger
1 tablespoon rice vinegar
2 scallions (white and green parts), trimmed and thinly sliced

CHIX PICKS

A roast chicken prepared with Soy-Ginger Brine (p. 9) will stay juicy in these ravioli, or try the pleasant spice of Chinese Salt and Pepper Roast Chicken (p. 52).

1. In a large nonstick skillet heat the garlic with the canola oil until it starts to sizzle steadily, about 1½ minutes. Add the mushrooms, season with salt and pepper, and cook, stirring, until softened and browned in places, about 3 minutes. Add the spinach and cook, stirring, until it wilts, about 2 minutes. Stir in the chicken, 1 tablespoon of the soy sauce, and the sesame oil. Remove from the heat and let cool.

2. Set 8 of the wonton skins on a cutting board. Top with a couple tablespoons of the chicken mixture. Press down so the filling lays flat. Brush the edges of the wonton with the egg, top with another wonton skin, and crimp with the tines of a fork so the top and bottom wrappers stick together. Repeat with the remaining wonton wrappers and filling.

3. Fill a medium saucepan with water and bring to a boil.

4. Meanwhile, in another medium saucepan, bring the broth, vinegar, ginger, and the remaining 2 tablespoons soy sauce to a boil, then reduce to a simmer.

5. Add several tablespoons of salt to the boiling water, add the ravioli, and cook until just tender, about 3 minutes. Using a slotted spoon, transfer the ravioli to the soy-ginger broth and simmer for 5 minutes. Divide the broth and ravioli evenly between bowls, and serve immediately sprinkled with the scallions.

Cold Peanut Noodles with Chicken, Carrots, and Mint

Serves 6 to 8

Peanut noodles are my idea of summer buffet food. Set them out with some grilled vegetables, a salad, and a steak or some burgers and you'll find that your guests will bypass the other offerings and come back for seconds on the noodles. You also can serve this dish as a refreshing weeknight dinner paired with some stir-fried green beans or broccoli.

Kosher salt
1 pound thin spaghetti
1/2 cup smooth, natural peanut butter
2 tablespoons soy sauce
2 tablespoons rice vinegar
2 tablespoons canola oil
2 tablespoons peeled and minced
  fresh ginger
2 teaspoons Thai chili paste (like sriracha),
  or your favorite hot sauce to taste
2 tablespoons water, more if needed
1/4 cup chopped fresh mint
3 scallions (white and green parts),
  trimmed and thinly sliced
2 cups thinly sliced leftover chicken
1 cup peeled and grated carrots
1/4 cup chopped dry-roasted peanuts

CHIX PICKS

A grill-roasted chicken goes nicely with this dish, like Grill-Roasted Thai Chicken with Lemongrass (p. 53) or Grilled Chicken Teriyaki with Scallions (p. 70); fold any leftover scallions into the pasta.

1. Bring a large pot of water to a boil. Add a couple of tablespoons of salt and cook the pasta, stirring occasionally, until it's just tender to the tooth, about 7 minutes. Drain and rinse under cold running water until the pasta is room temperature.

2. Meanwhile, make the sauce. Combine the peanut butter, soy sauce, vinegar, oil, ginger, and chili paste in a food processor and process until smooth. With the machine running, pour the water through the feed tube to thin the mixture to a pourable consistency. Transfer the sauce to a small bowl and stir in half the mint and scallions.

3. Add the pasta to a large serving bowl and toss with the chicken and carrots and half the peanut sauce. Drizzle with the remaining sauce and sprinkle with the remaining scallions and mint and the peanuts. Serve immediately.

Singapore Noodles with Chicken and Scallions

Serves 2

This dish is a staple of Chinese-American restaurant menus. The noodles balance the aromatic spice of curry powder with the crunch of stir-fried vegetables and sliced chicken or pork. Although it's hard to replicate the smoky flavor of high-heat wok cooking in restaurants, a nonstick skillet does a fine job of crisping up the noodles (with no fear of sticking).

¼ pound thin rice noodles
   or vermicelli
1 inner celery stalk
1 large carrot
1 teaspoon hot curry powder
1 teaspoon sugar
Kosher salt
3 tablespoons vegetable oil
4 scallions, greens cut into
   1-inch pieces and whites
   thinly sliced
1 tablespoon peeled
   and minced fresh ginger
2½ cups thinly sliced leftover chicken
1 tablespoon soy sauce

> ## CHIX PICKS
>
> A spice-rubbed bird, like one coated with Southwestern Chile Spice Rub (p. 11) or a grill-roasted bird like Grill-Roasted Tandoori Chicken (p. 62) will match the big flavors in this stir-fry.

1. Bring a medium pot of water to a boil. Remove from the heat, add the noodles, and soak until just tender, about 10 minutes. Drain well and set on a plate lined with paper towels.

2. Cut the celery into 4-inch lengths, then slice them lengthwise into thin julienne strips. Peel the carrot, then use the peeler to shave the carrot into thin strips.

3. Combine the curry powder, sugar, and ½ teaspoon salt in a small bowl and set aside. Heat the oil in a large, heavy-based nonstick skillet over medium-high heat until shimmering hot, about 1½ minutes. Add the scallion whites and the ginger and cook, stirring, for 30 seconds. Add the chicken, curry spice mix, carrot, celery, and scallion greens and stir-fry for 30 seconds to soften slightly. Add the noodles and cook, tossing, until they've soaked up the spice mix and are hot throughout, about 3 minutes. Toss with the soy sauce, taste for salt, and serve immediately.

Couscous with Chicken, Orange, and Roasted Butternut Squash

Serves 4

Whenever I roast chicken, I'll often make couscous for lunch the next day. Only, instead of waiting until the following day to throw it together, I like to make the couscous as I'm finishing off dinner. Before doing the dishes and tidying up, I'll cook up some plain couscous, which only takes about 5 minutes, then stir in any vegetables and chicken that remain from the meal. The resulting couscous is great served cold, though I like pulling it out a half hour before eating so the flavors perk up a bit.

In this version, roasted butternut squash accompanies the chicken. If you have any other roasted vegetables on hand—like onions, sweet potatoes, or asparagus—feel free to toss them in.

1 pound butternut squash, peeled, seeded, and cut into 1-inch pieces
3 tablespoons olive oil
1 teaspoon brown sugar
Large pinch of ground cinnamon
Kosher salt and freshly ground black pepper
2¼ cups water
2 cups couscous
1 teaspoon ground cumin
1 large navel orange
2 cups diced leftover chicken
1½ cups canned chickpeas, drained and rinsed well
¼ cup chopped fresh cilantro
2 scallions (white and green parts), trimmed and finely sliced

CHIX PICKS

Not surprisingly, a chicken coated with the Moroccan Spice Rub (p. 12) is a good fit, though any bird with a bright, citrus flavor would go nicely, like a roast chicken brushed with Orange-Apricot Glaze (p. 14).

1. Preheat the oven to 450°F.

2. In a large bowl, toss the squash with 1 tablespoon of the oil, the brown sugar, cinnamon, 1 teaspoon salt, and ½ teaspoon pepper, then transfer to a large, heavy baking sheet lined with aluminum foil, arranging the pieces in a single layer. Roast, tossing after 10 minutes, until the squash is browned and tender, about 15 minutes.

3. Meanwhile, bring the water to a boil in a medium saucepan. Stir in the couscous, cumin, the remaining 2 tablespoons oil, and 1 teaspoon salt. Cover, reduce the heat to low, and simmer for 5 minutes. Remove from the heat and let rest for 5 minutes with the cover on.

4. Finely grate the rind of the orange (removing just the orange, not the white pith below) and set aside. Peel the orange, then cut off all the white pith surrounding it so only the flesh is visible. Using a paring knife, cut between the membranes of the orange so you remove thin segments of the orange. Set aside.

5. Transfer the couscous to a large bowl, fluff with a fork, then toss with the squash, chicken, chickpeas, cilantro, scallions, and the orange zest and segments. Season with salt and pepper to taste and serve immediately or refrigerate, covered tightly, for up to a couple of days (bring to room temperature before serving).

Couscous with Spice-Crusted Grilled Vegetables and Chicken

Serves 4

The grill fuels the base for this couscous. I try to plan ahead and grill extra vegetables and chicken for this dish. If you're not able to, follow the instructions below.

¼ cup olive oil
1 teaspoon ground cumin
1 teaspoon chili powder
Large pinch of ground cinnamon
Kosher salt and freshly ground black pepper
1 red bell pepper, cored, seeded, and cut into 4 pieces
1 medium-size red onion, cut into ½-inch-thick slices
1 medium-size zucchini, cut lengthwise into ½-inch-thick slices
2¼ cups water
2 cups couscous
2 cups diced leftover chicken
¼ cup chopped fresh cilantro
2 tablespoons chopped fresh mint

CHIX PICKS

Since you'll be grilling the vegetables for the this couscous, it only makes sense to use a grill-roasted bird like Grill-Roasted Jamaican Jerk Chicken (p. 74) or one that's been cooked with any of the spice rubs, particularly Moroccan Spice Rub (p. 12).

1. Prepare a charcoal fire or heat up the gas grill (heat all burners to medium-high). For a charcoal fire, pile a couple of layers of briquettes on one side and a single layer of charcoal on the other so you end up with a medium hot to hot zone and a moderate to cool zone. Your fire is ready when the briquettes are mostly gray (or red hot if you're using hardwood).

2. In a small bowl, whisk together 2 tablespoons of the oil, the cumin, chili powder, cinnamon, 1½ teaspoons salt, and 1 teaspoon black pepper. Brush this all over the bell pepper, onion, and zucchini. Set the vegetables on the grill (on the hot side of the charcoal fire). Grill the peppers and zucchini, flipping occasionally, until browned and just tender, about 8 minutes. Transfer to a large cutting board to cool. Reduce the heat to medium on a gas grill or move the red onions to a cooler part of the charcoal fire. Cover and cook until the onions are just tender (they should still have some bite), about 6 minutes. Remove from the grill and coarsely chop along with the red pepper and zucchini.

3. Bring the water to a boil in a medium saucepan. Stir in the couscous, the remaining 2 tablespoons oil, and 1 teaspoon salt. Cover, reduce the heat to low, and simmer for 5 minutes. Remove from the heat and let rest for 5 minutes with the cover on.

4. Transfer to a large serving bowl and gently fluff with a fork. Fold in the vegetables, chicken, cilantro, and mint. Season with salt and pepper to taste and serve immediately or refrigerate, covered tightly, for up to a couple of days. Bring to room temperature before serving.

Chicken Fried Rice

Serves 3 to 4

I'm always amazed by the transformation of leftover rice from its hard, refrigerated state to its lively presence in fried rice. Leftover chicken undergoes a similar renaissance in fried rice. Thus a perfect leftover dish is born, especially convenient if you made some steamed rice with the roast chicken the night before. The other components for the rice—peas, ham, and eggs—are often on hand in the cupboard. In about 15 minutes, you have a wonderful, warming meal that's great on its own or as an accompaniment to stir-fried vegetables or meats. Don't make this with warm rice—the rice will have a soft, soggy texture. Either use cold leftover rice or fresh rice that you've let cool on a baking sheet for about an hour.

2 tablespoons peeled and minced
 fresh ginger
1 large clove garlic, minced
2 tablespoons canola or peanut oil
4 cups cold leftover white rice,
 crumbled into individual grains
2 cups diced leftover chicken
1/2 pound ham steak, cut into
 1/4-inch dice (2 cups)
1 cup frozen petite peas
2 large eggs, beaten together
 with 1 tablespoon dry sherry
2 teaspoons toasted sesame oil
Kosher salt

CHIX PICKS

Try a roast chicken with Asian flavors like Chinese Salt and Pepper Roast Chicken (p. 52) or Grilled Chicken Teriyaki with Scallions (p. 70).

1. In a large nonstick skillet over medium heat, heat the ginger and garlic with the canola oil until they start to sizzle steadily, about 2 minutes. Add the rice and cook, stirring often, until it softens and heats through, about 3 minutes. Add the chicken, ham, and peas and cook until heated though, about 2 minutes.

2. Make a well in the center of the rice and add the eggs. Cook, stirring a few times, until the egg starts to set, then break it up with a spatula into small pieces. Stir the mixture together, drizzle with the sesame oil, season with salt to taste, toss well, and serve immediately.

Coconut Rice with Ginger, Chicken, and Scallions

Serves 6

The addition of coconut milk to steamed rice adds richness (think butter but sweeter) and helps the grains cook evenly without sticking. While the rice steams, prepare a quick stir-fry using leftover chicken and a sweet soy mixture.

2 tablespoons peeled and minced fresh ginger

1/4 cup canola oil or peanut oil

2 1/2 cups long-grain rice (preferably jasmine), rinsed

One 14-ounce can unsweetened coconut milk

2 1/2 cups water

Kosher salt

4 scallions (white and green parts), trimmed and thinly sliced

1 jalapeño, seeded and finely diced

3 cups diced leftover chicken

1/2 cup low-salt chicken broth

2 tablespoons soy sauce

1 tablespoon rice vinegar

2 teaspoons light brown sugar

1/4 cup chopped fresh cilantro, plus more for sprinkling

2 teaspoons cornstarch

1 lime, cut into wedges, for serving

CHIX PICKS

The perfect pairing for this dish is Grill-Roasted Thai Chicken with Lemongrass (p. 53), though the spice of Grill-Roasted Tandoori Chicken (p. 62) also will go nicely.

1. Heat 1 tablespoon of the ginger with 2 tablespoons of the oil in a large saucepan over medium-high heat until it begins to sizzle steadily and becomes fragrant, about 2 minutes. Add the rice and cook, stirring, until the grains become opaque and start to brown in places, about 2 minutes. Add the coconut milk, water, and 1 teaspoon salt. Bring to a boil, then reduce the heat to low, cover, and cook for 20 minutes. Remove from the heat and let rest for 5 minutes.

2. Meanwhile, in a large skillet over medium-high heat add the remaining 1 tablespoon ginger and 2 tablespoons oil and cook until it just starts to sizzle, about 1 minute. Add the scallions and jalapeño and cook until softened and browned in places, about 2 minutes. Add the chicken, broth, soy sauce, vinegar, brown sugar, and cilantro and cook, tossing, until the chicken heats through, about 2 minutes. Stir the cornstarch together with 2 tablespoons water, add to the sauce, bring to a boil so the mixture thickens, then remove from the heat.

3. Fluff the rice with a fork before placing a mound on each plate and topping with the chicken. Sprinkle with cilantro and serve with a lime wedge for squeezing.

Paella with Chicken and Chorizo

Serves 4

I've been fortunate to spend quite a few years in Spain, first as a student and later as a tour guide and teacher for visiting American students. My favorite memories are of the long, hot summer days at the beach. The Spanish have perfected the art of beach-going. Beautiful, shaded chairs are available for rent, there's nicely groomed sand, and, of course, the warm, calm waters of the Mediterranean await the occasional swim. Over the years, I learned how to set up my beach day: laze in a beach chair and read the sports pages in the morning, then head to one of the beachside paella restaurants for lunch.

Pimenton de la vera is a smoky paprika produced in the western part of Spain. It's available in most gourmet food markets, or you can use Hungarian hot paprika—you'll just miss that smoky essence.

2 tablespoons olive oil

½ pound chorizo, cut into ½-inch pieces

3 cloves garlic, minced

1 large Spanish onion, finely diced

Kosher salt

2 cups medium-grain Spanish rice

½ teaspoon pimenton de la vera or hot paprika

Large pinch of saffron threads

4 cups low-salt chicken broth

2 cups diced leftover chicken

2 bay leaves

2 jarred roasted red peppers, cut into strips

1 cup frozen petite peas, thawed

1 lemon, cut into wedges, for serving

CHIX PICKS

A Mediterranean-style roast chicken with garlic and lemon pairs nicely with this rice. Try Bistro Roast Chicken with Lemon and Thyme (p. 34) or Greek Roast Chicken with Lemon, Black Olives, and Potatoes (p. 56).

1. Heat the oil in a large paella pan or a 12-inch skillet over medium-high heat until shimmering hot, about 1½ minutes. Reduce the heat to medium, add the chorizo, and cook, stirring a few times, until it browns, about 2 minutes. Add the garlic and onion, sprinkle with salt (about 1 teaspoon) and cook, stirring, until the onion softens and becomes translucent, about 6 minutes. Add the rice, pimenton, and saffron and cook, stirring, for 1 minute. Add the broth and bring to a boil. Stir in the chicken and bay leaves. Reduce the heat to a simmer and cook until the rice is tender and all the liquid is completely absorbed, about 20 minutes.

2. Top with the roasted red peppers and peas, cover, and let rest for 5 minutes, then serve with the lemon wedges for squeezing over the rice.

Arroz con Pollo

Serves 4 to 6

This dish is derivative of its Spanish counterpart, paella. One difference between the two is the Cuban substitution of turmeric to color the rice instead of the expensive (but flavorful) Spanish saffron. Also, mild Italian sausage takes the place of chorizo.

2 tablespoons olive oil

¾ pound sweet Italian sausage,
   removed from casings and cut into
   1½-inch chunks

3 cloves garlic, minced

1 large Spanish onion,
   finely diced

1 green bell pepper, cored,
   seeded, and finely diced

Kosher salt

3 cups medium-grain
   Spanish rice

1 teaspoon ground cumin

1 teaspoon turmeric

1 teaspoon sweet paprika

¾ cup canned diced tomatoes, drained

3 cups low-salt chicken broth

2 cups chopped leftover chicken

2 limes, cut into wedges, for serving

> ## CHIX PICKS
>
> A spice-rubbed bird, whether grill-roasted or just roasted, will punch up this rice. Try Sweet Southern Spice Rub (p. 12) or Southwestern Chile Spice Rub (p. 11).

1. Heat the oil in a large Dutch oven or casserole over medium-high heat until shimmering hot. Add the sausage and cook, stirring every couple of minutes, until well browned, about 6 minutes. Transfer to a large plate using a slotted spoon.

2. Reduce the heat to medium, add the garlic, onion, and pepper to the pan, sprinkle generously with salt and cook, stirring often, until the onion softens and browns in places, about 6 minutes. Add the rice and cook, stirring, for 1 minute. Add the cumin, turmeric, and paprika and cook, stirring, for 1 minute. Add the tomatoes and broth and bring to a boil. Reduce the heat to a simmer, stir in the sausage, cover, and cook until the rice is tender and all the liquid is completely absorbed, about 20 minutes.

3. Stir in the chicken and let sit for 5 minutes, uncovered, then serve with the lime wedges for squeezing.

Chinese Sticky Rice with Chicken and Sausage

Serves 4

I love dim sum, the Chinese brunch that consists of little bites of noodles and dumplings. One of my favorite dishes is sticky rice wrapped in lotus leaves, which are loaded with tiny morsels of Chinese sausage and dried mushrooms (The Chinese sausage is available at Asian markets; if you can't find it, substitute Italian sausage.)

For this recipe, you will need to pick up glutinous rice (or "sweet rice," as it's often labeled in Asian specialty stores). Other types of rice simply will not acquire the needed stickiness. Note: The long soaking time for the rice necessitates some planning ahead.

2½ cups sweet rice

2 tablespoons canola or peanut oil

6 ounces Chinese sausage, cut into ½-inch-thick pieces or ¾ pound Italian sausage, (removed from its casing and cut into ½-inch pieces)

5 scallions, trimmed and thinly sliced, white and green parts separated

3½ ounces shiitake mushrooms, stemmed and caps thinly sliced

¼ cup dry sherry

2 cups low-salt chicken broth

3 tablespoons soy sauce

2 tablespoons Chinese oyster sauce

2 tablespoons rice vinegar

1 teaspoon toasted sesame oil

2 cups diced leftover chicken

CHIX PICKS

Try a roast chicken with sweet Asian flavors like Grilled Chicken Teriyaki with Scallions (p. 70) or a roast chicken coated with Asian Barbecue Glaze (p. 14).

---

1. Set the rice in a large bowl, cover with cold water, and let sit for at least 3 hours and up to 8 hours at room temperature. Drain well and rinse. Set aside.

2. Heat the canola oil in a large Dutch oven over medium-high heat until shimmering hot, about 1½ minutes. Add the sausage and the white part of the scallions and cook, stirring, until the sausage and scallions brown, about 4 minutes. Add the shiitakes and cook, stirring a few times, until they soften and brown, about 3 minutes. Add the sherry and cook until it almost completely reduces, about 2 minutes. Stir in the broth, soy sauce, oyster sauce, vinegar, and sesame oil until well combined.

3. Add the rice and chicken, bring to a boil, then reduce the heat to low. Cover and cook until the rice is tender and has completely absorbed all of the liquid, about 20 minutes. Let rest, covered, for 5 minutes. Sprinkle with the scallion greens and serve.

Jambalaya with Shrimp, Chicken, and Andouille Sausage

Serves 4

This dish follows the theme of pairing rice with some sort of sausage, chicken, and plenty of spice. Here the cuisine is Cajun: smoky andouille sausage and the thickening power of okra. I generally prefer regular long-grain rice, though the parboiled grains of Uncle Ben's® work best for this jambalaya, as they hold up well in the brothy stew.

2 tablespoons olive oil

½ pound andouille sausage or chorizo sausage,
    cut into ¾-inch pieces

1 green bell pepper, cored, seeded,
    and cut into ¾-inch dice

1 jalapeño, seeded and coarsely chopped

Kosher salt

6 ounces okra, trimmed and thinly sliced

One 14.5-ounce can diced tomatoes
    and their juices

3 cups low-salt chicken broth

1 cup converted long-grain rice
    (I like Uncle Ben's)

1 pound large shrimp, peeled and deveined

Freshly ground black pepper

2 cups diced leftover chicken

3 scallions (white and green parts), trimmed and thinly sliced

> ## CHIX PICKS
>
> Try a roast chicken with plenty of spice and heat like Southern Spiced Chicken with Chipotle-Honey BBQ Sauce (p. 76) or Roast Chicken with Southwestern Rub and Cornbread and Jalapeño Stuffing (p. 48). For an extra hit of flavor, melt a pat or two of Smoky Chipotle Butter (p. 61) on top.

1. Heat the oil in a large Dutch oven over medium-high heat until shimmering hot, about 1½ minutes. Add the sausage, bell pepper, and jalapeño, sprinkle with 1 teaspoon of salt and cook, stirring, until the vegetables are softened and browned, about 6 minutes. Add the okra, tomatoes and their juices, broth, and rice and bring to a boil. Reduce the heat to a simmer, cover with the lid slightly askew, and cook for 15 minutes, until the rice is tender but the mixture is still brothy.

2. Season the shrimp with ¾ teaspoon salt and a few generous grinds of black pepper. Raise the heat under the Dutch oven to medium, add the shrimp and chicken and cook, stirring occasionally, until the shrimp are firm and a uniform pink color, about 5 minutes. Season generously with salt and pepper to taste.

3. Serve in shallow soup bowls sprinkled with the scallions.

Dirty Rice with Chicken

Serves 4

This Southern dish is a great way to use up the giblets—the heart, gizzard, and liver—that come in the cavity of a whole chicken. I will admit that the first time I tried to make dirty rice, I left out the giblets. The dish lacked that oomph—the richness and intensity—of the rice I had liked so much in other cooks' versions. I learned my lesson and sautéed the giblets the next time I made the rice. Take my advice and try them, too.

2½ cups converted long-grain rice
4½ cups low-salt chicken broth
2 bay leaves
2 tablespoons olive oil
Giblets from 1 chicken (optional), rinsed well and patted dry
Kosher salt and freshly ground black pepper
½ pound ground beef (preferably 85% lean chuck)
1 large Spanish onion, finely diced
1 green bell pepper, cored, seeded, and diced
3 cloves garlic, minced
2 cups finely chopped leftover chicken

1. Rinse the rice in a fine sieve until the water runs clear. Drain well and transfer to a large saucepan along with the broth and bay leaves. Bring to a boil, then cover, and cook until the rice is tender and all the water is absorbed, about 20 minutes. Remove from the heat.

2. Meanwhile, heat the oil in a large, heavy skillet over medium-high heat until shimmering hot, about 1½ minutes. Sprinkle the giblets (if using) generously with salt and pepper (about ½ teaspoon each) and cook, stirring, until well browned, about 5 minutes. Transfer to a large plate. Add the ground beef to the skillet and cook, stirring a few times, until it loses its raw color, about 3 minutes. Transfer to the plate with the giblets.

CHIX PICKS

Try a roast chicken with plenty of spice and heat like Southern Spiced Chicken with Chipotle-Honey Barbecue Sauce (p. 76) or Grill-Roasted Jamaican Jerk Chicken (p. 74).

3. Reduce the heat to medium, add the onion, bell pepper, and garlic to the pan, sprinkle generously with salt and cook, stirring often, until the onion becomes translucent and softens, about 6 minutes. Remove from the heat.

4. Chop up the giblets, then add them, the beef, the vegetable mixture, and the chicken to the rice. Stir well and let sit for 5 minutes, season with salt and pepper to taste, and serve.

Korean Bibimbap with Sesame Chicken and Stir-Fried Vegetables

Serves 4

My love for bibimbap, the big-bowl Korean rice dish, has grown in large part from frequent visits to Seoul Food, a tiny restaurant on a busy strip near Harvard Square in Cambridge, Massachusetts. Clara Byun runs the restaurant with her husband, constantly shifting between the kitchen, the cozy dining room, and the cash register. Clara is fiercely protective of her recipes, so I would never dare ask her the secret to her bibimbap. I have visited her restaurant enough times to have a general idea, though.

The key is to prepare a couple of intensely seasoned and colorful toppings. Here, carrots, stir-fried zucchini, and chicken adorn the rice, each of them infused with sesame oil. While Clara likes to come over to your table and stir the rice up for you, I like eating the different parts of the bibimbap in stages so I can enjoy each individually. Feel free to eat it as you see fit.

1 cup peeled and grated carrots
Kosher salt
1 tablespoon toasted sesame oil
3 tablespoons canola or peanut oil
2 medium zucchini, cut in half lengthwise,
   then cut into ¼-inch-thick slices
1 clove garlic, minced
6 ounces shiitake mushrooms,
   stemmed and caps thinly sliced
3 cups thinly sliced leftover chicken
1 tablespoon soy sauce
6 cups hot steamed medium-grain rice (long-grain also works fine)
3 tablespoons sesame seeds, toasted in a dry skillet over
   medium heat until lightly browned and fragrant
4 scallions (white and green parts), trimmed and thinly sliced
Spicy Korean red bean paste or Thai chili paste
   (available in Asian markets; optional)

> ## CHIX PICKS
>
> Try Chinese Salt and Pepper Roast Chicken (p. 52) or a bird marinated in Soy-Ginger Brine (p. 9) or Cinnamon and Cider Brine (p. 9).

1. In a small bowl, toss the carrots with ½ teaspoon salt and 1 teaspoon of the sesame oil.

2. Heat 1½ tablespoons of the canola oil in a large nonstick skillet over medium-high heat until shimmering hot. Add the zucchini, sprinkle with about ½ teaspoon salt and 1 teaspoon of the sesame oil and cook, stirring a few times, until it browns in places and becomes tender, about 4 minutes. Transfer to a large plate.

3. Return the skillet to the heat and add the remaining 1½ tablespoons canola oil and the garlic. Once it begins to sizzle, add the mushrooms and cook, stirring, until tender and starting to brown, about 3 minutes. Add the chicken and cook, tossing, until heated through, about 2 minutes. Stir in the soy sauce and the remaining 1 teaspoon sesame oil and cook for 1 minute. Remove from the heat.

4. Fluff the rice with a fork and divide it between 4 large bowls. Top each serving with the zucchini on one side, the carrots on the other, and some of the chicken mixture in the middle. Sprinkle with the sesame seeds, then the scallions. Serve immediately with the spicy bean paste if you like.

Risotto with Chicken, Peas, and Mushrooms

Serves 4 to 6

People get intimidated by risotto. Maybe it's the name (which sounds more complicated than "rice") or perhaps it's the thought of all that stirring. The truth is that risotto takes the same amount of time to make as long-grain rice—about 20 minutes. And the stirring, though important, is about as demanding as mashing potatoes. The key to risotto is adding the broth in 1-cup intervals, so the rice slowly absorbs the liquid and maintains its toothy texture.

1 ounce dried shiitake mushrooms
¾ ounce dried porcini or cépes
2 cups boiling water
4 cups low-salt chicken both
2 tablespoons unsalted butter
1 medium-size yellow onion, finely diced
Kosher salt and freshly ground black pepper
2 cups imported Carnaroli or arborio rice
⅓ cup dry white wine
2 cups diced leftover chicken
1½ cups frozen petite peas, thawed
1 cup freshly grated Parmesan cheese
1 tablespoon balsamic vinegar
3 tablespoons chopped fresh mint
1½ teaspoons chopped fresh thyme

> ## CHIX PICKS
>
> A bird with an Italian bent, like Sear-Roasted Chicken with Tomatoes and Rosemary (p. 78) or Roast Chicken with Fennel and Mushroom Dressing (p. 47), goes nicely in this risotto.

1. Soak the mushrooms in the water until tender, about 20 minutes. Remove from the water using a slotted spoon, pat dry, and chop. Strain the soaking liquid through a coffee filter. Heat the broth and the soaking liquid together in a medium saucepan over medium heat.

2. In another medium saucepan over medium heat, melt the butter. Add the onion and a sprinkling of salt and cook, stirring, until it's soft and slightly browned, about 5 minutes. Add the rice and cook, stirring, for 1 minute to coat the grains with the butter. Add the mushrooms and cook, stirring, for 1 minute. Add the wine and cook, stirring, until it's almost completely reduced, about 1 minute. Add 1 cup of the broth and cook, stirring, until it's almost completely absorbed. Continue adding the broth 1 cup at a time, stirring, until no more broth remains and the rice has a pleasant chewy texture. (The broth should simmer steadily; if it seems to simmer too rapidly, lower the heat a bit.)

3. Stir in the chicken, peas, Parmesan, vinegar, and half the mint and thyme. Season with salt and pepper to taste and serve immediately, sprinkled with the remaining mint and thyme.

Summery Risotto of Chicken, Tomatoes, and Sweet Corn

Serves 4 to 6

Risotto is often thought of as a wintry dish and, of course, it is warming and filling, but risotto can shine in the summer, too, filled with garden vegetables. Serve this dish on a cool, late August night when tomatoes and corn tend to be at their sweetest.

1 pint ripe cherry or grape tomatoes (like 100 Sweets), cut in half
Kosher salt and freshly ground black pepper
6 cups low-salt chicken both
2 tablespoons unsalted butter
1 medium-size yellow onion, finely diced
2 cups imported Carnaroli or arborio rice
1/2 cup dry white wine
Kernels cut from 3 ears corn
2 cups diced leftover chicken
3/4 cup freshly grated Parmesan cheese, plus more for sprinkling
1 tablespoon sherry vinegar or balsamic vinegar
1/4 cup packed fresh basil leaves, torn into smallish pieces, plus more for garnish

1. Sprinkle the tomatoes with 1 teaspoon salt and 1/2 teaspoon pepper.

2. In a medium saucepan over medium heat, heat the broth.

3. In another medium saucepan over medium heat, melt the butter. Add the onion and a sprinkling of salt and cook, stirring, until it's soft and slightly browned, about 5 minutes. Add the rice and cook, stirring, for 1 minute. Add the wine and cook, stirring, until it's almost completely reduced, about 1 minute. Add 1 cup of the broth and cook, stirring, until it's almost completely absorbed. Continue adding the broth 1 cup at a time, stirring, until all of the broth has been absorbed and the rice has a pleasant chewy texture. (The broth should simmer steadily; if it seems to simmer too rapidly, lower the heat a bit.)

4. Stir in the tomatoes (and any juices), corn, chicken, Parmesan, vinegar, and basil and cook, stirring, for a couple of minutes. Season with salt and pepper to taste and serve immediately with a sprinkling of Parmesan.

CHIX PICKS

Any mildly flavored roast chicken with plenty of herbs will do for this risotto. Try Bistro Roast Chicken with Lemon and Thyme (p. 34) or Italian Grilled Chicken Under a Brick with Smoky Balsamic Tomatoes (p. 68).

Bulgur Salad with Chicken, Tomatoes, and Mint

Serves 4 as a main course

Bulgur, a staple in the Middle East, may be most recognizable to Americans as the grain in tabbouleh. Processed from wheat kernels that are steamed, dried, and then cracked, bulgur is available in fine, medium, and coarse grinds. I prefer the delicate texture of fine bulgur for this salad. It cooks quickly and forms a light salad with the leftover chicken, diced tomatoes, and fresh herbs.

2 cups water
2 cups fine bulgur
2 cups diced leftover chicken
2 tablespoons olive oil
Kosher salt and freshly ground
    black pepper
2 cups diced ripe tomatoes
    (about 2 large)
1/4 pound feta cheese, crumbled
4 scallions (white and green parts),
    trimmed and thinly sliced
1/3 cup chopped fresh mint
2 tablespoons fresh lemon juice,
    more to taste

> ## CHIX PICKS
>
> Stir a mild, lemony chicken into this bulgur salad, like one roasted with Lemon-Herb Rub (p. 13) or try Greek Roast Chicken with Lemon, Black Olives, and Potatoes (p. 56).

1. Bring the water to a boil in a large saucepan.

2. Remove from the heat. Stir in the bulgur, chicken, oil, and 1 teaspoon salt. Cover and let sit until the bulgur has absorbed all the liquid and is just tender, about 10 minutes.

3. Pour the mixture out onto a large sheet pan and let cool to room temperature, then transfer to a large serving bowl and toss with the tomatoes, feta, scallions, mint, and lemon juice. Season as desired with salt, pepper, and more lemon juice, to taste. Serve immediately or refrigerate, tightly covered, for up to 2 days; let come to room temperature before serving.

Warm Farro Salad with Wild Mushrooms, Spinach, and Chicken

Serves 4

The antique grain farro, a predecessor to wheat, has undergone a revival of sorts in Italy. It is now increasingly available in large supermarkets and Italian specialty stores here in the U.S. Farro is similar to barley in appearance and flavor. You can cook it like a risotto, slowly stirring it while adding broth, or boil it and toss with bright ingredients to form a warm salad, as in this dish.

Kosher salt

2 cups farro (preferably *semi-perlato* or semi-pearled)

2 tablespoons olive oil

3½ ounces shiitake mushrooms, stemmed and caps thinly sliced

½ pound cremini mushrooms, thinly sliced

2 cloves garlic, minced

¼ cup dry sherry

10 ounces baby spinach

2½ cups diced leftover chicken

2 teaspoons chopped fresh thyme

Freshly ground black pepper

⅔ cup freshly grated Parmesan cheese

1 tablespoon sherry vinegar or balsamic vinegar

> ## CHIX PICKS
>
> Try using a mild roast chicken, like Roast Chicken with Fennel and Mushroom Dressing (p. 47) or Balsamic-Glazed Rosemary Chicken with Bacon and Pearl Onions (p. 36)—add any leftover onions to the salad.

1. Bring a large pot of water to a boil. Stir in a couple of tablespoons of salt, add the farro and cook, stirring, until it's just tender, about 12 minutes. Drain well and transfer to a large serving bowl.

2. Meanwhile, heat the oil in a large skillet over medium-high heat until shimmering hot, about 1½ minutes. Add the mushrooms, sprinkle generously with salt, and cook, stirring a few times, until browned and softened, about 4 minutes. Add the garlic and cook, stirring, for 1 minute. Add the sherry and cook until it almost completely reduces, about 2 minutes. Stir in the spinach, chicken, and thyme and cook, stirring, until the spinach wilts and the chicken heats through, about 3 minutes. Season with salt and pepper to taste. Pour the mixture over the farro, add three-quarters of the Parmesan and vinegar, and toss well. Season with salt and pepper to taste and serve immediately sprinkled with the remaining Parmesan.

Wheatberry Salad with Chicken and Dried Fruit

Serves 6 to 8

Wheatberries, the whole, unprocessed kernels of wheat, have a pleasant, chewy texture that is great in salads. I like pairing the grain with plenty of fresh herbs and diced fruit like apples or pears.

2 cups wheatberries
Kosher salt
3 tablespoons olive oil
¾ cup dried cherries
½ cup raisins
1 cup apple juice, warmed up
    on the stovetop
3 cups diced leftover chicken
1 Granny Smith apple, peeled,
    cored, and cut into ½-inch dice
½ cup chopped walnuts, toasted
    on a baking sheet at 375°F until
    lightly browned and fragrant
½ cup chopped fresh mint
¼ cup thinly sliced fresh chives
Freshly ground black pepper

CHIX PICKS

For this salad, use a roast chicken with plenty of sweetness and herbs, like Jerrod's Roast Chicken with Vermont Maple Glaze, Sweet Potatoes, and Sage (p. 35) or a bird brushed with Orange-Apricot Glaze (p. 14).

1. Bring a large pot of water to a boil. Add the wheatberries and 2 tablespoons salt, reduce the heat to a gentle simmer, cover and cook, stirring occasionally, until the grains are just tender, about 1 hour. Drain well, toss with 1 tablespoon of the oil, and transfer to a large baking sheet to cool to room temperature.

2. Meanwhile, let the cherries and raisins steep in a small bowl with the apple juice until they plump up nicely, about 20 minutes. Drain off any remaining apple juice.

3. Transfer the wheatberries to a large serving bowl. Toss with the remaining 2 tablespoons oil and the cherries and raisins, the chicken, apple, walnuts, mint, and chives. Taste for salt and pepper and serve immediately or refrigerate for up to 2 days; let it come to room temperature before serving.

Barley Risotto with Asparagus and Chicken

Serves 4

In this dish, the asparagus is slowly sautéed in butter, caramelizing its flavor so it becomes soft and sweet. In many ways, barley is more forgiving than rice in this risotto-style method, maintaining its texture even if it's overcooked a bit.

6 cups low-salt chicken broth

¼ cup (½ stick) unsalted butter

¾ pound asparagus, bottoms snapped off, peeled if thick, and cut into 1½-inch pieces

Kosher salt and freshly ground black pepper

1 small yellow onion, finely diced

2 cups pearl barley, rinsed and drained well

½ cup freshly grated Parmesan cheese, plus more for sprinkling

2 cups finely diced leftover chicken

Grated zest of 1 lemon

1 teaspoon chopped fresh thyme

CHIX PICKS

Sear-Roasted Chicken with Spring Onions and Asparagus (p. 86) is an obvious choice as you can fold in any leftover veggies. Or try something simple like Roast Chicken with Rosemary-Mustard Crust and Browned Onions (p. 30).

1. Heat the broth in a medium saucepan over medium-low heat.

2. Heat 2 tablespoons of the butter in a large skillet over medium heat until its foam begins to cook off. Add the asparagus, sprinkle generously with salt and pepper (about ½ teaspoon of each), reduce the heat to medium-low, and cook, stirring, until just tender, about 15 minutes.

3. Meanwhile, heat the remaining 2 tablespoons butter in a large saucepan over medium heat until it melts. Add the onion, sprinkle generously with salt and cook, stirring, until translucent and softened, about 6 minutes. Add the barley and cook, stirring, for 2 minutes to lightly brown the grains and coat with the butter. Add 1 cup of the hot broth and cook, stirring, until it's almost completely absorbed. Continue adding the broth, 1 cup at a time, until it's been completely absorbed, and the barley has a pleasant chewy texture, about 20 minutes.

4. Stir in the asparagus, Parmesan, chicken, lemon zest, and thyme. Taste for salt and pepper and serve immediately with an additional sprinkling of Parmesan.

Quinoa with Mozzarella, Tomatoes, Chicken, and Corn

Serves 4

The staple grain of the Incan empire, quinoa has finally begun to make the trek northward into the American culinary mainstream. The grain's recent rise in popularity in this country could be due in large part to its extraordinary nutritional values; it's high in protein and low in carbohydrates. More importantly, the grain is quite tasty, with a flavor and texture that are a cross between bulgur and couscous. In this dish, ripe tomatoes, sweet corn, and fresh mozzarella accompany the warm quinoa. I like the corn raw, though you can sauté it with a little oil first if you prefer.

2½ cups quinoa, rinsed and drained well

4 cups water

Kosher salt

3 tablespoon extra-virgin olive oil

2 large ripe tomatoes, cut into small dice

2 cups diced leftover chicken

Kernels cut from 3 ears fresh sweet corn

6 ounces fresh mozzarella cheese, cut into small dice

3 scallions (white and green parts), trimmed and thinly sliced

16 fresh basil leaves, torn into small pieces

1 tablespoon sherry vinegar or balsamic vinegar

> ## CHIX PICKS
>
> Try a roast chicken with a prominent herb flavor like Roast Chicken with Rosemary-Mustard Crust and Browned Onions (p. 30) or a bird with some sweetness like one brushed with Maple-Mustard Glaze (p. 14).

1. Bring the quinoa, water, 1 teaspoon salt, and 1 tablespoon of the olive oil to a boil in a medium saucepan. Reduce the heat to a gentle simmer, cover, and cook until the grains soften and appear to unravel, about 20 minutes.

2. Meanwhile, in a large serving bowl, toss together the tomatoes, chicken, corn, mozzarella, scallions, half the basil, the remaining 2 tablespoons oil, and the vinegar.

3. Drain the quinoa using a fine-mesh strainer. Add the quinoa to the serving bowl and toss well. Season generously with salt and pepper to taste. Serve immediately sprinkled with the remaining basil, or serve at room temperature.

Chicken and Wild Rice Salad

Serves 6

Wild rice is actually not a rice but the seed of a tall marsh grass harvested in the northern states along the Great Lakes. As exotic as this might sound, wild rice is relatively affordable and easy to cook. Although wild rice is often served exclusively at the holiday table, it's great in salads like this one.

1 pound wild rice (about 3 cups)
Kosher salt
1 cup dried cherries
1/3 cup orange juice
2 cups diced leftover chicken
2 tablespoons pure maple syrup
3 tablespoon balsamic vinegar
Freshly ground black pepper
1 1/2 teaspoons Dijon mustard
1/2 cup olive oil
1 cup pine nuts, toasted on
   a baking sheet at 375°F
   until lightly browned
3/4 cup chopped fresh parsley
2 teaspoons chopped fresh thyme

CHIX PICKS

Try a mildly flavored roast chicken with some sweetness like Jerrod's Roast Chicken with Vermont Maple Glaze, Sweet Potatoes, and Sage (p. 35) or a roast chicken brushed with Rosemary-Balsamic Glaze (p. 13) or Orange-Apricot Glaze (p. 14).

1. Rinse the rice in a colander under cold running water, then drain. Transfer to a large Dutch oven and cover with 2 inches of cold water. Sprinkle generously with salt. Bring to a boil, then reduce the heat to a simmer, cover, and cook until tender (most of the grains should just start to split open), about 1 hour. Transfer to a colander, rinse under cold running water, and drain well.

2. Meanwhile, in a small cup, toss the cherries with the orange juice and let soak for 20 minutes. In another small bowl, toss the chicken with the maple syrup and 1 tablespoon of the vinegar and sprinkle with salt and pepper to taste. In another small bowl, make a balsamic vinaigrette by whisking together the mustard and the remaining 2 tablespoons vinegar. Still whisking, slowly drizzle in the olive oil.

3. In a large serving bowl, toss the rice with the cherries, chicken, pine nuts, parsley, thyme, and balsamic vinaigrette. Serve immediately, or refrigerate for up to 2 days and serve cold (let come to room temperature before serving).

Chapter 6

Comforting Casseroles

Casseroles have long been the destination

of choice for leftover chicken and with good reason. These dishes rely on gentle heat and a measure of richness and substance, which fit perfectly with leftover chicken.

This chapter covers many of the old standbys: There's a trio of pot pies, chicken tetrazzini, and, of course, a chicken and broccoli casserole. But we also go to some new and exiting places with these dishes, like Baked Philippine-Style Chicken Adobo with Rice and Bok Choy, Mexican Lasagna with Spiced Chicken and Beans, and Grandma Pauline's Chicken Paprikash with Herb Dumplings.

Whether familiar friends or new introductions, all of these casseroles are hearty dishes that you'll enjoy serving on a chilly night when you've got an appetite. So crank up the stove and get ready to eat.

Potato-Crusted Chicken Pie with Mushrooms and Rosemary

Serves 6

A cross between a shepherd's pie and a pot pie, this casserole is perfect for those occasions when you happen to have both leftover mashed potatoes and roast chicken in the refrigerator. If you don't have any leftover potatoes, you can make them fresh; for straight up simple, go with Your Basic Mashed Potatoes (p. 84) or try Leek and Parmesan Mashed Potatoes (p. 85) for an extra layer of flavor. If making them fresh, then skip step 2 below and proceed with the recipe.

3 tablespoons unsalted butter, melted, plus more for greasing
5 cups leftover mashed potatoes
1 tablespoon chopped fresh rosemary
1/4 cup milk (don't use skim), more if needed
Kosher salt and freshly ground black pepper
2 tablespoons olive oil
1 large Spanish onion, finely diced
10 ounces white mushrooms, quartered
3 cups diced leftover chicken
2 cups frozen petite peas
10 oil-packed sun-dried tomatoes, thinly sliced
1 cup low-salt chicken broth
1 tablespoon balsamic vinegar

> ## CHIX PICKS
>
> Any basic roast chicken goes nicely in this casserole, particularly one with a prominent rosemary flavor like Balsamic-Glazed Rosemary Chicken with Bacon and Pearl Onions (p. 36) or Roast Chicken with Rosemary-Mustard Crust and Browned Onions (p. 30)—add any leftover onions from either chicken to the mix.

1. Preheat the oven to 400°F. Grease a 9 by 13-inch baking dish.

2. In a large saucepan over medium-low heat, combine the potatoes, half the rosemary, and the milk. Cook, gently mashing and stirring, until the potatoes are warmed through, about 10 minutes. Add a couple more tablespoons of milk if the potatoes are still dry. Season with salt and pepper to taste.

3. Meanwhile, heat the oil in a large skillet over medium heat until shimmering hot, about 2 minutes. Add the onion and a generous sprinkling of salt and cook, stirring, until it softens and begins to brown, about 8 minutes. Add the mushrooms, sprinkle with 1/2 teaspoon salt and cook, stirring, until they start to soften, about 4 minutes. Stir in the chicken, peas, tomatoes, broth, vinegar, and the remaining rosemary. Bring to a boil, then remove from the heat and let sit for a couple of minutes. Season generously with salt and pepper to taste.

4. Transfer the chicken mixture to the prepared baking dish. Spread the potatoes evenly over the top and drizzle with the melted butter. Bake until the top browns and the filling is hot throughout, about 20 minutes. Let rest for a couple of minutes, then serve.

Old-Fashioned Chicken Pot Pie with Peas and Carrots

Serves 6 to 8

What would a book on leftover chicken be without a pot pie? Not much, so this was one of the first recipes I started working on. It's a catchall recipe, a combination of a couple of my favorite versions. If you want to dress it up, add some mushrooms, potatoes, or any other vegetable you like.

2 tablespoons unsalted butter, more for greasing
1 large Spanish onion, finely diced
2 stalks celery, finely diced
2 medium carrots, diced
Kosher salt and freshly ground black pepper
3 tablespoons all-purpose flour
3½ cups low-salt chicken broth
1 tablespoon cider vinegar
1 tablespoon chopped fresh thyme
3 cups diced leftover chicken
2 cup frozen petite peas
1 Basic Pie Crust (p. 188)
2 tablespoons heavy cream or whole milk

CHIX PICKS

Keep it simple with a roast chicken that won't overpower the plain flavors in this dish. Try Roast Chicken with Caramelized Shallots and Fingerling Potatoes (p. 38) or Sear-Roasted Chicken with Spring Onions and Asparagus (p. 86)—you can throw in any leftover potatoes, asparagus, or onions.

1. Preheat the oven to 375°F. Grease a 9 by 13-inch baking dish.

2. Melt the butter in a large Dutch oven over medium heat. Add the onion, celery, and carrots, sprinkle generously with salt (about 1 teaspoon) and cook, stirring, until the vegetables soften and brown in places, about 8 minutes. Reduce the heat to medium-low, add the flour and cook, stirring, until it coats the vegetables and they color a light brown, about 5 minutes. Add the broth, vinegar, and thyme and bring to a boil (the mixture should thicken). Reduce the heat to a simmer, add the chicken and peas, and cook until just heated through, about 5 minutes. Let cool for a couple of minutes.

3. Roll the pie crust dough out into a rectangular shape slightly larger than the baking dish, about 10 by 14 inches (it should be between ¼ inch and ½ inch thick).

4. Pour the chicken mixture into the dish, then cover it with the crust. Using your thumb and forefinger, crimp the dough around the edges so it forms a pretty pattern. With the tip of a paring knife, make a couple of slits in the top of the crust so steam can escape during baking. Brush with the cream. Bake until the top of the pastry is golden all over and the filling is bubbling hot, about 35 minutes. Let cool for a couple of minutes, then and serve.

Basic Pie Crust

Makes enough for 1 pot pie or 1 quiche.

> 2½ cups all-purpose flour
> ½ teaspoon salt
> 10 tablespoons chilled unsalted butter, cut into pieces
> ¼ cup vegetable shortening
> 6 tablespoons ice water

1. Combine the flour and salt in a food processor and pulse once to blend. Add the butter and shortening and pulse until the mixture has a coarse texture about the size of peas. Pulse in ¼ cup of the water—the mixture should form coarse clumps—if it still needs more water, pulse in 1 or 2 more tablespoons.

2. Flip the dough out onto a piece of plastic wrap. Form it into a disk, wrap it, and refrigerate for at least half an hour and up to 2 days.

Curried Chicken Pie

Serves 6

I love curried meat pies so it was only natural to take curried chicken and put it into a pot pie.

2 tablespoons canola or vegetable oil, plus more for greasing
1 small yellow onion, finely diced
2 small carrots, cut into ¼-inch dice
1 jalapeño, cored, seeded, and finely diced
2 tablespoons peeled and minced fresh ginger
Kosher salt
2 teaspoons curry powder
2 teaspoons sweet paprika
Freshly ground black pepper
2 medium-size russet potatoes, peeled and cut into 1-inch chunks
1½ cups low-salt chicken broth
½ cup plus 2 tablespoons unsweetened coconut milk
2½ cups diced leftover chicken
½ cup chopped fresh cilantro
1 cup frozen petite peas
1 tablespoon cider vinegar
1 Basic Pie Crust (see recipe, facing page)
1 lime, cut into wedges, for serving

> ## CHIX PICKS
>
> A bird with plenty of spice complements the curry in this pot pie. Try E.G.'s Roast Chicken with Tarragon and Whole-Grain Mustard (p. 46) or a bird coated with Moroccan Spice Rub (p. 12).

1. Preheat the oven to 375°F. Grease an 8-inch-square baking dish.

2. Heat the oil in a large Dutch oven over medium-high heat until shimmering hot, about 1½ minutes. Reduce to medium heat, add the onion, carrots, jalapeño, and ginger, sprinkle with ½ teaspoon salt, and cook, stirring often, until the onion is softened, about 8 minutes. Add the curry powder and paprika, sprinkle generously with salt and pepper (about ¾ teaspoon of each) and cook, stirring, for 1 minute. Add the potatoes, broth, and ½ cup of the coconut milk, bring to a boil, then reduce the heat to a simmer. Cover and cook with the lid askew until the potatoes are just tender, about 15 minutes. Stir in the chicken, cilantro, peas, and vinegar, and cook for 5 minutes to heat through. Season with salt and pepper to taste.

3. Roll the pie crust dough out slightly larger than the baking dish (it should be about ¼ to ½ inch larger than the baking dish). Pour the chicken into the baking dish and cover it with the crust. With thumb and forefinger, crimp the dough around the edges to it form a pretty pattern. With the tip of a paring knife, make a couple of slits in the top so steam can escape. Brush with the remaining 2 tablespoons coconut milk. Bake until the top is golden and the filling bubbling hot, about 35 minutes. Let cool a couple of minutes, then serve with the lime wedges.

Chicken, Spinach, and Mushroom Pie with a Phyllo Crust

Serves 4 to 6

The buttery crispness of phyllo (which serves as the top crust for this pie) goes great with the mushrooms and spinach in this pie.

6 tablespoons (¾ stick) unsalted butter, plus more for greasing
10 ounces cremini or white mushrooms, thinly sliced
3½ ounces shiitake mushrooms, stemmed and caps thinly sliced
Kosher salt
10 ounces spinach, heavy stems removed, washed well and spun dry
2 tablespoons all-purpose flour
1½ cups low-salt chicken broth
1½ tablespoons sherry vinegar or balsamic vinegar
1 tablespoon chopped fresh rosemary
3 cups diced leftover chicken
2 tablespoons heavy cream
6 sheets phyllo, thawed and covered with a damp towel

CHIX PICKS

The flavors in Mom's Hungarian Roast Chicken with Wild Mushrooms and Buttered Egg Noodles (p. 40) and Roast Chicken with Fennel and Mushroom Dressing (p. 47) both complement this dish—you can toss any leftover mushrooms or dressing into the filling for this pie.

1. Preheat the oven to 400°F. Grease an 8-inch-square baking dish. Melt 2 tablespoons of the butter in a large sauté pan over medium-high heat. Add the mushrooms, sprinkle with 1 teaspoon salt and cook, stirring a few times, until softened and browned in places, about 4 minutes. Add the spinach and cook, stirring, until just wilted, about 3 minutes. Transfer to a large baking sheet to cool.

2. Wipe the pan with a paper towel, reduce the heat to medium, and melt another 2 tablespoons of the butter. Add the flour and cook, stirring, until it colors golden brown, about 2 minutes. Whisk in the broth, vinegar, and 2 teaspoons of the rosemary and bring to a boil. Reduce the heat to a simmer, stir in the chicken, mushroom mixture, and cream, and cook for 5 minutes. Let cool for a couple of minutes, then pour into the baking dish.

3. Melt the remaining 2 tablespoons butter. Brush one of the sheets of phyllo with the butter, sprinkle with some of the remaining rosemary and a little salt, and gently place over the top of the baking dish, crimping it to fit around the dish. Repeat with the remaining sheets of phyllo. Bake until the top of the pastry is golden all over, about 25 minutes. Let cool for a couple of minutes, then cut and serve.

Chicken Florentine

Serves 4

This was always one of my favorite meals at the red sauce eateries my family frequented in Boston's North End years ago. Though sautéed chicken is the norm for this Italian-American dish, sliced leftover chicken stands in nicely.

1 clove garlic, minced, and 1 clove garlic, smashed
3 tablespoons olive oil
10 ounces spinach, heavy stems removed, soaked and spun dry
Kosher salt
1 teaspoon dried oregano
1/4 teaspoon crushed red pepper flakes
One 28-ounce can diced tomatoes and their juices
Freshly ground black pepper
3 cups thinly sliced leftover chicken
6 ounces fresh mozzarella cheese, thinly sliced
1/2 cup freshly grated Parmesan cheese

1. Preheat the oven to 425°F.

2. Heat the minced garlic in 1½ tablespoons of the oil in a large ovenproof sauté pan over medium heat until it sizzles steadily and starts to brown around the edges, about 2 minutes. Add the spinach, sprinkle with ½ teaspoon salt and cook, tossing, until it just wilts, about 3 minutes. Transfer to a large plate.

3. Add the remaining 1½ tablespoons oil and the smashed garlic clove to the pan and cook, tossing, until the garlic starts to brown and become very fragrant, about 2 minutes. Add the oregano and red pepper flakes and cook, stirring, for 1 minute. Add the tomatoes and their juices, and bring to a boil. Reduce the heat to a simmer, cover, and cook for 5 minutes to meld the different flavors. Season generously with salt and black pepper to taste.

4. Evenly scatter the chicken, spinach, mozzarella, and Parmesan on top of the sauce. Transfer to the oven and bake until the cheese melts and browns, about 15 minutes. Serve immediately.

CHIX PICKS

Sear-Roasted Chicken with Tomatoes and Rosemary (p. 78) complements the tomatoes in this casserole (and you can add any leftover sauce to the dish). Or try a simple bird with Mediterranean flavors like Greek Roast Chicken with Lemon, Black Olives, and Potatoes (p. 56).

Grandma Pauline's Chicken Paprikash with Herb Dumplings

Serves 4

I've taken some liberties with my grandmother Pauline's Hungarian paprikash to turn it into a casserole—no worries, I got her ok. Crisped bacon adds richness while mushrooms and fresh herbs infuse and intensify the broth.

DUMPLINGS:

1½ cups all-purpose flour
1 teaspoon kosher salt
½ teaspoon freshly ground black pepper
½ teaspoon baking soda
1 large egg, beaten
1¼ cups water, or as needed
6 tablespoons thinly sliced fresh chives
1½ tablespoons chopped fresh dill

CASSEROLE:

¼ pound bacon (about 4 slices), cut into thin strips
1 large Spanish onion, finely diced
Kosher salt
1 tablespoon sweet Hungarian paprika
10 ounces white mushrooms, thinly sliced
1½ cups low-salt chicken broth
3 cups diced leftover chicken
1 cup sour cream
3 tablespoons thinly sliced fresh chives
Freshly ground black pepper

1. Preheat the oven to 375°F.

2. Prepare the dumpling batter: In a large bowl, gently stirring, combine the flour, salt, pepper, and the baking soda, and then add the egg and water until the mixture has a uniform texture similar to that of thick pancake batter. Add up to ¼ cup more water, if needed, to achieve this consistency. Stir in the chives and dill and set aside.

3. Bring a large pot of water to a boil.

4. Meanwhile, cook the bacon in a large Dutch oven over medium heat, stirring occasionally, until it browns and renders much of its fat, about 6 minutes. Transfer to a plate lined with paper towels.

5. Add the onion to the pot, sprinkle with ½ teaspoon salt and cook, stirring occasionally, until softened and browned in places, about 6 minutes. Add the paprika and cook, stirring, for 30 seconds. Turn the heat to medium-high, add the mushrooms, and season with ½ teaspoon salt. Cook, stirring occasionally, until the mushrooms brown and soften, about 4 minutes. Add the broth and bring to a boil. Reduce the heat to a simmer, stir in the chicken, and cook for 10 minutes to heat through.

6. Meanwhile, add a couple of tablespoons of salt to the boiling water. Working in two batches, add the batter in heaping 1-tablespoon portions to the water and cook until they float and start to firm up, about 5 minutes. Strain and then stir the dumplings into the chicken mixture, cover with the lid askew, and transfer to the oven. Bake for 25 minutes so the dumplings finish cooking and the broth thickens.

7. Stir the sour cream into the casserole, season with salt and pepper to taste, and serve immediately with a sprinkling of the crisped bacon and chives.

CHIX PICKS

This works nicely with a chicken that has some paprika in it, like one coated with All-Purpose Poultry Spice Rub (p. 11), or Mom's Hungarian Roast Chicken with Wild Mushrooms and Buttered Egg Noodles (p. 40). If you have any Wild Mushroom and Herb Jus (p. 33), stir it into the sauce.

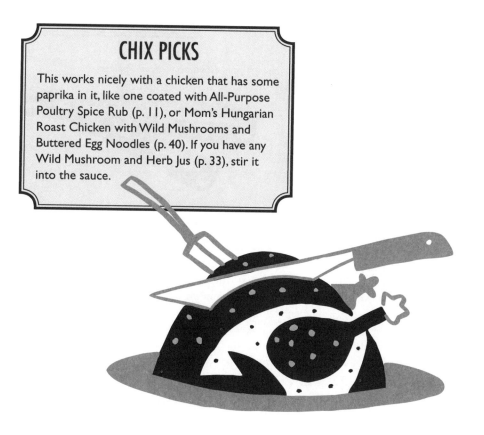

Chicken with Sage and Cornmeal Dumplings

Serves 4

This chicken and dumpling dish has more of a Southern feel, the cornmeal and Cheddar in the dumplings reminiscent of grits.

DUMPLINGS:

¾ cup all-purpose flour
⅓ cup cornmeal
½ teaspoon baking powder
½ teaspoon kosher salt
½ teaspoon freshly ground black pepper
¾ cup whole milk
1 large egg, beaten
½ cup shredded sharp Cheddar cheese,
1 teaspoon chopped fresh sage

CASSEROLE:

2 tablespoons unsalted butter
2 medium leeks (white and light green parts), finely diced, soaked, and patted dry
2 medium carrots, cut into ½-inch-thick rounds
2 stalks celery, sliced ½ inch thick
Kosher salt
1 teaspoon sweet Hungarian paprika
3 cups low-salt chicken broth
1 tablespoon cider vinegar
3 cups diced leftover chicken

> ## CHIX PICKS
>
> A roast chicken with some sweetness and spice punches up the simple broth in this casserole. Try Southern Spiced Chicken with Chipotle-Honey BBQ Sauce (p. 76) or a bird tossed with Smoky Chipotle Butter (p. 61).

1. Preheat the oven to 375°F. In a large bowl, combine the flour, cornmeal, baking powder, salt, and pepper. Stirring, add the milk and egg so it forms an even batter. Fold in the cheese and sage and set aside.

2. Melt the butter in a large ovenproof skillet over medium heat. Add the leeks, carrots, and celery, sprinkle with 1 teaspoon salt, and cook, stirring, until softened, about 10 minutes. Add the paprika and cook, stirring, for 30 seconds. Add the broth and vinegar and bring to a boil. Reduce the heat to a simmer, add the chicken, and cook until the vegetables are completely tender, about 10 minutes. Add heaping 1-tablespoon portions of the batter to the chicken mixture, spacing them as best you can. Cook, without touching, until the tops start to firm up, about 10 minutes, then gently flip them over.

3. Transfer the skillet to the oven, cover with the lid askew, and bake until the dumplings are completely cooked through, about 20 minutes. Serve immediately.

Mexican Lasagna with Spiced Chicken and Beans

Serves 6

Tortillas take the place of pasta in this Mexican casserole and spiced chicken, kidney beans, and cheese form the filling. This dish only gets better after a day in the fridge.

2 tablespoons olive oil, plus more for greasing
1 large Spanish onion, cut in half and thinly sliced into half moons
Kosher salt and freshly ground black pepper
1½ tablespoons chili powder
1 tablespoon ground cumin
1 cup beer (I prefer a light lager)
One 28-ounce can diced tomatoes and their juices
One 15-ounce can kidney beans, drained and rinsed
3 cups thinly sliced leftover chicken
½ cup jarred sliced jalapeños, drained and chopped
6 burrito-size (about 12 inches wide) flour tortillas
¾ cup chopped fresh cilantro
½ pound sharp Cheddar cheese, shredded (about 2 cups)
¼ pound shredded Monterey Jack cheese (about 1 cup)
1 cup sour cream

> ## CHIX PICKS
>
> The intense flavor of a grill-roasted bird works well with this Tex-Mex casserole. Try Italian Grilled Chicken Under a Brick with Smoky Balsamic Tomatoes (p. 68) or Grill-Roasted Chicken with Tex-Mex Spice Crust and Grilled Corn Salsa (p. 58)—you can add any leftover salsa from either bird to the casserole.

1. Preheat the oven to 425°F. Grease a 9 by 13-inch baking dish.

2. Heat the oil in a large skillet over medium-high heat until shimmering hot, about 1½ minutes. Reduce the heat to medium, add the onion, sprinkle with 1 teaspoon salt and cook, stirring often, until softened and browned, about 8 minutes. Add the chili powder and cumin and cook, stirring, for 1 minute to intensify the flavors. Add the beer and cook, stirring, until it almost completely reduces, about 4 minutes. Add the tomatoes and their juices and beans and bring to a boil. Reduce the heat to a simmer and cook for 10 minutes to meld the flavors. Stir in the chicken and jalapeños and cook for 5 minutes to heat through.

3. Set 3 of the tortillas so they cover the bottom of the baking dish. Top with half the chicken-tomato mixture, half the cilantro, and half the Cheddar and Monterey Jack. Repeat with the remaining tortillas, chicken-tomato mixture, cilantro, and cheeses. Bake until the cheeses melt and brown and the casserole heats through, about 20 minutes. Let cool for 5 minutes, then cut into pieces and serve with the sour cream.

Mushroom Chicken Tetrazzini

Serves 4

Tetrazzini has long been the king of leftover chicken and turkey preparations. I like to dress my version up with a touch of sherry, some fresh herbs and a medley of mushrooms. Serve over a bed of buttered egg noodles.

¼ cup (½ stick) unsalted butter

10 ounces cremini or white mushrooms, thinly sliced

3½ ounces shiitake mushrooms, stemmed and thinly sliced

Kosher salt

2 tablespoons all-purpose flour

¼ cup dry sherry

2 cups low-salt chicken broth

3 cups diced leftover chicken

3 tablespoons heavy cream

Freshly ground black pepper

½ cup thinly sliced fresh chives

½ cup freshly grated Parmesan cheese

1. Preheat the oven to 400°F. Melt 2 tablespoons of the butter in a large ovenproof sauté pan over medium-high heat. Add the mushrooms, sprinkle with 1 teaspoon salt and cook, stirring occasionally, until the mushrooms are softened and browned in places, about 5 minutes.

2. Reduce the heat to medium and push the mushrooms to the side of the pan. Add the remaining 2 tablespoons of butter and melt. Add the flour and cook, stirring, until it colors a golden brown and acquires a nutty fragrance, about 2 minutes. Add the sherry and cook, until it almost completely reduces, about 2 minutes. Stir in the broth and bring to a boil—the mixture should start to thicken. Reduce the heat to a simmer, stir in the chicken and cream, and cook for 5 minutes.

3. Season with salt and pepper to taste and stir in half the chives. Sprinkle with the Parmesan, transfer to the oven, and bake until the cheese is browned, about 20 minutes. Let rest for a couple of minutes, then serve sprinkled with the remaining chives.

CHIX PICKS

The sweetness of a glazed bird complements the sherry in this tetrazzini. Try Rosemary-Balsamic Glaze (p. 13) or Orange-Apricot Glaze (p. 14).

THE IMPORTANCE OF BLACK PEPPER

For many cooks, black pepper is an afterthought, a spice that can just as easily be added at the dinner table from a shaker as from a mill during cooking. This approach misses the strength of this spice. When added in a measured but generous manner, black pepper gives a dish an edge that sharpens the other flavors around it. That is not to say that black pepper belongs in every dish. Rather, when seasoning with black pepper, make sure to add enough so that it asserts its presence.

One good way to do this is to use freshly ground black pepper. Grinding pepper just before adding it to a dish activates the tiny berries' volatile oils and consequently perks up their flavors. Pre-ground pepper, on the other hand, has less of this vibrancy and a heavier, dull flavor.

Southwestern Chicken and Corn Casserole

Serves 4

This casserole is kind of like a lazy enchilada. Instead of wrapping the filling in tortillas, you layer the ingredients in a skillet, top with the tortillas, sprinkle with cheese, and bake. Note that the piquancy of jalapeños can vary quite a bit. If you're a fan of hot food, you may want to up the amount by one or two peppers.

2 tablespoons olive oil
1 large Spanish onion, cut in 1/4-inch dice
1 red bell pepper, cored, seeded, and cut in 1/4-inch dice
1 jalapeño, thinly sliced
Kosher salt
3 cups diced leftover chicken
3 cups fresh or frozen corn kernels
1/2 cup low-salt chicken broth
1/4 cup chopped fresh cilantro
Freshly ground black pepper
4 corn tortillas
1 cup shredded Monterey jack cheese (1/4 pound)
1 cup shredded sharp Cheddar cheese (1/4 pound)
1 cup Tomatillo-Chipotle Salsa (see Chicken and Spinach Enchiladas, p. 244) or your favorite salsa

> ## CHIX PICKS
>
> The flavors in Grill-Roasted Jamaican Jerk Chicken (p. 74) or Grill-Roasted Chicken with Tex-Mex Spice Crust and Grilled Corn Salsa (p. 58) meld nicely with the spice and heat of this casserole. Fold any leftover salsa from the latter into the filling.

1. Preheat the oven to 425°F

2. Heat the oil over medium-high heat in a large ovenproof skillet (preferably cast iron) until shimmering hot, about 1½ minutes. Reduce the heat to medium, add the onion, bell pepper, and jalapeño, sprinkle with 1 teaspoon salt and cook, stirring, until softened and browned in places, about 8 minutes. Stir in the chicken, corn, and broth and bring to a boil, stirring occasionally.

3. Stir in the cilantro and one-quarter of the cheeses and season with salt and pepper to taste. Top with the tortillas, overlapping them, so they cover the skillet. Sprinkle evenly with the remaining cheeses. Bake until the cheese melts and browns, about 15 minutes. Let sit for a few minutes, then cut into pieces and serve immediately with a spoonful of the salsa.

Stuffed Peppers with Chicken, Chorizo, and Rice

Serves 4 to 6

Stuffed peppers are one of those dishes that seem like they should be tough to make, but they're really not. Here, the peppers are stuffed with a well-spiced mixture of rice (leftover works fine), chorizo, and Monterey Jack cheese. If you can't find chorizo, substitute hot Italian sausage.

3 tablespoons olive oil, plus more for greasing
¾ pound chorizo, cut into ½-inch dice
2 cloves garlic, minced
1 tablespoon chili powder
One 14.5-ounce can diced tomatoes
  and their juices
3 cups diced leftover chicken
4 cups cooked white rice
4 scallions (white and green parts),
  trimmed and thinly sliced
½ pound Monterey Jack or sharp Cheddar
  cheese, shredded (2 cups)
Kosher salt and freshly ground black pepper
6 red bell peppers, cored

CHIX PICKS

A bird tossed with a spice rub—like Southwestern Chile Spice Rub (p. 11) or Sweet Southern Spice Rub (p. 12)—will perk up the rice filling nicely.

1. Preheat the oven to 375°F. Grease a 9 by 13-inch baking dish.

2. Heat 2 tablespoons of the oil in a large skillet over medium-high heat until shimmering hot, about 1½ minutes. Reduce the heat to medium, add the chorizo, and cook, stirring occasionally, until browned, about 6 minutes. Add the garlic and cook, stirring, until it sizzles for 30 seconds and becomes aromatic. Add the chili powder and cook, stirring, for 30 seconds. Add the tomatoes and their juices and bring to a boil, then stir in the chicken and cook for 5 minutes to heat through. Fold in the rice, scallions, and half the cheese. Season with salt and pepper to taste.

3. Toss the peppers with the remaining 1 tablespoon oil and sprinkle (inside and out) with a total of ¾ teaspoon salt and ½ teaspoon pepper. Fill the peppers with the rice filling. Set the peppers in the prepared baking dish and bake until softened and browned in places, about 30 minutes. Top with the remaining cheese and bake until melted and browned, about another 10 minutes. Let cool for a couple of minutes, then serve.

Chicken Divan with Seared Asparagus

Serves 4

Chicken Divan is thought to have originated at a New York restaurant—the Divan Parisienne—back in the 1950s. The dish usually contains thin pieces of chicken breast and broccoli florets, which are tossed with a creamy sauce and then broiled. I like to substitute asparagus for the broccoli, which gives the casserole a little dressiness. Serve with buttered egg noodles or rice pilaf.

2 tablespoons unsalted butter

1 tablespoon olive oil

1 1/2 pounds thick asparagus, bottoms snapped off, cut into 3-inch lengths

Kosher salt

3 tablespoons all-purpose flour

1 1/2 cups low-salt chicken broth

3 cups thinly sliced leftover chicken

1 tablespoon heavy cream

Juice of 1/2 lemon

Freshly ground black pepper

6 ounces fontina or mozzarella cheese, shredded (1 1/2 cups)

CHIX PICKS

Layer any leftover asparagus or onions from Sear-Roasted Chicken with Spring Onions and Asparagus (p. 86) into this casserole. Or try Balsamic-Glazed Rosemary Chicken with Bacon and Pearl Onions (p. 36). The bacon and onions will act as a nice foil to the creaminess of the dish.

1. Preheat the oven broiler to high and set a rack so it's 6 inches away from the heating element.

2. Melt 1 tablespoon of the butter with the oil in a large ovenproof sauté pan over medium-high heat until it starts to foam and brown, about 1 1/2 minutes. Reduce the heat to medium, add the asparagus, sprinkle with 1/2 teaspoon salt and cook, tossing occasionally, until it browns in places and starts to soften, about 4 minutes.

3. Add the remaining 1 tablespoon butter and the flour and cook, tossing, until the flour coats the asparagus and turns a light golden brown, about 1 1/2 minutes. Stir in broth and bring to a boil, then reduce the heat to a simmer. Cook, stirring, until the mixture thickens, about 5 minutes. Stir in the chicken and cream and cook for 5 minutes to heat through. Stir in the lemon juice and season generously with salt and pepper to taste.

4. Sprinkle with the cheese, transfer to the oven, and broil until it browns and the mixture bubbles all along the sides, 3 to 5 minutes. Serve immediately.

Chicken Posole with Hominy and Chiles

Serves 4

Hominy is made of dried corn kernels (either white or yellow) that have had their hulls and germ removed. It's most frequently availabie canned in its rehydrated form. Like canned beans, you can stir hominy into spicy stews, as I do here, where it will absorb all the different flavors and add a pleasant, chewy texture.

2 tablespoons olive oil
1 medium-size yellow onion, finely diced
1 green bell pepper, cored, seeded, and cut into 1/4-inch dice
1 jalapeño, thinly sliced
Kosher salt
1 tablespoon chili powder
1 teaspoon ground ancho chile powder (or more chili powder)
One 29-ounce can white hominy, drained and rinsed
One 14.5-ounce can diced tomatoes with their juices
1 1/2 cups low-salt chicken broth
Freshly ground black pepper
3 cups 2-inch pieces leftover chicken
Juice of 1 lime
1/2 cup chopped fresh cilantro
1 cup crumbled queso fresco or feta cheese

CHIX PICKS

Try a bird coated with a spice rub like All-Purpose Poultry Spice Rub (p. 11) or go with a full-flavored chicken like Grill-Roasted Tandoori Chicken (p. 62).

1. Preheat the oven to 350°F.

2. Heat the oil in a large Dutch oven over medium-high heat until shimmering hot, about 1 1/2 minutes. Reduce the heat to medium, add the onion, bell pepper, and jalapeño, sprinkle with 1 teaspoon salt, and cook, stirring, until the onion softens and browns, about 8 minutes. Add the chili powder and ground ancho and cook, stirring, for 30 seconds. Stir in the hominy, tomatoes and their juices, and the broth and bring to a boil. Reduce the heat to a simmer, cover, and cook for 10 minutes. Season with salt and black pepper to taste.

3. Stir in the chicken, cover, and transfer to the oven. Bake with the lid askew until the flavors mix and meld and the vegetables become completely tender, about 30 minutes.

4. Stir in half the lime juice and half the cilantro. Taste for salt and pepper and more lime juice. Serve sprinkled with the cheese and the remaining cilantro.

Moroccan Chicken and Carrot Casserole

Serves 4

This is a riff on the chicken tagines popular at Moroccan restaurants. Braise some diced leftover chicken with carrots, oranges, saffron, and spices, then serve over a bed of Couscous with Red Peppers and Orange (p. 85) or your own couscous recipe. Though butter isn't a traditional finishing touch to a Mediterranean braise, here it gives the broth a touch of richness and covers up any dryness in the chicken.

1 large navel orange
Large pinch of saffron threads
2 tablespoons olive oil
1 large onion, cut in half and thinly sliced into half moons
Kosher salt
1 pound carrots, cut on the diagonal into ¼-inch pieces
2 teaspoons ground cumin
1 teaspoon chili powder
¼ teaspoon ground cinnamon
1 cup low-salt chicken broth
3 cups large-dice leftover chicken
½ cup chopped fresh cilantro
2 tablespoons unsalted butter
Freshly ground black pepper

CHIX PICKS

Any spice-rubbed roast chicken goes nicely with this casserole—try Moroccan Spice Rub (p. 12) or All-Purpose Poultry Spice Rub (p. 11). Moroccan Spiced Chicken Roasted over a Bed of Couscous and Apricots (p. 54) is a perfect fit as well.

1. Preheat the oven to 375°F.

2. Using a peeler, shave 1-inch strips of zest from the orange (take care to peel only the orange zest and not the inner white pith). Juice the orange and mix with the zest and saffron in a small bowl. Let sit for 10 minutes.

3. Heat the oil in a large ovenproof sauté pan over medium heat until shimmering hot, about 2 minutes. Add the onion, sprinkle with 1 teaspoon salt, and cook, stirring occasionally, until it completely wilts and browns in places, about 8 minutes. Add the carrots, cumin, chili powder, cinnamon, and ½ teaspoon salt and cook, stirring, for 1 minute. Add the broth and orange juice mixture and bring to a boil. Reduce the heat to a simmer, cover, and cook until the carrots are just tender to the tooth, about 10 minutes. Stir in the chicken, cover with the lid askew, transfer to the oven, and bake until the carrots are tender, about 30 minutes.

4. Stir in half the cilantro and the butter, season generously with salt and pepper, and serve immediately, sprinkled with the remaining cilantro.

Chicken and Stuffing Casserole with Sherry and Mushrooms

Serves 4

This casserole is the perfect solution for leftover chicken and stuffing, which are often hanging around in the refrigerator at the same time.

2 tablespoons unsalted butter
10 ounces white mushrooms, thinly sliced
3½ ounces shiitake mushrooms, stemmed and thinly sliced
Kosher salt
¼ cup dry sherry
1 cup low-salt chicken broth
2 teaspoons chopped fresh thyme
3 cups diced leftover chicken
3 tablespoons heavy cream
6 cups cooked leftover stuffing, broken into small pieces
½ cup freshly grated Parmesan cheese
Freshly ground black pepper

> ## CHIX PICKS
>
> Use any leftover stuffing along with the chicken from Roast Chicken with Rosemary-Garlic Croutons (p. 44) or Roast Chicken with Fennel and Mushroom Dressing (p. 47).

1. Preheat the oven to 400°F.

2. Melt the butter in a large ovenproof sauté pan over medium-high heat. Add the mushrooms, sprinkle with ½ teaspoon salt and cook, stirring occasionally, until softened and browned in places, about 4 minutes. Add the sherry and cook, stirring, until it almost completely cooks off, about 2 minutes. Stir in the broth and thyme and bring to a boil. Reduce the heat to a simmer, stir in the chicken, cream, stuffing, and half the Parmesan, and cook for 5 minutes to heat through. Season with salt and pepper to taste and sprinkle with the remaining Parmesan.

3. Transfer the pan to the oven and bake until the top of the stuffing browns, about 25 minutes. Let cool for a couple of minutes, then cut and serve.

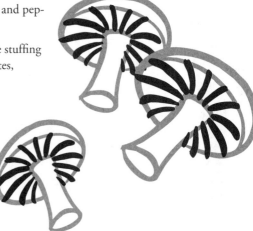

Glazed Chicken and Sweet Potato Hash

Serves 4

This is a great brunch accompaniment for eggs or French toast. Hash is a forgiving dish—it'll hold for an hour or so in a low oven before serving.

1/4 pound bacon (about 4 slices),
cut into thin strips
1 large Spanish onion, finely diced
Kosher salt
2 cloves garlic, minced
1 teaspoon chili powder
2 medium-size sweet potatoes,
cut into 1-inch dice
1 medium-size russet potato,
cut into 1/2-inch dice
2 1/2 cups diced leftover chicken
2 teaspoons chopped fresh thyme
1/2 cup maple syrup
Freshly ground black pepper

CHIX PICKS

Try a roast chicken with some sweetness and spice—most any glazed bird will do. Or you can dice up any leftover potatoes from either Roast Chicken with Caramelized Shallots and Fingerling Potatoes (p. 38) or Jerrod's Roast Chicken with Vermont Maple Glaze, Sweet Potato, and Sage (p. 35). Just toss them into the pan as you transfer it to the oven.

1. Preheat the oven to 425°F.

2. Brown the bacon in a large, heavy skillet (I use my cast-iron) over medium heat until it crisps and renders much of its fat, about 6 minutes. Transfer to a plate lined with paper towels.

3. Add the onion to the bacon fat, sprinkle with salt (about 1/2 teaspoon) and cook, stirring, until the onion softens and starts to brown in places, about 6 minutes. Add the garlic and chili powder and cook, stirring, for 1 minute. Add the potatoes, sprinkle with 1 teaspoon salt and cook, stirring, for a couple of minutes. Stir in the chicken, thyme, and maple syrup and toss well.

4. Transfer to the oven and bake, tossing occasionally, until the potatoes are browned and tender, about 30 minutes.

5. Fold in the bacon, season with salt and pepper to taste, and serve immediately.

Chicken, Cauliflower, and Roasted Red Pepper Casserole

Serves 4 to 6

This is a dressed-up version of a creamy cauliflower casserole. A sprinkling of Parmesan imparts richness and a few drops of Tabasco, a little heat.

2 tablespoons olive oil

1 medium head cauliflower (about 1½ pounds), stems and florets cut into 1½-inch pieces

Kosher salt

2 cloves garlic, minced

¾ cup low-salt chicken broth

2½ cups thinly sliced leftover chicken

2 cups Béchamel Sauce (see recipe, facing page)

3 jarred roasted red peppers, thinly sliced

¾ cup freshly grated Parmesan cheese

2 teaspoons chopped fresh thyme

¼ teaspoon Tabasco sauce

Freshly ground black pepper

½ cup Garlic-Thyme Breadcrumbs (p. 205) or other coarse breadcrumbs

> ## CHIX PICKS
>
> The simpler the roast chicken, the better for this casserole. Try Roast Chicken with Rosemary-Garlic Croutons (p. 44)—chop up any leftover croutons and scatter them on top of the casserole instead of the breadcrumbs— or a roast chicken coated with Lemon-Herb Rub (p. 13).

1. Preheat the oven to 400°F.

2. Heat the oil in a large, ovenproof sauté pan over medium-high heat until shimmering hot, about 1½ minutes. Reduce the heat to medium, add the cauliflower, sprinkle with 1 teaspoon salt and cook, stirring, until it browns in places and starts to soften, about 5 minutes. Add the garlic and cook, stirring, for 1 minute. Add the broth, cover, and cook until the cauliflower is just tender, 5 to 8 minutes.

3. Stir in the chicken, béchamel, red peppers, Parmesan, thyme, and Tabasco. Season with salt and pepper to taste and sprinkle with the breadcrumbs. Transfer to the oven and bake until the breadcrumbs brown and the sauce bubbles around the sides, about 25 minutes. Let sit for a couple of minutes, then serve.

Garlic-Thyme Breadcrumbs

Makes about 3 cups

6 ounces thick, crusty bread, cut into large cubes
2 tablespoons extra-virgin olive oil
2 cloves garlic, minced
2 teaspoons chopped fresh thyme
Kosher salt

Set the bread in a food processor and pulse until it forms coarse crumbs. Meanwhile, heat the oil and garlic in a large, heavy skillet over medium heat until the garlic begins to sizzle steadily and becomes very fragrant, about 3 minutes. Add the breadcrumbs and thyme, sprinkle generously with salt (about ½ teaspoon), and cook, stirring occasionally, until the crumbs turn a light brown and crisp, about 6 minutes. Transfer to a large baking sheet to cool and then store in an air-tight container for up to 1 day.

Béchamel Sauce

Makes about 3 cups

3 cups whole milk
¼ cup (½ stick) unsalted butter
¼ cup all-purpose flour

1. Heat the milk in a small saucepan over low heat.

2. Meanwhile, heat the butter in a medium saucepan over medium-low heat until it begins to foam. Add the flour and cook, stirring well, until the mixture is smooth and a light golden color, about 2 minutes. Whisk in the warm milk and heat, whisking often, until the mixture thickens (it should just come to a boil), about 10 minutes. Use immediately or let cool to room temperature and refrigerate for up to 3 days.

Italian Chicken Polpette with Spicy Tomato Sauce

Serves 4

Polpette is a catch-all Italian term for meatballs. The *polpette* in this version are like croquettes, only with potatoes as the base for the filling instead of a thickened béchamel sauce. The potatoes are riced (that is, cooked and then passed through a potato ricer or food mill), then mixed with shredded leftover chicken and some prosciutto or pancetta. This filling is formed into golf-ball-sized rounds which are breaded, fried, topped with a simple tomato sauce and some cheese, and baked. I'll admit that this dish takes longer than most in this book (about 1½ hours), but it's worth it. Serve them over pasta as though they were giant meatballs, or on their own with some good, crusty bread.

2 tablespoons olive oil, plus more for greasing
2 cloves garlic, minced
1 teaspoon dried oregano
¼ teaspoon crushed red pepper flakes
One 28-ounce can diced tomatoes and their juices
Kosher salt and freshly ground black pepper
1½ pounds russet potatoes, peeled and
    cut into 1½-inch dice
2 cups shredded leftover chicken
4 large eggs, beaten
2 ounces prosciutto, finely chopped
½ cup freshly grated Parmesan cheese
1 cup all-purpose flour for dredging
3 cups fine fresh breadcrumbs
Canola or olive oil for frying
6 ounces mozzarella cheese, shredded (1½ cups)

1. Preheat the oven to 425°F. Grease a 9 by 13-inch baking dish.

2. In a large sauté pan over medium heat, heat the olive oil, garlic, oregano, and red pepper flakes together, stirring, until the garlic sizzles steadily for about 1 minute and just begins to brown around the edges. Add the tomatoes and their juices and bring to a boil. Reduce the heat to a simmer and cook for 5 minutes. Season generously with salt and black pepper to taste. Purée the tomatoes with an immersion blender or in an upright blender and set aside.

3. Meanwhile, prepare the *polpette*. Put the potatoes and a generous sprinkling of salt (about 1 tablespoon) in a medium-size pot with water to cover by about 2 inches and bring to a boil. Reduce the heat to a simmer and cook until the potatoes are fork tender, about 20 minutes. Drain well and let cool for a couple of minutes.

4. Pass the potatoes through a ricer or a food mill and transfer to a large bowl. Gently fold in the chicken, half of the eggs, the prosciutto, half the Parmesan, and ¼ teaspoon each of salt and black pepper.

5. Set the flour, the remaining eggs, and the breadcrumbs in separate shallow bowls. Drop about ¼-cup scoops of the chicken mixture onto a large baking sheet. Form them into balls, then lightly dredge in the flour, dip in the egg, and press to coat completely with the bread-crumbs. You should end up with about 16 *polpette*.

6. Fill a large saucepan or Dutch oven with 2 inches (about 3 cups) of oil and heat over medium heat to 350°F, about 5 minutes. Line a large plate with paper towels.

CHIX PICKS

The flavor of Lemon-Herb Rub (p. 13) brightens up these polpette. Or go with a more predictable Italian pairing, like Italian Grilled Chicken under a Brick with Smoky Balsamic Tomatoes (p. 68) or Sear-Roasted Chicken with Tomatoes and Rosemary (p. 78).

7. Carefully add half the *polpette* to the oil and cook, flipping them after about 2 minutes, until browned all over, about 4 minutes total. Transfer to the plate and sprinkle with salt. Cook the remaining polpette in the same manner.

8. Transfer to the baking dish, top with the tomato sauce, mozzarella, and the remaining Parmesan and bake until the cheese melts, about 15 minutes. Let sit for a couple of minutes, then serve.

Baked Philippine-Style Chicken Adobo with Rice and Bok Choy

Serves 4 to 6

Chicken adobo is a traditional Filipino dish in which chicken is marinated in soy, garlic, and vinegar and then grilled. I've taken those standard elements and tossed them into a casserole. Diced leftover chicken (preferably grilled) is simmered in an intense mixture of soy sauce and rice vinegar, then transferred to a baking dish, covered with white rice, and baked. Though it's not traditional, I like folding in sautéed baby bok choy. If you can't find it, substitute diced large bok choy or Napa cabbage.

2 cloves garlic, minced

5 tablespoons canola oil

½ cup water

⅓ cup rice vinegar

¼ cup soy sauce

1 teaspoon light brown sugar

½ teaspoon freshly ground black pepper

2 bay leaves

1 pound baby bok choy, cut in half, washed well, and patted dry

½ teaspoon kosher salt

3 cups diced leftover chicken

4 scallions (white and green parts), trimmed and thinly sliced

6 cups cooked rice (reheated leftover rice is fine)

1 lime, cut into wedges, for serving

> ## CHIX PICKS
>
> In keeping with the adobo theme, try a grill-roasted bird, preferably one with Asian flavors, like Grill-Roasted Thai Chicken with Lemongrass (p. 53) or Grilled Chicken Teriyaki with Scallions (p. 70).

1. Preheat the oven to 400°F.

2. Place the garlic and 2 tablespoons of the oil in a medium saucepan over medium heat and cook, stirring occasionally, until the garlic sizzles steadily for about 1 minute and just begins to brown around the edges. Add the water, vinegar, soy sauce, brown sugar, pepper, and bay leaves and bring to a boil. Reduce the heat to a simmer and cook for 15 minutes to infuse the flavor of the bay leaves.

3. Meanwhile, heat another 2 tablespoons of the oil in a large skillet over medium-high heat until shimmering hot, about 1½ minutes. Reduce the heat to medium, add the bok choy, sprinkle with the salt, and cook, stirring, until the bok choy starts to brown in places, about 3 minutes. Add a couple of tablespoons of water, cover, and cook until just tender, about 2 minutes. Set aside to cool.

4. Remove the soy-vinegar mixture from the heat, discard the bay leaves, and stir in the chicken. Let sit for about 15 minutes.

5. Spread the bok choy and the chicken and soy mixture on the bottom of a 9 by 13-inch baking dish, sprinkle with half the scallions, and top with the rice. Cover with aluminum foil and bake for 20 minutes to heat through, then raise the oven temperature to 450°F, remove the foil, drizzle the rice with the remaining 1 tablespoon oil, and bake until the top of the rice crisps and just starts to brown, about 10 minutes.

6. Remove the casserole from the oven and let sit for 5 minutes, then serve, sprinkled with the remaining scallions and the lime wedges for squeezing.

Baked Chicken Cordon Bleu

Serves 4

After writing all the recipes for this book, I'll admit that, at times, my mind got to wandering, trying to dream up new and different ways to use roast chicken. I've always liked chicken cordon bleu, so it seemed natural to try this pairing—and I'm glad I did. A layer of thick crusty bread serves as the base for the casserole, which is then topped with ham, Swiss cheese, a spoonful of béchamel sauce, and some coarse breadcrumbs. The whole thing amounts to a warm, open-faced sandwich, sort of like a croque monsieur, without the top.

Unsalted butter for greasing (about 1 tablespoon)

¾ pound good crusty bread, cut into 1-inch-thick slices and lightly toasted (you can do this on a baking sheet in a moderate oven)

3 cups thinly sliced leftover chicken

1½ cups Béchamel Sauce (p. 205), warmed

¼ pound thinly sliced ham

6 ounces sliced Gruyère or Swiss cheese

1½ cups Garlic-Thyme Breadcrumbs (p. 205) or other coarse breadcrumbs

CHIX PICKS

The sweetness of a glazed bird pairs well with the cheese and ham. Try Maple-Mustard Glaze (p. 14) or Rosemary-Balsamic Glaze (p. 13).

1. Preheat the oven to 425°F. Grease a 9 by 13-inch dish.

2. Fit the bread into the dish so it forms one even layer on the bottom—cut the pieces to fit, if you need to. Top evenly with the chicken, then the béchamel, then the ham and cheese. Sprinkle evenly with the breadcrumbs. Bake until the cheese melts and the breadcrumbs brown, about 20 minutes. Let rest for a couple of minutes, then cut into pieces and serve.

Hungarian Chicken Goulash

Serves 4

Thanks to my father's Hungarian roots, in addition to chicken paprikash, we also grew up eating beef goulash, a thick stew with potatoes, peppers, and caraway seeds. In this version, I've subbed out the beef for leftover chicken.

2 tablespoons olive oil

1 large Spanish onion, finely diced

1 red bell pepper, cored, seeded, and finely diced

Kosher salt and freshly ground black pepper

1 tablespoon all-purpose flour

1 tablespoon sweet Hungarian paprika

2 teaspoons caraway seeds

3½ cups low-salt chicken broth

1 large russet potato, peeled and cut into 1-inch dice

2 teaspoons tomato paste

3 cups diced leftover chicken

Freshly ground black pepper

¾ cup sour cream

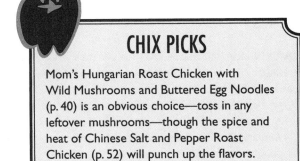

CHIX PICKS

Mom's Hungarian Roast Chicken with Wild Mushrooms and Buttered Egg Noodles (p. 40) is an obvious choice—toss in any leftover mushrooms—though the spice and heat of Chinese Salt and Pepper Roast Chicken (p. 52) will punch up the flavors.

1. Preheat the oven to 375°F.

2. Heat the oil in a large ovenproof sauté pan over medium heat until shimmering hot, about 2 minutes. Add the onion and bell pepper, sprinkle with 1 teaspoon salt and cook, stirring occasionally, until softened and browned in places, about 8 minutes. Add the flour, paprika, and caraway and cook, stirring, for 1 minute. Stir in the broth, potato, and tomato paste and bring to a boil. Reduce the heat to a simmer, cover, and cook until the potato is just tender, about 15 minutes.

3. Stir in the chicken and season with salt and black pepper to taste. Cover the pan with the lid askew and transfer to the oven. Bake until the potatoes are completely softened and the broth thickens a bit, about 25 minutes. Serve immediately with a dollop of the sour cream.

Pulled Barbecue Chicken and Cornbread Casserole

Serves 6

This casserole has its own built-in top crust of cornbread, which bakes up as the casserole heats up. Serve with some Braised Garlicky Collard Greens (p. 43) or Spicy Black Beans (p. 241).

- ¼ cup canola or vegetable oil, plus more for greasing
- 1 recipe Carolina BBQ Sauce (p. 61)
- 3 cups shredded leftover chicken
- 1 cup all-purpose flour
- 1 cup yellow cornmeal
- 1½ teaspoons baking soda
- 1 teaspoon baking powder
- 1 teaspoon kosher salt
- ¾ cup buttermilk
- 2 large eggs, beaten
- 2 tablespoons sugar
- 6 ounces Monterey jack cheese, shredded (1½ cups)
- 2 scallions (white and green parts), trimmed and thinly sliced
- 1 jalapeño, thinly sliced

CHIX PICKS

A spice-rubbed or grill-roasted bird (or both) will match the heat of the BBQ sauce and the cornbread in this recipe. Try Grill-Roasted Chicken with Tex-Mex Spice Crust and Grilled Corn Salsa (p. 58)—you can fold any leftover salsa into the cornbread—or a bird coated with Sweet Southern Spice Rub (p. 12) or Southwestern Chile Spice Rub (p. 11).

1. Preheat the oven to 425°F. Grease a 9 by 13-inch baking dish.

2. Heat the BBQ sauce in a medium saucepan over medium-low heat, stirring. Once it's hot, add the chicken and simmer until warmed through, about 5 minutes.

3. In a large bowl, whisk together the flour, cornmeal, baking soda, baking powder, and the salt. In a medium bowl, whisk together the buttermilk, eggs, oil, and sugar. Gently stir the wet ingredients into the dry, then fold in the cheese, scallions, and jalapeño.

4. Pour the chicken mixture into the baking dish, spreading it evenly, then top with the cornbread batter, also spreading it evenly. Transfer to the oven and bake until the top of the cornbread lightly browns and becomes firm to the touch and a toothpick inserted into the center comes out clean, about 25 minutes. Let cool for 5 minutes, then cut into pieces and serve.

Chicken Cassoulet

Serves 4

This preparation resembles a traditional French cassoulet (a heavy mix of beans, sausages, and preserved duck or goose) in spirit more than anything else—it's lighter and takes less time to make and, of course, has chicken as its centerpiece.

¼ pound bacon (about 4 strips), thinly sliced crosswise

1 pound sweet Italian sausage, cut into 1-inch-thick rounds

2 cloves garlic, minced

1 cup beer (preferably a light lager)

3 cups low-salt chicken broth

One 29-ounce or two 15-ounce can(s) cannellini beans, drained and rinsed

2 teaspoons chopped fresh rosemary

2 cups diced leftover chicken

½ cup freshly grated Parmesan cheese

Kosher salt and freshly ground black pepper

2 cups Garlic-Thyme Breadcrumbs (p. 205) or other coarse breadcrumbs

> ## CHIX PICKS
>
> From one bistro classic to another, try Sear-Roasted Chicken with Lots of Garlic (p. 82)—purée any leftover garlic cloves and serve them on toasts—or go with Roast Chicken with Rosemary-Mustard Crust and Browned Onions (p. 30).

1. Preheat the oven to 400°F.

2. Brown the bacon in a large ovenproof sauté pan over medium heat until it crisps and renders much of its fat, about 6 minutes. Transfer to a plate lined with paper towels.

3. Add the sausage to the pan and cook, stirring occasionally, until well browned, about 8 minutes. Add the garlic and cook, stirring, until it sizzles steadily but doesn't quite brown, about 1 minute. Add the beer and cook, stirring, until it almost completely reduces, about 2 minutes. Add the broth and bring to a boil. Reduce the heat to a simmer, stir in the beans, rosemary, and chicken and simmer for 5 minutes to heat through.

4. Stir in the Parmesan, season with salt and pepper to taste, and sprinkle evenly with the breadcrumbs. Transfer to the oven and bake until the crumbs brown and crisp, about 25 minutes. Let sit for a couple of minutes, then serve immediately with a sprinkling of the bacon.

Thai Chicken Curry with Green Beans and Tofu

Serves 4

As opposed to the standard yellow spice mix that most of us know as curry, Thai curries are either red or green pastes, which contain chiles, lemongrass, and galangal. The difference in the color is due to the chiles used—green curry paste contains fresh green bird chiles, while red curry paste is made from dried red chiles. Both are intensely flavored (a little goes a long way) and spicy. For this casserole, pick up some Thai red curry paste, which is now increasingly available at supermarkets.

2 tablespoons canola oil
1/2 pound green beans, trimmed and cut into 2-inch lengths
I medium-size yellow onion, thinly sliced in half moons
I red bell pepper, cored, seeded, and cut into 1/2-inch-wide strips
1/2 teaspoon kosher salt
One 14-ounce can unsweetened coconut milk, whisked to blend
2 teaspoons Thai red curry paste
2 1/2 cups diced leftover chicken
10 ounces firm tofu, cut into 1 1/2-inch cubes
I tablespoon light brown sugar
I tablespoon Thai fish sauce
I ripe tomato, cored and finely diced
2 tablespoons thinly sliced fresh Thai basil or 1/4 cup thinly sliced fresh basil
I tablespoon fresh lime juice
Steamed jasmine or white rice for serving

> ## CHIX PICKS
>
> A grilled bird with plenty of spice like Grill-Roasted Thai Chicken with Lemongrass (p. 53) or Grill-Roasted Tandoori Chicken (p. 62) matches the heat of this curried chicken.

1. Preheat the oven to 375°F.

2. Heat the oil in a large ovenproof skillet over medium-high heat until shimmering hot, about 1 1/2 minutes. Add the green beans, onion, and bell pepper, sprinkle with the salt and cook, stirring occasionally, until they start to soften and brown in places, about 4 minutes. Add the coconut milk and curry paste and bring to a boil, whisking constantly. Stir in the chicken, tofu, brown sugar, and fish sauce, reduce the heat to a simmer, and cook until heated through, about 5 minutes.

3. Cover the skillet, transfer to the oven, and cook with the lid askew until the beans are soft and tender, about 25 minutes.

4. Stir in the tomato, basil, and lime juice and serve immediately, spooned over the rice.

Ryan's Chicken and Broccoli Casserole

Serves 4

My friend Ryan Becze is a chef at Masa in New York, an elegant, acclaimed, and over-whelmingly expensive Japanese restaurant. Though I still have yet to eat at Masa—the cost of the meal would most likely preclude me from sending my kids to college—I do get to cook with Ryan every now and then. Despite his tremendous abilities with fancy food, Ryan is a native Iowan who likes making casseroles from back home—like this one—on his days off.

Kosher salt
¾ pound broccoli crowns, cut into 1½-inch florets (about 6 cups)
1 recipe Béchamel Sauce (p. 205)
¾ cup low-salt chicken broth
2 tablespoons olive oil
10 ounces white mushrooms, thinly sliced
2 cloves garlic, minced
2½ cups thinly sliced leftover chicken
1½ teaspoons balsamic vinegar
1 cup freshly grated Parmesan cheese
Freshly ground black pepper
1 cup Garlic-Thyme Breadcrumbs (p. 205)
   or other coarse breadcrumbs

1. Preheat the oven to 400°F.

2. Bring a medium pot of water to a boil. Add a couple table-spoons of salt and blanch the broccoli until it turns bright green and softens to a pleasant crunch, about 1½ minutes. Drain and cool under cold running water. Set aside.

3. Whisk together the béchamel and broth in a small saucepan and warm over medium-low heat, stirring occasionally.

4. Meanwhile, heat the oil in a large ovenproof sauté pan over medium-high heat until shimmering hot, about 1½ minutes. Add the mushrooms and cook, stirring occasionally, until browned in places and softened, about 4 minutes. Push the mushrooms to the side of the pan and add the garlic. Cook, stirring, until it just starts to brown around the edges, about 30 seconds. Stir together with the mushrooms and cook for 1 minute. Stir in the chicken, béchamel mixture, broccoli, vinegar, and Parmesan. Season generously with salt and pepper to taste.

5. Sprinkle evenly with the breadcrumbs and bake until the crumbs brown and the casserole bubbles around the sides, about 20 minutes. Let rest for a couple of minutes and then serve immediately.

CHIX PICKS

The prominence of garlic in Sear-Roasted Chicken with Lots of Garlic (p. 82) or herbs in Bistro Roast Chicken with Lemon and Thyme (p. 34) pairs nicely with the broccoli and chicken.

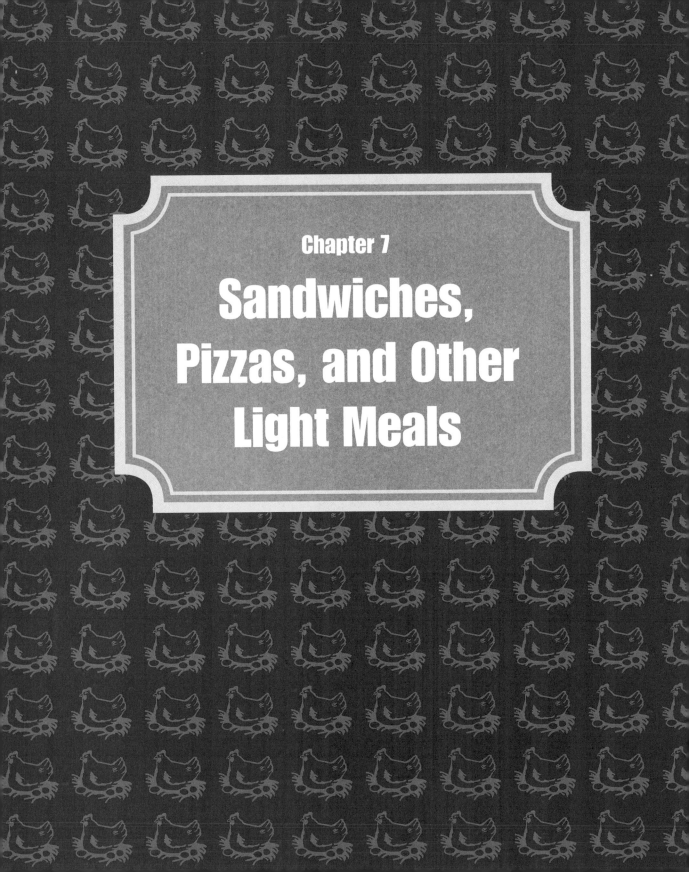

Chapter 7
Sandwiches, Pizzas, and Other Light Meals

These preparations are some of my

favorites—the ones I like turning to when I get home late and have to get dinner on the table quickly. Or easy meals for serving up as a rainy day lunch or for toting to the beach or on a hike.

In my house, sandwiches are an any-time-of-day affair (I'll eat one for breakfast if nobody's looking). Though I don't get fussy about their constructions, I do like to go beyond the basic lettuce-and-tomato route. It's not hard to get creative, especially with leftover chicken as the base. Just flip through the cupboard for a few accompaniments to layer with the bread or to roll into the wrap.

I also like to top leftover chicken on pizza or to tuck it into a calzone. It works well in egg dishes like frittatas or quiches, which are great for brunch or as a weeknight meal accompanied by a salad. And then there are chicken quesadillas and chicken croquettes which are equally good as a light nibble for company or as a midweek change of pace.

Shredded Carolina Barbecue Chicken Sandwich with Tangy Slaw

Serves 4

This sandwich is loosely based on pulled pork sandwiches. The only trick to assembling it is to properly shred the chicken (I prefer using dark meat, which holds up better). I use my fingers to pull the meat into long, thin strips. Then I toss the chicken in a vinegar-heavy, Carolina-style barbecue sauce and pair it with a slaw of green cabbage and scallions. I like adding grilled red onions to this slaw, though I leave them optional in case you don't have the time.

Serve this chicken sandwich with some pickle spears and a handful of potato chips. Also, make sure to keep a bottle of hot sauce on hand in case the spirit moves you.

1 cup Carolina BBQ Sauce (p. 61)
3 cups shredded leftover chicken
4 cups thinly sliced green cabbage
   (about 1/2 pound)
1 cup grated carrots
1 cup Grilled Red Onions
   (see recipe, facing page)
2 scallions (white and green parts),
   trimmed and thinly sliced
1 teaspoon light brown sugar
1 teaspoon kosher salt
1/2 teaspoon freshly ground black pepper
2 tablespoons olive oil
1 tablespoon cider vinegar
4 bulky rolls, lightly toasted
2 tablespoons ketchup

CHIX PICKS

Try a full-flavored grill-roasted chicken with some spice in this sandwich, like Southern Spiced Chicken with Chipotle-Honey BBQ Sauce (p. 76) or Grill-Roasted Chicken with Tex-Mex Spice Crust and Grilled Corn Salsa (p. 58).

1. Heat the BBQ sauce in a medium saucepan over medium-low heat, stirring. Once it's hot, add the chicken and simmer until warmed through, about 5 minutes.

2. Meanwhile, combine the cabbage, carrots, onions (if using), scallions, and brown sugar in a large bowl. Sprinkle with the salt and pepper, drizzle with the oil and vinegar, and toss well.

3. Spread the rolls lightly with the ketchup, top with the chicken and coleslaw, and serve.

Grilled Red Onions

3 to 4 onions will make about 2½ cups

Very rarely do I choose to take the long route when I cook at home. My method for grilling red onions is one of the few departures from this policy. Instead of simply grilling the onions, I favor a two-part method, finishing the onions in a sauté pan on the stovetop after grilling. This slow sauté helps the onions soften and intensify in flavor.

The extra work is worth it. These grilled red onions have a sweetness similar to caramelized onions and an intense smokiness that makes them the vegetarian equivalent of bacon: great in sandwiches (you'll find them in many recipes in this chapter), pastas, and salads or simply as a condiment for grilled or roast chicken (or other meats or fish).

One piece of equipment you will need for this method is a cooling rack, preferably an inexpensive one that you don't mind beating up a bit. I like to set this rack over the grill (so it runs perpendicular to the grill grates) to prevent the onions from falling in. (I don't have the patience for skewering the onions.) If you have a large grill basket, you can just use it instead. I would suggest making a relatively large batch—at least 3 or 4 onions—as the grilled onions will store well in the refrigerator for up to 5 days.

Red onion, sliced ½ inch thick
Olive oil for drizzling
Kosher salt and freshly ground black pepper
¼ cup water, more if needed

1. Prepare a charcoal fire or heat up the gas grill (heat all burners to medium-high). For a charcoal fire, pile a couple of layers of briquettes so that you end up with a medium-hot fire. Your fire should be ready when the briquettes are mostly gray (or, if you're using hardwood, when they are red hot). Set a cooling rack or grill basket on the grill.

2. In a large bowl, toss the onions with a generous drizzle of oil and salt and pepper.

3. Grill the onions, flipping every 5 minutes, until well browned and charred in places, about 15 minutes.

4. Using tongs and a metal spatula, transfer the onions to a sauté pan and set over medium heat on the stovetop. Cook, stirring, until the onion starts to soften and stick to the bottom of the pan, about 10 minutes. Add the water, toss well, and continue to cook until the onion softens completely and becomes just tender, 15 to 20 minutes. Add more water if the onion starts to burn at any point. Let cool to room temperature and then serve, or refrigerate for up to 5 days before using.

Spicy Southwest Chicken Sandwich with Avocado and Bacon

Serves 4

I love chipotles. The smoky heat of these smoked and dried chiles is sweet and balanced. Here, chipotles are puréed into a paste with sun-dried tomatoes, olive oil, and balsamic vinegar, then layered into a sandwich with avocado, onions, and chicken. Note: If you have the time or inclination, substitute the raw sliced red onions with 1 cup of Grilled Red Onions (p. 219). Serve with tortilla chips and some guacamole.

6 oil-packed sun-dried tomatoes, chopped
1 canned chipotle chile, plus 2 tablespoons of the adobo sauce
¼ cup olive oil
1 tablespoon balsamic vinegar
2 teaspoons Dijon mustard
1 teaspoon light brown sugar
2 tablespoons water
Kosher salt and freshly ground black pepper
1 ripe avocado, pitted
¼ cup chopped fresh cilantro
Juice of 1 lime
2½ cups thinly sliced leftover chicken
4 thick slices bacon, cooked until crisp
1 large ripe tomato, cored and thinly sliced
½ red onion, thinly sliced
8 slices focaccia or sourdough bread, lightly toasted

CHIX PICKS

A leftover chicken with plenty of spice and heat suits this sandwich, like Grill-Roasted Jamaican Jerk Chicken (p. 74) or Grill-Roasted Chicken with Tex-Mex Spice Crust and Grilled Corn Salsa (p. 58)—add any leftover salsa to the sandwich.

1. In a blender, mini-chop, or food processor, pulse the sun-dried tomatoes, chipotle, adobo sauce, oil, vinegar, mustard, and brown sugar together until smooth, and then add the water while processing. Season with salt and pepper to taste and pulse again. Transfer to a small bowl.

2. In another small bowl, mash the avocado with half the cilantro and lime juice. Season generously with salt and pepper and more lime juice to taste.

3. Spread 4 of the slices of bread with the avocado mixture. Spread the remaining 4 pieces of bread with the sun-dried tomato-and-chipotle mixture, then layer on the chicken, bacon, tomato, onion, the remaining cilantro, and the bread. Cut in half and serve immediately.

SWEET, SMOKY CHIPOTLES

As our interest in Mexican food has advanced past the nacho-and-fajita stage, authentic Mexican ingredients have started to enter the American culinary mainstream. Perhaps my favorite of the lot are chipotle chiles.

Chipotles are jalapeños that have been smoked and dried. The smoking not only helps preserve the fleshy jalapeños, but also gives them a smoky richness and intensity. Chipotles take three basic forms at the local market—whole and dried, ground into a fine powder, or canned. I prefer the latter—chipotle en adobo sauce—which I find it to be the most convenient of the bunch. Not only are the chipotles rehydrated, so they're easy to chop and throw into stews and braises, but the adobo sauce (a sweet and spicy tomato mixture consisting of garlic, onions, and herbs) is also great in vinaigrettes and salsas.

Hoisin Chicken Sandwiches with Cucumbers and Scallions

Serves 4

This was one of our original sandwiches at b.good, a group of healthy fast-food restaurants I helped start up in the Boston area a couple of years ago. The flavors are simple but dressy. Scallions and hoisin are a classic pairing (think Peking duck), while the cucumbers give the sandwich a pleasant crunch. Make sure to use a premium brand of hoisin sauce (try Koon Chun or Lee Kum Kee)—you'll taste the difference.

¼ cup hoisin sauce
1 tablespoon soy sauce
1 tablespoon rice vinegar
1 teaspoon toasted sesame oil
2 cups thinly sliced leftover chicken
8 slices focaccia, toasted
2 scallions (white and green parts), trimmed and thinly sliced
½ English cucumber, thinly sliced

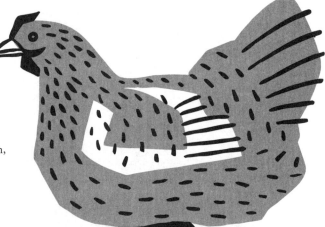

1. In a medium bowl, whisk together the hoisin, soy sauce, vinegar, and sesame oil. Add the chicken and toss well to coat.

2. Set the chicken on 4 slices of the focaccia. Sprinkle with the scallions, then top with the cucumber. Top with the remaining bread, slice in half, and serve.

CHIX PICKS

Try to use a leftover chicken that has some sweetness (like a glaze) or an Asian accent, or both, like a roast chicken brushed with Asian Barbecue Glaze (p. 14) or Grilled Chicken Teriyaki with Scallions (p. 70)—substitute any leftover grilled scallions for the raw ones in this recipe.

Chicken Sandwiches with Pesto, Baby Spinach, and Sun-Dried Tomatoes

Serves 4

This sandwich is perfect picnic fare. The flavors and textures hold well for a couple of hours (chilled for safety's sake, of course); just make sure to toast the bread a little longer so it doesn't get soggy. If you want to embellish a bit, add some sliced tomatoes, marinated black olives, or a handful of fresh herbs from the garden.

2$\frac{1}{2}$ cups thinly sliced leftover chicken
1 tablespoon olive oil
1 teaspoon chopped fresh thyme
$\frac{1}{4}$ teaspoon kosher salt
$\frac{1}{4}$ teaspoon freshly ground black pepper
$\frac{1}{2}$ cup pesto (see Rotini with Pesto, Chicken, and Green Beans, p. 143)
8 slices focaccia or crusty peasant bread, toasted
2 cups baby spinach
6 oil-packed sun-dried tomatoes, thinly sliced
$\frac{1}{3}$ cup freshly grated Parmesan cheese

1. Toss the chicken with the oil and thyme and sprinkle with the salt and pepper.

2. Spread the pesto on 4 slices of the bread. Top with the chicken, spinach, tomatoes, Parmesan, and the remaining bread. Cut in half and serve.

CHIX PICKS

The smokiness of a grill-roasted chicken perks up the relatively mild flavors in this sandwich. Try Anago's Garlicky Grill-Roasted Split Chickens with Lemon and Herbs (p. 66) or a grill-roasted bird coated with All-Purpose Poultry Spice Rub (p. 11).

Chicken and Tarragon Tea Sandwiches

Serves 4 to 6

I must admit that I've never served afternoon tea, but when I do, these sandwiches will be on the menu. They're simple but elegant, just as good packed into a lunchbox as they are on a platter for company.

½ cup mayonnaise

3 tablespoons chopped fresh tarragon

Finely grated zest of 1 lemon

¼ teaspoon kosher salt

¼ teaspoon freshly ground black pepper

8 large slices 7-grain or whole wheat bread, toasted and crusts trimmed

2½ cups thinly sliced leftover chicken

1 cup Grilled Red Onions (p. 219) or ½ red onion, thinly sliced

CHIX PICKS

E.G.'s Roast Chicken with Tarragon and Whole-Grain Mustard (p. 46) shares the same herb as this sandwich and the curry will spice up the flavors. You also can try a roast chicken brushed with Rosemary-Balsamic Glaze (p. 13).

1. In a small bowl, whisk together the mayonnaise, tarragon, and lemon zest and season with the salt and pepper.

2. Spread the mayonnaise on one side of each of the pieces of bread. Top 4 of the slices with the chicken, onion, and the remaining slices of bread. Set 4 toothpicks into each of the sandwiches and slice each into 4 square pieces. Serve immediately or cover with plastic wrap and refrigerate for up to 2 hours.

Smothered Chicken and Onion Sandwiches

Serves 4

The components in this sandwich form the traditional base for a steak sandwich, but they're equally good with leftover chicken. The method is simple: Brown strips of onions over moderate heat, then simmer with a mixture of soy sauce, ketchup, and Worcestershire. Stir in some sliced leftover chicken and serve on a toasted baguette with Cheddar. You can build on this basic method by adding peppers, mushrooms, and other types of cheeses or whatever else comes to mind.

2 tablespoons olive oil
1 large or 2 medium Spanish onion(s), thinly sliced
Kosher salt
1/4 cup ketchup
2 tablespoons cider vinegar
2 tablespoons soy sauce
1 tablespoon Worcestershire sauce
1/3 cup water
2 1/2 cups thinly sliced leftover chicken
6 ounces sharp Cheddar cheese, shredded (1 1/2 cups)
1 crusty baguette, split and cut into 4 pieces, or 4 crusty sub rolls

CHIX PICKS

A roast chicken with a vibrant spice rub like All-Purpose Poultry Spice Rub (p. 11) or Sweet Southern Spice Rub (p. 12) pairs well with the tanginess of the Worcestershire and ketchup in this sandwich.

1. Preheat the oven to 425°F.

2. Heat the oil in a large skillet over medium-high heat until shimmering hot, about 1 1/2 minutes. Reduce the heat to medium, add the onion, sprinkle with 1 teaspoon salt, and cook, stirring often, until the onion is wilted and nicely browned, about 10 minutes.

3. In a small bowl, stir together the ketchup, vinegar, soy sauce, Worcestershire, and water. Add to the onions and stir well for 1 minute, scraping the bottom of the pan with a wooden spoon to get up any browned bits. Add the chicken, reduce the heat to low, and cook, stirring, until it warms through, about 5 minutes.

4. Stuff the baguette with the chicken-and-onion mixture and top with the cheese. Set on a baking sheet and bake until the cheese just melts, about 8 minutes. Cut in half and serve immediately.

Chicken, Tapenade, and Herbed Goat Cheese Sandwich

Serves 4

Tapenade is a thick olive paste from the south of France, traditionally used as a spread for breads and as a topping for meats and fish. The version in this sandwich eschews anchovies and capers in favor of bright herbs like chopped mint and rosemary. If you like, you can serve this combination atop toast points as an appetizer. It's also a nice candidate for a picnic. If you're going to hold it for a few hours before serving, toast the bread a little longer.

1 cup pitted kalamata olives, drained
2 tablespoons chopped fresh mint
2 teaspoons chopped fresh rosemary
1/4 cup extra-virgin olive oil
1/4 pound goat cheese
Grated zest of 1 lemon
1/4 teaspoon kosher salt
1/4 teaspoon freshly ground black pepper
8 slices crusty peasant bread or sourdough, toasted
2 1/2 cups thinly sliced leftover chicken
6 oil-packed sun-dried tomatoes, thinly sliced
2 scallions (white and green parts), trimmed and thinly sliced

> ## CHIX PICKS
>
> A simple roast chicken with plenty of herbs goes nicely in this sandwich. Try one with a Mediterranean accent like Moroccan Spiced Chicken Roasted over a Bed of Couscous and Apricots (p. 54) or a grilled bird topped with a vinaigrette like Black Olive and Sherry Vinaigrette (p. 60).

1. Combine the olives, mint, and half the rosemary in a food processor and pulse until they form a paste. With the machine running, slowly drizzle in the olive oil. Transfer to a medium bowl.

2. In a small bowl, mash the goat cheese with the remaining rosemary, the lemon zest, and the salt and pepper.

3. Spread 4 slices of bread with the tapenade. Spread the remaining 4 slices of bread with the goat cheese mixture. Sandwich one of each type of bread with the chicken, sun-dried tomatoes, and scallions in the middle. Cut in half and serve.

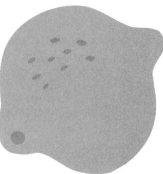

Curried Chicken Sandwiches with Lime-Cilantro Mayonnaise and Grilled Red Onions

Serves 4

Mayonnaise, curry, and lime form a happy mix of bright and spice. If you have the time or inclination, add some grilled red onions to this sandwich—they add a wonderful, smoky kick.

⅔ cup mayonnaise

¼ cup chopped fresh cilantro

Grated zest of 1 lime

¼ teaspoon kosher salt

¼ teaspoon freshly ground black pepper

2 teaspoons peeled and minced fresh ginger

¾ teaspoon curry powder

2½ cups thinly sliced leftover chicken

8 slices sourdough or other crusty bread, toasted

2 cups baby spinach

1 large ripe tomato, thinly sliced

1 cup Grilled Red Onions (p. 219) or ½ red onion, thinly sliced

1. In a small bowl, combine the mayonnaise, cilantro, lime zest, salt, and pepper. Spoon ¼ cup of the mayonnaise mixture into a large bowl. Stir in the ginger and curry powder and toss well with the chicken.

2. Spread the remaining mayonnaise mixture over one side of each slice of bread. Top 4 of the bread slices with the chicken, spinach, tomato, and onion, and the remaining bread. Cut in half and serve.

CHIX PICKS

Though any well spiced bird will do, try using a roast chicken with an Indian accent, like Grill-Roasted Tandoori Chicken (p. 62) or E.G.'s Roast Chicken with Tarragon and Whole-Grain Mustard (p. 46).

Chicken Monte Cristo with Cranberries and Thyme

Serves 3

A cross between French toast and a grilled ham and cheese, a Monte Cristo is not your standard sandwich. They are wonderfully tasty, great served for brunch on a lazy Sunday.

I've crafted the recipe to serve three only because that's all you can make in one pan at a time. If you're cooking for a crowd, just double the recipe and hold the sandwiches in a 300°F oven until ready to serve.

3 large eggs, beaten
1/4 cup whole milk
1/4 teaspoon kosher salt
1/4 teaspoon freshly ground black pepper
3 tablespoons unsalted butter
6 slices whole-wheat bread
1/4 cup cranberry sauce
2 cups thinly sliced leftover chicken
6 ounces thinly sliced ham
3 ounces sliced Swiss cheese
3 tablespoons Dijon mustard
3 tablespoons maple syrup

> ### CHIX PICKS
> A mildly flavored bird brushed with a sweet glaze like Orange-Apricot Glaze (p. 14) or Maple-Mustard Glaze (p. 14) complements the maple syrup on this sandwich.

1. In a medium bowl, whisk together the eggs, milk, salt, and pepper.

2. Melt 1½ tablespoons of the butter in a heavy 12-inch skillet (either cast-iron or non-stick) over medium heat. Dip 3 slices of the bread in the egg mixture and set in the skillet. Cook until browned, about 2 minutes. Flip and cook the other side until browned, too, about 2 more minutes. Transfer to a large plate.

3. Melt the remaining 1½ tablespoons butter in the skillet, dip the remaining 3 slices of bread in the egg mixture and cook until browned, about 2 minutes. Flip the bread and top with the cranberry sauce, chicken, ham, and Swiss. Spread the remaining slices of bread with the mustard and set on top. Reduce the heat to medium-low and cook, flipping once or twice and pressing down with a metal spatula to flatten the sandwiches, until the cheese is melted, about 5 minutes.

4. Cut in half and serve with a drizzle of the maple syrup.

Chicken, Roasted Red Pepper, and Smoked Mozzarella Panini

Serves 4

Though panini can be a catchall term for sandwiches in Italy, my favorites ones are grilled, which melds together the flavors and textures of the filling. You don't need a panini press to make this sandwich. You can use a well-seasoned cast-iron pan or a nonstick skillet and set something bulky over the sandwiches to weigh them down—another skillet will do. Or simply pull out your George Foreman® grill, if you have one.

    8 slices focaccia bread
    3 tablespoons olive oil
    2½ cups thinly sliced leftover chicken
    2 jarred roasted red peppers, cut into 2-inch pieces
    6 ounces smoked mozzarella cheese, cut into ¼-inch-thick slices
    3 ounces baby arugula
    Kosher salt and freshly ground black pepper
    I teaspoon chopped fresh rosemary

1. Preheat the oven to 300°F. Heat a large cast-iron skillet or heavy non-stick skillet over medium heat.

2. Meanwhile, brush both sides of the bread with the oil. Top 4 of the slices with the chicken, red peppers, mozzarella, and arugula. Sprinkle with salt and pepper and the rosemary and top with the remaining focaccia.

3. Set 2 of the sandwiches in the hot skillet. Set another heavy skillet or a heavy plate on top of the sandwiches and cook until browned, about 3 minutes. Flip and cook until the other side browns, again placing weight on it, about another 3 minutes. Transfer the sandwiches to a baking sheet and keep warm in the oven. Cook the remaining sandwiches in the same manner. Cut in half and serve immediately.

CHIX PICKS

Any mildly flavored grill-roasted (or roast) chicken will go nicely in this sandwich. Try one with plenty of herbs like Roast Chicken with Rosemary-Mustard Crust and Browned Onions (p. 30) or Greek Roast Chicken with Lemon, Black Olives, and Potatoes (p. 56).

Grilled Cheese with Chicken and Herbed Tomatoes

Serves 4

I'm sure my memory is skewed but it seems like a grilled cheese sandwich and a bowl of soup accompanied almost every rainy day of my youth. Even if that's stretching the truth a bit, it's certain that the moment I was old enough to take over the fry pan, I started making my own grilled cheese and I've been doing so ever since. Leftover chicken is particularly well suited to this preparation.

1 large ripe tomato, cored and thinly sliced
Kosher salt and freshly ground black pepper
2 teaspoons chopped fresh thyme
2 cups thinly sliced leftover chicken
1 tablespoon olive oil
1 tablespoon balsamic vinegar
3 tablespoons unsalted butter, softened
8 thick slices 7-grain or peasant wheat bread
½ pound extra-sharp Cheddar cheese, thinly sliced

CHIX PICKS

The bright, acidic tang of Bistro Roast Chicken with Lemon and Thyme (p. 34) or Balsamic-Glazed Rosemary Chicken with Bacon and Pearl Onions (p. 36) pairs nicely with this grilled cheese—toss any leftover bacon or onions from the latter into the sandwich.

1. Preheat the oven to 300°F.

2. Set the tomato on a large plate and sprinkle generously with salt and pepper (about 1 teaspoon and ½ teaspoon, respectively) and the thyme. Let sit for 10 minutes.

3. In a small bowl, toss the chicken with the oil and vinegar and sprinkle lightly with salt and pepper.

4. Set a large, heavy skillet (either cast-iron or non-stick) over medium heat for 2 minutes.

5. Meanwhile, butter both sides of each piece of bread. Top 4 of the slices with the tomato, Cheddar, chicken, and the remaining slices of bread.

6. Set two of the sandwiches in the skillet. Weigh them down with another skillet or a heavy plate and cook until browned, about 3 minutes. Flip and cook until the other side browns and the cheese begins to melt out through the sides, about another 3 minutes. Transfer the sandwiches to a baking sheet and keep warm in the oven while you cook the other two sandwiches.

7. Cut in half and serve.

Chicken Reuben

Serves 4

I'm a Reuben guy. I like to get one at a diner every couple of months—it's good for clogging up the arteries. Here, thinly sliced leftover chicken healthfully stands in for the corned beef. It's a substitution I'm sure my prospective cardiologist will appreciate.

> 8 slices rye bread or pumpernickel
> 3 tablespoons unsalted butter, softened
> 1/2 cup Thousand Island dressing
> 2 cups thinly sliced leftover chicken
> 3/4 cup sauerkraut, drained well
> 4 thick slices Swiss or Gruyère cheese

1. Preheat the oven to 300°F.

2. Set a large, heavy skillet (either cast-iron or non-stick) over medium heat for 2 minutes.

3. Meanwhile, spread one side of each piece of bread with the butter and the other side with the Thousand Island dressing. Top 4 of the slices of bread, on the Thousand Island side, with the chicken, sauerkraut, cheese and the remaining bread.

4. Set two of the sandwiches in the hot skillet and cook, gently pressing with a metal spatula to flatten, until well browned, about 4 minutes. Flip and cook until the other side is browned, too, about another 4 minutes. Transfer to a baking sheet and set in the oven to keep warm while you cook the other two sandwiches.

5. Cut in half and serve immediately.

CHIX PICKS

A roast chicken with plenty of herbs goes wonderfully in this sandwich, like Italian Grilled Chicken Under a Brick with Smoky Balsamic Tomatoes (p. 68) or Roast Chicken with a Rosemary-Mustard Crust and Browned Onions (p. 30)—add any leftover onions from the latter to the reuben.

Buffalo Chicken Wrap

Serves 4

I love buffalo chicken. Though wings are the standard, sliced leftover chicken stands in nicely in this wrap. I like adding leftover rice to the mixture to give it some substance but you can go without if you like.

3 tablespoons unsalted butter
½ cup Original Frank's Hot Sauce or your favorite brand
1 teaspoon chopped fresh rosemary
3 cups thinly sliced leftover chicken
¼ pound blue cheese, crumbled
¾ cup plain yogurt
Kosher salt and freshly ground black pepper
4 pieces lavash or large flour tortillas, warmed
2 cups hot cooked rice (optional)
3 cups shredded iceberg lettuce
2 ribs celery, cut in half and sliced lengthwise into very thin strips

CHIX PICKS

The lemon in Bistro Roast Chicken with Lemon and Thyme (p. 34) or the garlic in Sear-Roasted Chicken with Lots of Garlic (p. 82) will complement the heat of the sauce in this wrap.

1. Combine the butter, hot sauce, and rosemary in a medium saucepan over medium heat and bring to a simmer, stirring occasionally. Stir in the chicken and remove from the heat.

2. In a food processor, pulse the blue cheese and yogurt together until they form a uniform, thick paste. Season generously with salt and pepper to taste.

3. Set a piece of the lavash on a cutting board. Top with one quarter of the rice (if using), chicken, lettuce, celery, and blue cheese dressing. Roll up and wrap, and repeat with the remaining lavash and filling. Cut in half and serve.

Chicken Mu-Shu Wrap

Serves 4

If you've never tried one, mu-shu is sort of like a crunchy Chinese version of a soft taco. Substituting flour tortillas for fresh Chinese pancakes would be considered blasphemy by purists, but the tortillas stand in admirably and are convenient obviously. While exotic dried ingredients like wood ear mushrooms and golden needles give mu-shu its traditional crunch, in this version, fresh shiitake mushrooms, thinly sliced cabbage, and fried egg form a tasty tangle of textures and flavors.

5 cups thinly sliced green cabbage
2 teaspoons toasted sesame oil
1½ teaspoons kosher salt
3 tablespoons canola or peanut oil
2 large eggs, beaten
2 cloves garlic, minced
¼ pound shiitake mushrooms, stemmed, caps thinly sliced
4 scallions, green parts cut into 2-inch lengths and whites thinly sliced
2½ cups thinly sliced leftover chicken
1 tablespoon soy sauce
1 tablespoon rice vinegar
½ cup hoisin sauce
4 flour tortillas, warmed

> ## CHIX PICKS
>
> A mild roast chicken with a sweet glaze would work nicely. Try a roast chicken brushed with Asian Barbecue Glaze (p. 14) or Orange-Apricot Glaze (p. 14).

1. In a medium bowl, toss the cabbage with the sesame oil and 1 teaspoon of the salt.

2. Heat 1½ tablespoons of the canola oil in a large nonstick skillet or well-seasoned wok over medium-high heat until shimmering hot, about 1½ minutes. Add the eggs and cook, breaking them up with a wooden spoon into small pieces, until just set, about 1 minute. Transfer to a large plate and set aside.

3. Wipe the skillet or wok dry with a paper towel and set over medium-high heat. Add the garlic and remaining 1½ tablespoons canola oil and cook until the garlic starts to sizzle steadily, about 1 minute. Add the shiitakes and scallions, sprinkle with the remaining ½ teaspoon salt, and cook, stirring occasionally, until they soften and brown in places, about 3 minutes.

4. Add the seasoned cabbage and chicken and cook, stirring often, until the cabbage becomes just tender (it should have a softened crunch), about 2 minutes. Stir in the eggs, soy sauce, vinegar, and 2 tablespoons of the hoisin sauce and toss well.

5. Serve immediately: allow diners to assemble their own pancake by rolling the warm tortillas with the chicken filling and the remaining hoisin sauce.

Honey Mustard Chicken Wrap with Tomatoes and Swiss Cheese

Serves 4

This wrap is great for a brown bag lunch. If you have the foresight, pick up some lavash and cheese at the deli so that you can throw these sandwiches together the same night you roast the chicken.

⅓ cup whole-grain or brown mustard
¼ cup honey
2 teaspoons chopped fresh thyme
3 cups thinly sliced leftover chicken
1 large ripe tomato, cored and thinly sliced
Kosher salt and freshly ground black pepper
4 slices whole wheat lavash
½ romaine heart, cored and cut crosswise into
   3-inch-wide strips
½ red onion, thinly sliced
6 ounces sliced Swiss cheese

1. In a large bowl, combine the mustard, honey, and thyme. Add the chicken and toss well to coat.

2. Sprinkle the tomato with salt and pepper (about ½ teaspoon of each).

3. Set one of the pieces of lavash on a large cutting board. Top with one quarter of the chicken, tomato, lettuce, onion, and Swiss. Roll and wrap. Repeat with the remaining lavash and filling. Cut in half and serve.

CHIX PICKS

A glazed roast chicken goes nicely with the sweet mustard in this wrap. Try Jerrod's Roast Chicken with Vermont Maple Glaze, Sweet Potatoes, and Sage (p. 35) or a roast chicken brushed with Maple-Mustard Glaze (p. 14).

Cucumber, Cherry Tomato, and Grilled Chicken Pita Wrap

Serves 4

While I do like stuffing pita, I also like using it as a wrap, rolling it up as I would lavash bread or a tortilla. Here, pita serves as a wrap for a salad of chopped cucumbers, cherry tomatoes, and chicken. Make sure to use pitas at least 10 inches wide—bread any smaller will be hard to wrap.

1 English cucumber, cut into ½-inch dice
¾ pound cherry tomatoes, cut in half
½ red onion, finely diced
¼ cup freshly grated Parmesan
Kosher salt and freshly ground
　black pepper
2 tablespoons olive oil
1 tablespoon red wine vinegar
2½ cups diced leftover chicken
2 tablespoons chopped fresh mint
1 teaspoon chopped fresh thyme
4 large pitas (at least 10 inches)

CHIX PICKS

A grilled bird will punch up the simple flavors in this wrap. Try Italian Grilled Chicken Under a Brick with Smoky Balsamic Tomatoes (p. 68) or one coated with Lemon-Herb Rub (p. 13).

1. Combine the cucumber, tomatoes, onion, and Parmesan in a large bowl, sprinkle generously with salt and pepper (about 1 teaspoon and ½ teaspoon, respectively), and toss well. Add the oil, vinegar, chicken, mint, and thyme and toss well again.

2. Set a pita on a cutting board. Top with about one quarter of the cucumber salad, and roll it up. Repeat with the remaining pitas and cucumber salad. Cut in half and serve.

Pitas with Spiced Chickpea-Chicken Fritters

Serves 4

I'm a sucker for street food from any point on the globe and falafel has long been one of my favorites. Adding leftover chicken to the chickpea mixture adds a bit more substance. Traditionally these fritters are deep-fried, but I prefer the healthfulness and simplicity of pan-frying them, then finishing them in the oven.

6 tablespoons olive oil
1 small yellow onion, finely chopped
Kosher salt
2 cloves garlic, minced
1 tablespoon ground cumin
½ teaspoon ground coriander
One 15-ounce can chickpeas,
    drained and rinsed well
Freshly ground black pepper
1½ cups shredded leftover chicken
¾ cup breadcrumbs,
    plus more if needed
½ cup chopped fresh cilantro
1 cup plain yogurt
Grated zest of 1 lemon
10 drops Tabasco sauce
4 large pitas (at least 10 inches wide), warmed
1 large ripe tomato, cored and thinly sliced
1 heart of romaine, bottom trimmed and separated into leaves

> ## CHIX PICKS
>
> Try using a roast chicken with plenty of spice, like Moroccan Spiced Chicken Roasted over a Bed of Couscous and Apricots (p. 54) or one sprinkled with All-Purpose Poultry Spice Rub (p. 11) or Southwestern Chile Spice Rub (p. 11).

1. Preheat the oven to 400°F.

2. Heat 2 tablespoons of the oil in a large nonstick skillet over medium heat. Add the onion, sprinkle with 1 teaspoon salt and cook, stirring occasionally, until it softens and becomes translucent, about 8 minutes. Add the garlic, cumin, and coriander and cook, stirring, for 1 minute. Add a couple of tablespoons of water and stir well to scrape up any browned bits on the bottom of the pan.

3. Transfer the onion mixture and the chickpeas to a food processor and process into a thick paste. Season with salt and pepper to taste (about 1 teaspoon and ½ teaspoon, respectively) and pulse one more time.

4. Transfer the mixture to a large bowl. Fold in the chicken, breadcrumbs, and half the cilantro. You should be able to pack this mixture into a ball shape—if the mixture is still wet, mix in a couple more tablespoons of breadcrumbs. Form into small patties, about 2 heaping tablespoons each—you should have about 16.

5. Using a paper towel, wipe the skillet clean. Add 2 tablespoons of the oil and heat over medium-high heat until shimmering hot, about 1½ minutes. Add half the chickpea fritters to the skillet and brown, about 2 minutes. Flip and cook the other side until browned, about 2 minutes. Transfer to a large baking sheet and sprinkle generously with salt and pepper. Repeat with the remaining oil and fritters, then transfer the fritters to the oven to finish cooking through, 10 to 15 minutes.

6. Meanwhile, combine the yogurt, the remaining cilantro, the lemon zest, and Tabasco in a small bowl. Season with salt and pepper to taste, about ¼ teaspoon of each.

7. Set a pita on a cutting board. Top with 4 of the fritters, one quarter of the tomato and lettuce, and a generous drizzle of the yogurt dressing. Roll up and repeat with the remaining ingredients. Serve immediately.

Pita Stuffed with Greek Salad and Herbed Chicken

Serves 4

This is a Greek salad in a pita. I like constructing it in two stages so all the toppings are evenly distributed: First, toss the greens with the feta and some of the vinaigrette and set in the warmed pitas. Then, toss the tomatoes, cucumbers, and chicken with the remaining vinaigrette and stuff in the bread as well.

1 tablespoon red wine vinegar
1 1/2 teaspoons Dijon mustard
1 teaspoon dried oregano
1/3 cup extra-virgin olive oil
2 tablespoons fresh lemon juice
Kosher salt and freshly ground black pepper.
4 large pitas, warmed
1 heart of romaine, bottom trimmed and cut
    across into 2-inch-wide strips
6 ounces feta cheese, crumbled
2 cups thinly sliced leftover chicken
1 large ripe tomato, cored and cut into
    thin wedges
1/2 English cucumber, thinly sliced
1/2 small red onion, thinly sliced into half moons
3/4 cup pitted kalamata olives, drained and coarsely chopped

> ## CHIX PICKS
>
> A roast chicken with Mediterranean flavorings will go nicely with this sandwich. The lemon and oregano in Greek Roast Chicken with Lemon, Black Olives, and Potatoes (p. 56) make it a good fit or try Anago's Garlicky Grill-Roasted Split Chickens with Lemon and Herbs (p. 66).

1. In a small bowl, whisk together the vinegar, mustard, and oregano. Still whisking, slowly drizzle in the oil so it forms a thick emulsion, then add the lemon juice. Season with salt and pepper to taste (about 3/4 teaspoon of each).

2. Cut 1 inch off the tip of each pita (you can throw these pieces out, though I like to nosh on them as I prepare the rest of the recipe). In a large bowl, toss the romaine with the feta and half the lemon vinaigrette dressing and stuff into the pitas. Combine the chicken, tomato, cucumber, onion, and olives in a bowl, drizzle with the remaining vinaigrette, and toss well. Gently pack the chicken mixture into the pitas as well and serve immediately.

Soft Chicken Tacos with Guacamole

Serves 4

The big flavors of Tex-Mex cooking really liven up leftover chicken. These tacos take no more than a half hour to throw together.

2 large ripe avocados, pitted
1 large Spanish onion, finely diced
2/3 cup chopped fresh cilantro
Juice of 1 lime
Kosher salt and freshly ground black pepper
2 tablespoons olive oil
1 large clove garlic, minced
1 tablespoon chili powder
1 teaspoon ground cumin
3 cups diced leftover chicken
4 oil-packed sun-dried tomatoes, finely diced
1/2 cup beer (I prefer a light lager)
6 ounces extra sharp Cheddar, shredded (1 1/2 cups)
4 large flour tortillas, warmed
1 lime, cut into wedges, for serving

CHIX PICKS

Try a roast or grill-roasted chicken with Tex-Mex flavorings like Grill-Roasted Chicken with Tex-Mex Spice Crust and Grilled Corn Salsa (p. 58)—fold any of the leftover salsa into the tacos—or Roast Chicken with Southwestern Rub and Cornbread and Jalapeño Stuffing (p. 48).

1. Make the guacamole. Mash the avocados, one quarter of the onion, half the cilantro, and half the lime juice together in a medium bowl. Season with salt and pepper to taste and add more of the lime juice, if you like. Set aside. (This will hold in the fridge, tightly covered, for up to 8 hours.)

2. Set a large, heavy skillet (I like a cast-iron pan) over medium-high heat. Add the oil and the remaining onion, sprinkle with salt (about 1/2 teaspoon), and cook, stirring, until softened and translucent, about 8 minutes. Add the garlic, chili powder, and cumin and cook, stirring, for 30 seconds. Add the chicken and tomatoes and cook, stirring, until warmed through, about 3 minutes. Add the beer and cook, stirring, until it almost completely evaporates, about 2 minutes. Remove from the heat.

3. Serve immediately. Allow diners to construct their own tacos by topping the tortillas with the chicken mixture, Cheddar, and guacamole, squirting with the lime wedges, and wrapping.

Chicken Burritos with Spicy Black Beans and Rice

Serves 4

Burritos have become quick comfort food in this country over the last couple of years. Though I do have a couple of favorite burrito spots, I like to make them myself, especially when I have some leftover chicken in the fridge. I generally use rice as a base for burritos (leftover rice is fine). It adds substance and soaks up all the different flavors. I also like to fill out these burritos with black beans that I've stewed quickly with garlic, spices, and tomatoes.

2 cloves garlic, smashed

2 tablespoons olive oil

1 teaspoon chili powder

1 teaspoon ground cumin

1/4 teaspoon ground chipotle chile powder

2 1/2 cups diced leftover chicken

1/4 cup low-salt chicken broth

4 large burrito-size flour tortillas, warmed

2 1/2 cups hot cooked rice (either brown or white)

1 1/2 cups Spicy Black Beans (p. 241)

1/2 pound extra-sharp Cheddar cheese, shredded (2 cups)

1 cup Pico de Gallo (p. 241) or your favorite salsa

> ## CHIX PICKS
>
> This recipe goes well with Tex-Mex flavorings like a roast chicken with Southwestern Chile Spice Rub (p. 11) or Grill-Roasted Chicken with Tex-Mex Spice Crust and Grilled Corn Salsa (p. 58)—fold any leftover corn salsa from the latter into the burrito.

1. Heat the garlic and oil together in a large, heavy skillet over medium-low heat, stirring occasionally, until the garlic becomes fragrant and starts to brown, about 3 minutes. Add the chili powder, cumin, and chipotle powder and cook, stirring, for 30 seconds. Add the chicken and cook, stirring, until just warmed through, about 2 minutes. Add the chicken broth, cover, and simmer for 5 minutes. Discard the garlic.

2. To construct the burritos, top each of the tortillas evenly with the rice, a spoonful of the chicken, black beans, cheese, and salsa. Roll the tortilla, tucking its edges over itself to form a tight bundle. Serve immediately.

Pico de Gallo

Makes about 3 cups

I like cutting all of the ingredients for this simple salsa by hand, though you can pulse them together in a food processor if you prefer.

2 large ripe tomatoes, cored and cut in ¼-inch dice
½ cup chopped fresh cilantro
I small red onion, finely diced
3 serrano chiles or 2 jalapeños, cored, seeded, and finely chopped
I lime, juiced
Kosher salt and freshly ground black pepper

Set the tomatoes, cilantro, red onion, and chiles in a large bowl, sprinkle with half the lime juice, 1 teaspoon salt, ½ teaspoon black pepper, and mix well. Season with more lime juice, salt, or pepper to taste. Let sit for at least 15 minutes at room temperature (or refrigerate for up to 1 day).

Spicy Black Beans

Makes about 6 cups

2 cloves garlic, finely chopped
2 tablespoons olive oil
2 teaspoons chili powder
2 teaspoons dried oregano
I teaspoon ground cumin
I teaspoon light brown sugar
One 29-ounce can black beans, drained and rinsed well
One 14.5-ounce can diced tomatoes and their juices
One canned chipotle, minced plus 2 tablespoons adobo sauce
I tablespoon cider vinegar, or more to taste
Kosher salt and freshly ground black pepper

1. Heat the garlic in the oil in a medium saucepan over medium heat until it sizzles steadily and becomes fragrant, about 2 minutes. Add the chili powder, oregano, cumin, and brown sugar, and stir for 30 seconds.

2. Stir in the black beans, tomatoes and their juices, chipotle and adobo sauce, and vinegar, bring to a boil, then reduce the heat to a simmer and cook for 10 minutes. Using an immersion blender, puree a couple of times so the mixture thickens, or in an upright blender, puree 1 cup of the broth and beans and then return to the saucepan. Cook a couple of minutes more to thicken slightly. Season generously with salt and pepper to taste and use immediately or let cool and refrigerate for up to 4 days.

Chicken Burritos with Three Cheeses and Tomatillo Salsa Verde

Serves 4

A tomatillo salsa verde livens up this burrito. This small, green fruit has a brownish, papery husk and a firm texture similar to an unripe tomato.

2 cloves garlic, smashed
2 tablespoons olive oil
1 teaspoon chili powder
1 teaspoon ground cumin
1/4 teaspoon ground chipotle
   chile powder
2 1/2 cups leftover diced chicken
1/4 cup low-salt chicken broth
4 large burrito-size flour
   tortillas, warmed
2 1/2 cups hot cooked rice
   (either brown or white;
   leftover rice is fine)
1 large ripe tomato, cored and diced
2 ounces Monterey jack cheese, shredded (1/2 cup)
2 ounces mozzarella cheese, shredded (1/2 cup)
1/4 pound extra-sharp Cheddar cheese, shredded (1 cup)
Tomatillo Salsa Verde (p. 243)

> ## CHIX PICKS
>
> Try using a chicken coated with Southwestern Chile Spice Rub (p. 11) or All-Purpose Poultry Spice Rub (p. 11).

1. Heat the garlic and oil together in a large, heavy skillet over medium-low heat, stirring occasionally, until the garlic becomes fragrant and starts to brown, about 3 minutes. Add the chili powder, cumin and chipotle powder and cook, stirring, for 30 seconds. Add the chicken and cook, stirring, until it just warms through, about 2 minutes. Add the chicken broth, cover, and simmer for 5 minutes. Discard the garlic.

2. To construct the burritos, top each of the tortillas evenly with the rice, chicken, tomato, the cheeses, and salsa. Roll the tortilla, tucking its edges over itself to form a tight bundle. Serve immediately.

Tomatillo Salsa Verde

Makes about 1 1/2 cups

3/4 pound tomatillos (about 6), husked, rinsed, and coarsely chopped
1 jalapeño, seeded and finely chopped
Juice of 1 lime
1/4 cup water
1 teaspoon kosher salt
1/2 teaspoon freshly ground black pepper
1 small yellow onion, finely diced
1/2 cup chopped fresh cilantro

1. Combine the tomatillos, jalapeño, lime juice, water, salt, and pepper in a food processor or blender and process until smooth.

2. Transfer to a medium bowl and stir in the onion and cilantro. Season with more salt and pepper to taste. Let sit at room temperature for half an hour, or store, tightly covered, for up to 24 hours in the refrigerator before serving to let the flavors develop.

Chicken and Spinach Enchiladas

Serves 4

Enchiladas are like tacos, only topped with salsa and cheese and baked. Here diced leftover chicken and baby spinach fill the wraps, which are then topped with chipotle salsa and shredded Cheddar.

TOMATO-CHIPOTLE SALSA:
One 14.5-ounce can diced tomatoes, drained
2 canned chipotle chiles, plus 2 tablespoons of the adobo sauce
¼ cup chopped fresh cilantro
1 tablespoon cider vinegar
2 teaspoons light brown sugar
½ teaspoon chili powder
Kosher salt and freshly ground black pepper

ENCHILADAS:
3 cups thinly sliced leftover chicken
¼ pound baby spinach, coarsely chopped
3 scallions (white and green parts), trimmed and thinly sliced
½ pound sharp Cheddar cheese, shredded (2 cups)
Kosher salt and freshly ground black pepper
4 large burrito-size flour tortillas
Olive oil for greasing

CHIX PICKS

Try a roast or grill-roasted chicken with plenty of heat like Grill-Roasted Jamaican Jerk Chicken (p. 74) or Chinese Salt and Pepper Roast Chicken (p. 52).

1. Preheat the oven to 425°F. Grease a 9 by 13-inch baking dish.

2. Make the salsa. Place all the ingredients with the exception of the salt and pepper in a food processor and process until smooth. Season generously with salt and pepper to taste.

3. Make the enchiladas. Toss the chicken with the spinach, scallions, half the Cheddar and half the tomato-chipotle salsa. Season with salt and pepper to taste.

4. Set one quarter of this mixture on one of the tortillas. Roll the tortilla, tucking its edges over itself to form a tight bundle. Repeat with the remaining tortillas and filling.

5. Transfer the stuffed tortillas to the baking dish, spoon the remaining tomato-chipotle salsa over the top, and sprinkle with the remaining cheese. Bake until the cheese melts and the filling is warmed through, 15 to 20 minutes. Serve immediately.

Nachos with Chicken, Cilantro-Lime Cream, and Pico de Gallo

Serves 4 to 6

It's arguable whether you really need a recipe for nachos, given how easy they are to make. This version has a few twists, though—chicken tossed with jalapeños and black beans, and topped with a homemade salsa and a cilantro-lime cream—which elevates it to another level.

2½ cups thinly sliced leftover chicken

1 cup jarred jalapeño slices, drained well

1 cup Spicy Black Beans (p. 241) or black beans, drained and rinsed well

¾ pound tortilla chips

6 ounces extra-sharp Cheddar, shredded (1½ cups)

6 ounces Monterey jack cheese, shredded (1½ cups)

1 cup Pico de Gallo (p. 241) or your favorite salsa

¾ cup Cilantro-Lime Cream (p. 112)

CHIX PICKS

A roast chicken coated with a vibrant spice rub stands up to the big flavors in nachos. Try the Sweet Southern Spice Rub (p. 12) or a bird topped with Smoky Chipotle Butter (p. 61).

1. Preheat the oven to 425°F.

2. In a medium bowl, toss the chicken with the jalapenos and black beans.

3. Line a heavy, rimmed baking sheet with aluminum foil. Cover with half the tortilla chips. Top with half the chicken mixture and half the Cheddar and Monterey jack cheeses. Layer with the remaining tortilla chips, chicken mixture, and cheeses. Bake until the cheeses melt and start to brown, 12 to 15 minutes.

4. Transfer to a large platter, top with the pico de gallo and cilantro-lime cream, and serve immediately.

Chipotle Chicken and Cheddar Quesadillas

Serves 4 to 6

Quesadillas are a great choice for leftover chicken, as the richness of the cheese compensates for any dryness in the chicken.

3 cups shredded leftover chicken

¼ cup chopped fresh cilantro

3 scallions (white and green parts), trimmed and thinly sliced

1 canned chipotle chile, minced, plus 2 tablespoons of the adobo sauce

¼ cup olive oil

1 tablespoon balsamic vinegar

1 teaspoon light brown sugar

Kosher salt and freshly ground black pepper

4 large burrito-size flour tortillas

½ pound sharp Cheddar cheese, shredded (2 cups)

1 cup Pico de Gallo (p. 241) or your favorite salsa

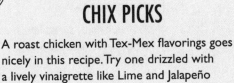

CHIX PICKS

A roast chicken with Tex-Mex flavorings goes nicely in this recipe. Try one drizzled with a lively vinaigrette like Lime and Jalapeño Vinaigrette (p. 60).

1. Preheat the oven to 325°F.

2. In a medium-size bowl, toss the chicken together with the cilantro, scallions, chipotle, adobo sauce, 1 tablespoon of the oil, the vinegar, and the brown sugar. Season with salt and pepper to taste.

3. Set one of the tortillas on a cutting board. Top half of the tortilla with about ¼ of the filling and cheese. Fold the tortilla over so it forms a half moon. Repeat with the remaining tortillas, filling, and cheese.

4. Heat 1½ tablespoons of the oil in a heavy 12-inch skillet over medium heat until shimmering hot, about 2 minutes. Place two of the stuffed tortillas in the hot pan—they should fit snugly. Cook, pressing down occasionally with a metal spatula, until the bottoms are nicely browned, about 3 minutes. Flip and cook until the other side is well browned and the cheese melts out the sides, 2 to 3 minutes.

5. Transfer to a baking sheet and keep warm in the oven while you cook the remaining quesadillas in the same manner. Serve immediately with the pico de gallo.

Grilled Chicken and Vegetable Quesadillas

Serves 4

When I grill-roast chicken, I like to throw any vegetables I have on hand on the grill as well. What I don't eat that night goes great in leftovers like this quesadilla. These flavors are more Mediterranean than south of the border, so you can use most any grilled vegetable you like.

1 red onion, cut into
½-inch-thick slices

2 medium-size zucchini,
cut lengthwise into
½-inch-thick slices

1 red bell pepper, cored,
seeded, and cut into 4 pieces

6 tablespoons olive oil

Kosher salt and freshly
ground black pepper

2½ cups thinly sliced
leftover chicken

1 tablespoon balsamic vinegar

6 ounces feta cheese, crumbled

2 teaspoons chopped fresh thyme

4 large burrito-size flour tortillas

CHIX PICKS

Try a grill-roasted chicken with Mediterranean flavors, like Anago's Garlicky Grill-Roasted Split Chickens with Lemon and Herbs (p. 66) or Italian Grilled Chicken Under a Brick with Smoky Balsamic Tomatoes (p. 68).

1. Prepare a charcoal fire or heat up the gas grill (heat all burners to medium-high). For a charcoal fire, pile a couple of layers of briquettes on one side and a single layer of charcoal on the other side of the grill so that you end up with medium-hot to hot zone and a moderate to cool zone. Your fire should be ready when the briquettes are mostly gray (or, if you're using hardwood, when they are red hot).

2. Drizzle the onion, zucchini, and pepper with 2 tablespoons of the oil and season generously with salt and pepper, about 1 teaspoon and ½ teaspoon, respectively.

3. Grill the vegetables (covered on the gas grill or starting in the hot zone if using charcoal) until browned, about 3 minutes. Flip them and cook the pepper and zucchini until browned on the other side and just tender, about 4 minutes. Transfer to a large plate.

4. Reduce the heat on the gas grill to medium-low or transfer the onion slices to the cooler part of the charcoal fire and cook, flipping occasionally, until they soften to a pleasant crunch, 6 to 10 minutes. Remove from the grill and let cool to room temperature.

continued

5. Pre-heat the oven to 325°. Chop the vegetables and toss with the chicken, 1 tablespoon oil, the vinegar, feta, and thyme. Season with salt and pepper to taste.

6. Set one of the tortillas on a cutting board and top half of it with a heaping one quarter cup of the filling. Fold the tortilla over so it forms a half moon. Repeat with the remaining tortillas and filling.

7. Heat 1½ tablespoons of the oil in a heavy 12-inch skillet over medium heat until shimmering hot, about 2 minutes. Place two of the stuffed tortillas in the pan—they should fit snugly. Cook, pressing down occasionally on the tortillas to flatten them, until the bottoms are nicely browned, about 3 minutes. Flip and cook until the other side is well browned, too, 2 to 3 minutes.

8. Set the cooked quesadillas on a baking sheet and keep warm in the oven while you cook the remaining quesadillas in the same manner. Serve immediately.

Fresh Spring Rolls with Grilled Chicken and Spicy Peanut Dipping Sauce

Serves 4 as main course or 6 as an appetizer

Spring-roll skins are one of those ingredients that, as my friend Amy Albert would point out, make you look like a bloody genius. The skins can be a little delicate to work with, but after you roll up a couple, you'll get the feel. They're a delicious change of pace for a light dinner or packed into a lunch bag for work.

SPRING ROLLS:
12 thin sheets rice paper (or spring-roll skins)
¼ pound rice vermicelli, soaked in hot water until tender (5 to 10 minutes) and drained
2 cups thinly sliced leftover chicken
½ cup fresh mint leaves, torn into large pieces
6 scallions (white and green parts), trimmed, cut in half lengthwise if thick, then crosswise into 2-inch lengths
1 red bell pepper, cored, seeded, and thinly sliced
2 medium carrots, shredded

PEANUT SAUCE:

1/2 cup peanut butter (preferably natural)
1/4 cup soy sauce
2 tablespoons rice vinegar
1 1/2 tablespoons Thai chili paste or 1/2 teaspoon Tabasco sauce
1/4 cup water

1. Fill a large bowl with cold water. Immerse 1 piece of rice paper in the water for about 5 seconds. Set on a clean dish towel on a large work space and let rest until pliable, about 20 seconds; if it's still tough, using your fingers, spread a little more water over it.

2. Top the rice paper with a small handful of noodles, some of the chicken, some mint, scallions, red pepper, and carrots. Roll the rice paper away from you, tucking the edges into the center so the paper wraps the filling into a tight, rectangular bundle. Set on a large platter and repeat with the remaining 11 sheets of rice paper and filling.

3. Place all the peanut sauce ingredients except the water in a food processor and process until combined. With the machine running, add the water and process until smooth.

4. To serve, slice the rolls in half on the diagonal. Set on a serving platter and serve with the peanut sauce for dipping.

CHIX PICKS

Use a roast chicken with some sweetness and some spice, like one brushed with Asian Barbecue Glaze (p. 14), or one with citrus, like Orange-Rosemary Pan Sauce (p. 32).

Crisp Spring Rolls with Chicken

Serves 4 as a main course or 8 as an appetizer

I'm not one to order fried spring rolls in a restaurant—there's just too many other options on a Chinese menu. But now and then when I have some leftover chicken, I will prepare spring rolls at home. They're easy to make and though I don't deep fry often, they're worth it. I've prepared all sorts of dipping sauces for these spring rolls, but I can't help but like the convenience and flavor of store-bought duck sauce the best. Try and pick up a good quality version at an Asian market (I like Koon Chun).

3 tablespoons canola oil, plus about 3 cups for frying

3½ ounces shiitake mushrooms, stemmed and caps thinly sliced

Kosher salt

1 large clove garlic, minced

2 cups thinly sliced Napa cabbage

1 cup grated carrot

2 cups shredded leftover chicken

2 tablespoons soy sauce

1 teaspoon toasted sesame oil

8 egg roll wrappers

1 cup duck sauce for dipping

CHIX PICKS

For these spring rolls, try a roast chicken with some Asian flavors like Grilled Chicken Teriyaki with Scallions (p. 70) or Chinese Salt and Pepper Roast Chicken (p. 52).

1. Heat 2 tablespoons of the oil in a large skillet over medium-high heat until shimmering hot. Add the shiitakes, sprinkle with ¼ teaspoon salt, and cook until browned and softened, about 3 minutes. Make a well in the center of the pan, add 1 tablespoon oil and the garlic and cook, stirring, until it starts to sizzle steadily, about 30 seconds. Stir in the cabbage, carrot, and chicken, sprinkle with another ¼ teaspoon salt and cook until the cabbage wilts a bit, about 2 minutes. Stir in the soy sauce and sesame oil and toss well.

2. Set one of the wrappers on a cutting board so a corner faces you (it should look like a diamond). Set a cup of cold water next to you. Place ¼ cup of the chicken mixture in the middle of the wrapper. Close the spring roll as though it were an envelope: fold the edge closest to you over the filling, then fold the sides together, and roll the wrapper away from you so it rolls into a tight cigar shape. Brush the final edge with some of the cold water so it becomes sticky and adheres. Fill and roll the remaining spring rolls the same way. (You can refrigerate them up to 24 hours before frying.)

3. Fill a large saucepan or medium pot with oil so it's 2 inches deep and heat over medium heat until it's 350°F, about 5 minutes.

4. Carefully add half the spring rolls to the hot oil and cook, gently flipping with tongs, until crisp all over, 4 to 6 minutes. Transfer to a plate lined with paper towels and gently sprinkle with salt. Cook the remaining spring rolls in the same manner, then serve immediately with the duck sauce.

Asian Sesame Chicken Wraps

Serves 4

Lettuce leaves are great as a wrap, particularly for dishes with Asian flavors. Lighter than lavash or tortillas, greens wraps are perfect summer finger food. I like to assemble all of the ingredients for the wraps in small bowls, then let guests wrap them with the lettuce leaves at the table.

2 tablespoons honey
2 tablespoons ketchup
2 tablespoons hoisin sauce
1 tablespoon rice vinegar
1 tablespoon soy sauce
2 teaspoons toasted
  sesame oil
3 cups shredded
  leftover chicken
12 Boston lettuce leaves
3 medium carrots, shredded
½ English cucumber, seeded and cut in julienne strips
3 scallions (white and green parts), trimmed and thinly sliced
1 tablespoon sesame seeds, toasted in a dry skillet
  over medium heat until light brown

CHIX PICKS

The spice of hoisin sauce in Asian Barbecue Glaze (p. 14) or the brightness of Orange-Apricot Glaze (p. 14) pairs well with the sweet sesame sauce in this wrap.

1. In a large bowl, whisk together the honey, ketchup, hoisin, vinegar, soy sauce, and sesame oil. Add the chicken and toss well. (This will keep in the refrigerator, tightly covered, up to 1 day.)

2. In different plates and bowls, set out the lettuce leaves, chicken, carrots, cucumber, scallions and sesame seeds and allow guests to form their own wraps.

Spiced Chicken Empanadas

Makes about 12 empanadas; serves 4 as a light meal or 8 as an appetizer

In most every Spanish-speaking country around the globe, empanadas are the pre-eminent snack, sort of a bundled-up sandwich for eating on the go. They have a half-moon shape similar to a calzone, only smaller. In Spain, empanadas are often baked in a light, puff pastry crust. In Central and South America, they have a thinner crust and are fried to crisp brownness.

The empanadas in this recipe are fried like their South American cousins, with thin wonton skins holding the filling. Also, for the sake of simplicity, I form these empanadas into rounds instead of folding them over into half-moons. I like to serve these with a chipotle salsa, but they're also great with guacamole.

2 cups shredded leftover chicken
I canned chipotle chile, minced, plus
   2 tablespoons of the adobo sauce
I tablespoon cider vinegar
I teaspoon light brown sugar
¼ cup chopped fresh cilantro
Kosher salt and freshly ground black pepper
24 round wonton skins
All-purpose flour
I large egg, beaten
Canola or vegetable oil for frying
I cup Tomato-Chipotle Salsa (p. 244)

> ## CHIX PICKS
>
> A roast chicken with some sweetness and spice matches the heat of the chipotles in this empanada. Try Southern Spiced Chicken with Chipotle-Honey BBQ Sauce (p. 76) or a bird sprinkled with Southwestern Chile Spice Rub (p. 11).

1. In a medium bowl, toss together the chicken, chipotle, adobo sauce, vinegar, brown sugar, and cilantro. Season generously with salt and pepper to taste.

2. Set 8 of the wonton skins on a lightly floured baking sheet. Using a pastry brush, lightly brush the edges of the wontons with the egg. Place about 3 tablespoons of the filling in the center of each wonton, taking care to pat it down. Top with one of the remaining wontons. Using the tines of a fork, press the edges down. Repeat with the remaining wonton wrappers and filling. (At this point, you can cover tightly and refrigerate for up to 24 hours before cooking.)

3. Fill a large saucepan or medium pot with oil so it's 2 inches deep and heat over medium heat to 350°F, about 5 minutes, then carefully add half the empanadas to the oil. Cook, flipping them after 2 minutes, until they're browned all over, about 4 minutes total. Using a slotted spoon, transfer them to a plate lined with paper towels and sprinkle with salt. Cook the remaining empanadas in the same way, then serve with the chipotle salsa for dipping.

Curried Chicken, Potato, and Pea Samosas

Makes about 16; serves 4 as a light meal or 8 as an appetizer

Samosas are the Indian version of an empanada—fried pockets of spiced meat or vegetables. I use store-bought wonton skins, then fry them quickly in hot oil. Serve as a light meal with steamed basmati rice and sautéed vegetables or as a jazzy appetizer.

1 medium-size russet potato, peeled and cut into 1/2-inch chunks
Kosher salt
2 tablespoons olive oil
1 medium-size yellow onion, finely diced
1 1/2 tablespoons curry powder
2 cups diced leftover chicken
1/2 cup low-salt chicken broth
1 cup frozen petite peas, thawed
Freshly ground black pepper
All-purpose flour
32 wonton skins
2 large eggs, beaten
Vegetable oil for frying (about 3 cups)
1 recipe Cilantro-Lime Cream (p. 112)

> ## CHIX PICKS
> Not surprisingly, this recipe pairs well with a roast chicken with some curry flavor, like Grill-Roasted Tandoori Chicken (p. 62) or E.G.'s Roast Chicken with Tarragon and Whole-Grain Mustard (p. 46).

1. Place the potato in a medium saucepan, add water to cover by about 2 inches, salt well, and bring to a boil. Reduce the heat to a simmer and cook until just tender, about 10 minutes. Drain and transfer to a large baking sheet to cool.

2. Heat the olive oil in a large sauté pan over medium heat for about 1 1/2 minutes. Add the onion, sprinkle with 1/2 teaspoon salt and cook, stirring, until softened and translucent, about 8 minutes. Stir in the curry powder and cook for 1 minute. Add the potato, chicken, and broth and cook, stirring, until the broth cooks off and the potato completely softens through. Stir in the peas and season with salt and pepper to taste.

3. Lightly flour a baking sheet and set 8 wonton skins on it. Use a pastry brush to brush their edges with the egg. Place 3 tablespoons of the filling in the center of each wonton, patting it down. Top with a remaining wonton. Use the tines of a fork to press the edges down. Repeat with the remaining wrappers. (You can refrigerate these, tightly covered, for up to 24 hours.)

4. Fill a large saucepan or medium pot with oil so it's 2 inches deep and heat over medium heat to 350°F, about 5 minutes. Carefully add half the samosas to the hot oil and cook, flipping after about 2 minutes, until browned all over, about 4 minutes total. Transfer to a plate lined with paper towels and sprinkle lightly with salt. Cook the remaining samosas in the same manner, then serve with the cilantro-lime cream for dipping.

Chicken, Spinach, and Sun-Dried Tomato Roulades

Serves 2 to 3 as a main course or 6 to 8 as an appetizer

These roulades are a wonderful meal served with a simple green salad, though they're also elegant enough to be thinly sliced and set out as an appetizer. If you've never cooked with phyllo, it takes a delicate hand. Because these sheets are very thin and brittle, it's important to keep them covered with a damp kitchen towel until the moment you work with them.

1 large clove garlic, minced
2 tablespoons olive oil
1 pound spinach, heavy stems removed, washed well and spun dry
Kosher salt
2 cups thinly sliced leftover chicken
6 ounces feta cheese, crumbled
1/3 cup pitted kalamata olives, drained and coarsely chopped
6 oil-packed sun-dried tomatoes, thinly sliced
Freshly ground black pepper
4 sheets frozen phyllo dough, thawed and covered with a damp kitchen towel
3 tablespoons unsalted butter, melted, plus more for greasing

> ## CHIX PICKS
>
> A roast chicken with a strong lemon flavor complements the spinach and feta in this Mediterranean roulade. Try Bistro Roast Chicken with Lemon and Thyme (p. 34) or Greek Roast Chicken with Lemon, Black Olives, and Potatoes (p. 56).

1. Preheat the oven to 400°F.

2. Heat the garlic in the oil in a large skillet over medium-high heat until it sizzles steadily for about 20 seconds. Add the spinach, sprinkle lightly with salt and cook, stirring often, until wilted, about 3 minutes. Remove from the heat and stir in the chicken, feta, olives, and tomatoes. Season with more salt and with pepper to taste; be careful—the feta and olives have quite a lot of salt.

3. Set one of the sheets of phyllo on a large cutting board running lengthwise away from you. Lightly brush with some of the melted butter and sprinkle lightly with salt. Set another sheet on top of the first and repeat the process. Repeat with the remaining 2 sheets of phyllo. Spread the spinach mixture over two thirds of the phyllo, in the area that's closest to you. Roll the phyllo over itself (away from you) so it forms a tight roll. Brush the outside with the remaining melted butter.

4. Grease a large baking sheet and set the roulade on top. Bake until crisp and a uniform brown, 15 to 20 minutes. Transfer the roulade to a cutting board and let rest for 5 minutes. Using a bread knife, gently slice into 2-inch pieces if serving as a main course or 1-inch pieces if serving as an appetizer.

Basic Pizza Dough

Makes about 2 pounds, enough for 2 large pizzas (about 12 inches each)

Sunday is pizza night in my house. Occasionally I'll phone out, but I generally prefer to make the pies myself. I'll mix a large batch of dough in the afternoon (the recipe follows), then assemble some toppings just before cooking, whatever I can patch together from the pantry or refrigerator. But feel free to pick up a premade dough at the market or a local pizzeria. These prepared doughs are usually quite good and cut down on your prep time.

1 package active dry yeast (about 2 1/2 teaspoons)
1 teaspoon granulated sugar
1 1/4 cups warm water
3 1/2 cups all-purpose flour
1 1/2 teaspoons kosher salt
2 tablespoons extra-virgin olive oil, plus more for oiling the bowl

1. Combine the yeast and sugar in a 2-cup measuring cup and add the water, stirring well. Let sit for 10 minutes; the mixture should bubble and become frothy. If it doesn't, the yeast isn't active and you need to start again.

2. *If making by hand:* Mix the flour and salt in a large bowl. Make a well in the center and stir in the oil with a wooden spoon. Slowly drizzle in the yeast mixture, stirring well. Using your hands, knead the dough for a minute or two against the side and bottom of the bowl until most all of the flour is incorporated and it forms a round mass; if the mixture is dry and the flour is not well incorporated, add a tablespoon or so of water and continue kneading until the remaining flour is absorbed.

   If using a stand mixer: Add the flour and salt to the bowl of a large stand mixer fitted with the dough hook. Whisking on low speed, add the oil, then add the yeast mixture in a steady stream until combined. Continue whisking on medium speed until the mixture becomes a uniform dough. If the mixture is dry and the flour is not well incorporated, add a tablespoon or so of water, and continue kneading until the remaining flour is absorbed.

3. Tip the dough onto a lightly floured work surface and knead until it forms a tight elastic ball, 5 to 10 minutes. Set in a large, lightly oiled bowl, cover with a kitchen towel, and let sit at room temperature until it doubles in size, about 1 hour. Punch the dough down, form into 2 balls, and use in one of the pizza recipes on p. 256. The dough will keep in a tightly closed plastic bag in the refrigerator up to 24 hours; it will keep in the freezer indefinitely.

Baked Pizza

You'll need two tools for this oven-baking method—a wooden pizza peel (those long-handled trays that pizza makers use to slide pizzas in and out of the oven) and a pizza stone at least 14 inches wide. Both are relatively cheap and go a long way to making great pizzas. If you don't have a pizza stone, you can pick one up at a kitchen store. Or you can always simply set the pizza on a well-oiled baking sheet.

1. Preheat the oven to 450°F. Set a large pizza stone on the middle rack.

2. Set the rolled-out dough on a lightly floured pizza peel and sprinkle with the toppings. (Shake the peel to make sure the dough isn't sticking.) Slide the pizza from the peel onto the pizza stone. Bake until the crust is well browned and crisp and the cheese or other toppings are browned, 10 to 12 minutes.

3. Transfer the pizza to a cutting board, let rest for a couple of minutes, then slice and serve.

Grilled Pizza

If you've never grilled pizza before, relax—it's easy. The trick is to maintain a moderate fire, which helps the pizzas cook evenly and uniformly. This is easier to do on a gas grill than it is with a charcoal fire—all you have to do is turn a knob. However, the intense heat of a charcoal fire, while hard to control, imparts a wonderful smokiness and crispness to the dough. Just make sure to build a modest fire with two clear zones—one medium heat and the other low—so you can transfer the pizzas to the cooler side if they start to burn. One other thing to note: as opposed to a baked pizza where the toppings are layered on the dough before cooking, for grilled pizza, it's necessary to grill the dough first before topping it—this ensures that it properly crisps and cooks through.

1. Heat a gas grill to medium-high or prepare a charcoal fire with a moderate and a low zone. To do so, set a couple of layers of charcoal on one side of the grill and a sparse single layer of charcoal on the other side.

2. Grease a large baking sheet with olive oil and set the rolled-out pizza dough on top.

3. Carry the dough and the toppings to the grill. Brush the top of the dough lightly with 1 tablespoon oil. Using both hands, set the pizza onto the grill grates (on the hotter part of the charcoal fire). Cook, covered on the gas grill, until the top of the pizza starts to bubble and the bottom gets nice grill marks (but does not burn), 2 to 3 minutes. If the dough appears to be burning, reduce the heat on the gas grill to medium or transfer the dough to the cooler part of the charcoal fire.

4. Flip the dough using tongs and a large metal spatula (one in each hand). Transfer it to the cooler part of the fire if cooking over a charcoal fire or reduce the heat to medium-low on a gas grill. Sprinkle with the toppings. Cook, covered, until the toppings heat through and any cheese melts, about 6 minutes.

5. Transfer the pizza to a cutting board, let rest for a couple of minutes, then slice and serve.

Pizza with Tomatoes, Rosemary, and Chicken

Serves 2 to 3

This is a nice plain pie to serve up for the family. I love fresh tomatoes on pizza but it's important to salt them well before cooking. The salt seasons them and gets rid of excess moisture so the crust doesn't get soggy.

1 large ripe tomato,
  cored and thinly sliced
2 teaspoons chopped fresh rosemary
Kosher salt and freshly ground
  black pepper
1½ cups thinly sliced leftover chicken
2 tablespoons olive oil
1 pound pizza dough (p. 255),
  stretched into a 12-inch round
½ pound fresh mozzarella cheese,
  thinly sliced
⅓ cup freshly grated Parmesan cheese

CHIX PICKS

For this pizza, you're best off using a roast chicken with an assertive herb flavor, like one brushed with Rosemary-Balsamic Glaze (p. 13) or Italian Grilled Chicken Under a Brick with Smoky Balsamic Tomatoes (p. 68)—you can substitute any leftover tomatoes from the chicken for those on the pizza.

1. Set the tomato on a large plate and sprinkle with half of the rosemary, 1 teaspoon salt, and ½ teaspoon black pepper. Let sit for 10 minutes, then discard the tomato juices.

2. In a medium bowl, toss the chicken with 1 tablespoon of the oil and the remaining 1 teaspoon rosemary and sprinkle lightly with salt and pepper, about ¼ teaspoon of each.

3. Brush the dough with the remaining 1 tablespoon olive oil. Either grill the pizza dough following the directions on the bottom of the facing page, top it with the tomatoes, chicken, and two cheeses and finish grilling, or top the dough first and then bake it following the directions on the top of the facing page.

Pizza with Grilled Vegetables, Chicken, and Goat Cheese

Serves 2 to 3

This is the perfect pizza to make when you have some leftover grilled vegetables and chicken. Rich and tangy, goat cheese pairs well with the smoky, intense flavors of this pizza.

1 pound pizza dough (p. 255), stretched into a 12-inch round
1 tablespoon olive oil
1½ cups grilled vegetables (p. 247), thinly sliced
1½ cups thinly sliced leftover chicken
1 teaspoon chopped fresh rosemary
6 ounces goat cheese, crumbled
Kosher salt and freshly ground black pepper

CHIX PICKS

Try using a grill-roasted chicken like Anago's Garlicky Grill-Roasted Split Chickens with Lemon and Herbs (p. 66) or Italian Grilled Chicken Under a Brick with Smoky Balsamic Tomatoes (p. 68).

1. Brush the dough with the olive oil.

2. Either grill the pizza dough following the directions on the bottom of p. 256, top it with the vegetables, chicken, rosemary, goat cheese, and a generous sprinkling of salt and pepper and finish grilling, or top the dough first and then bake it following the directions on the top of p. 256.

Grilled Pizza with Buffalo Chicken and Blue Cheese

Serves 2 to 3

It didn't take much imagination for me to come up with this pairing and just like with wings, the combination is great on pizza.

1½ cups thinly sliced
   leftover chicken

¼ cup Original Frank's Hot Sauce
   or your favorite brand

1 pound pizza dough (p. 255),
   stretched into a 12-inch round

1 tablespoon olive oil

6 ounces blue cheese,
   crumbled

Kosher salt and freshly
   ground black pepper

3 tablespoons thinly sliced
   fresh chives or scallion greens

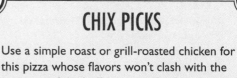

CHIX PICKS

Use a simple roast or grill-roasted chicken for this pizza whose flavors won't clash with the spiciness of the buffalo sauce. Try Sear-Roasted Chicken with Tomatoes and Rosemary (p. 78) or a grilled chicken prepared with All-Purpose Poultry Spice Rub (p. 11).

1. In a medium bowl, toss the chicken with the hot sauce.

2. Brush the dough with the olive oil. Either grill the pizza dough following the directions on the bottom of p. 256, then top it with the chicken, blue cheese, and a sprinkling of salt and pepper and finish grilling, or top the dough first and then bake it following the directions on the top of p. 256. Serve with a sprinkling of the chives or scallions.

 Sandwiches, Pizzas, and Other Light Meals 259

Pesto Pizza with Chicken and Fresh Mozzarella

Serves 2 to 3

This pizza is easy to put together if you have pesto in the fridge. Store-bought pesto works fine, but homemade is even better.

1 large ripe tomato, cored and thinly sliced
Kosher salt and freshly ground black pepper
1 pound pizza dough (p. 255), stretched
   into a 12-inch round
1 tablespoon olive oil
1 cup pesto, store-bought or homemade
   (see Rotini with Pesto, Chicken,
   and Green Beans, p. 143)
1½ cups thinly sliced leftover chicken
6 ounces fresh mozzarella cheese,
   thinly sliced

CHIX PICKS

A roast chicken with plenty of herbs like Bistro Roast Chicken with Lemon and Thyme (p. 34) or a roast chicken with Lemon-Herb Rub (p. 13) complements the pesto in this pizza.

1. Set the tomato on a large plate and sprinkle with 1 teaspoon salt and ½ teaspoon pepper. Let sit for 10 minutes, then drain away the tomato juice.

2. Brush the dough with the olive oil. Either grill the pizza dough following the directions on the bottom of p. 256, top it with the pesto, chicken, tomato, and mozzarella, sprinkle with salt and pepper and finish grilling, or top the dough first and then bake it following the directions on the top of p. 256.

Herbed Chicken, Roasted Red Pepper, and Artichoke Pizza

Serves 2 to 3

Roasted red peppers out of a jar and canned artichoke bottoms are two shortcuts worth taking. While I do prefer to make things from scratch, there's something to be said for pantry ingredients like these that you can stock in the cupboard and call upon at a moment's notice. Fontina (which is like mozzarella, only with a little more bite) and black olives join the red pepper and artichokes atop this colorful pie.

1 cup thinly sliced leftover chicken

1 cup canned diced tomatoes, drained well

2 tablespoons extra-virgin olive oil

2 teaspoons chopped fresh thyme

Large pinch of crushed red pepper flakes

Kosher salt and freshly ground black pepper

1 pound pizza dough (p. 255), stretched into a 12-inch round

3 canned artichoke bottoms, drained, rinsed, and thinly sliced

1 jarred roasted red pepper, thinly sliced

½ cup pitted black olives, drained and cut in half

¼ pound fontina cheese (preferably Italian), thinly sliced

1. In a medium bowl, toss the chicken with the tomatoes, 1 tablespoon of the oil, the thyme, red pepper flakes, and a light sprinkle of salt and black pepper (about ¼ teaspoon of each).

2. Brush the dough with the remaining 1 tablespoon olive oil. Either grill the pizza dough following the directions on the bottom of p. 256, top with the chicken mixture, artichokes, red peppers, olives, and fontina and finish grilling, or top the dough first and bake it following the directions on the top of p. 256.

CHIX PICKS

Pair with a mildly flavored bird like Roast Chicken with Rosemary-Garlic Croutons (p. 44) or a roast chicken brushed with Rosemary-Balsamic Glaze (p. 13).

Barbecued Chicken Pizza with Scallions and Three Cheeses

Serves 2 to 3

Like the buffalo chicken pizza, this pie transfers the elements of great bar food to a pizza. The barbecue sauce takes the place of tomatoes, and a medley of cheeses adds richness and melds nicely with the spicy sauce.

> 1½ cups thinly sliced leftover chicken
> 1 cup Slow-Cooked Chipotle-Honey BBQ Sauce (p. 77)
>   or your favorite bottled sauce
> 1 pound pizza dough (p. 255), stretched into a 12-inch round
> 1 tablespoon olive oil
> 2 scallions (white and green parts), trimmed
>   and thinly sliced
> 1 cup shredded extra-sharp Cheddar cheese
>   (about ¼ pound)
> 1 cup shredded fresh mozzarella cheese (about ¼ pound)
> ⅓ cup freshly grated Parmesan cheese

1. In a medium bowl, toss the chicken with half the barbecue sauce.

2. Brush the dough with the olive oil. Either grill the pizza dough following the directions on the bottom of p. 256, spread with the remaining barbecue sauce, top with the chicken, scallions, and cheeses and finish grilling, or top the pizza dough first and bake it following the directions on the top of p. 256.

CHIX PICKS

A roast chicken with barbecue flavor goes well with the sauce in this pizza. Try Southern Spiced Chicken with Chipotle-Honey BBQ Sauce (p. 76)—you can use any leftover sauce for the pizza—or Grilled Chicken Teriyaki with Scallions (p. 70), using any leftover scallions in place of the scallions in this recipe.

Marguerite's Chicken and Broccoli Calzone

Serves 2 to 3

This calzone is a go-to preparation for my fiance, Marguerite. Broccoli, chicken, and white wine are a classic combination. She likes to sauté the broccoli with some garlic, then add the chicken, sun-dried tomatoes, and wine and cook until all the flavors meld.

Note that the directions for making this calzone (and the one in the following recipe) are different than the pizza recipes so I've listed all the steps. As with pizzas, I prefer to bake calzones on a pizza stone. If you don't have a pizza stone, you can use a baking sheet. Line it with parchment paper or grease it with a tablespoon or so of olive oil.

3 tablespoons olive oil
3 cups 1½-inch broccoli florets
   (about ½ pound)
1 teaspoon kosher salt
2 cloves garlic, minced
¼ cup white wine
¼ cup low-salt chicken broth
2 cups thinly sliced leftover chicken
6 oil-packed sun-dried tomatoes,
   thinly sliced
1 pound pizza dough (p. 255),
   stretched into a 12-inch round
6 ounces fresh mozzarella cheese,
   thinly sliced
⅓ cup freshly grated Parmesan cheese
Generous ¼ teaspoon freshly ground black pepper

> ## CHIX PICKS
>
> Any simply flavored chicken will do, though I have found that a grill-roasted chicken really perks this up. Try Anago's Garlicky Grill-Roasted Split Chickens with Lemon and Herbs (p. 66) or Italian Grilled Chicken Under a Brick with Smoky Balsamic Tomatoes (p. 68), tossing any leftover tomato salsa into the filling.

1. Preheat the oven to 450°F and set a pizza stone on the middle rack.

2. Heat 2 tablespoons of the oil in a large skillet over medium-high heat until shimmering hot, about 2 minutes. Add the broccoli, sprinkle with ¾ teaspoon of the salt and cook, stirring, until it browns in places and turns bright green, about 3 minutes. Reduce the heat to medium low, stir in the garlic, and toss well for 15 seconds. Add the wine and cook until it completely reduces, about 1 minute. Add the broth, chicken, and tomatoes, cover, and cook until the broccoli is just tender to the tooth but still plenty crisp, about 3 minutes. Remove from the heat, uncover, and let cool.

continued

3. Set the dough on a lightly floured work surface. Using a slotted spoon, arrange the broccoli mixture over half the surface of the dough, top with the mozzarella and Parmesan, and sprinkle with the pepper.

4. Fold the empty side of the dough over the other so it forms a half moon shape. Using your fingers, crimp the dough so it forms a neat edge. Brush the top of the calzone with the remaining 1 tablespoon oil and sprinkle with the remaining ¼ teaspoon salt. Using a paring knife, make a couple of slits on the top of the calzone so that steam can escape.

5. Using a pizza peel, transfer the calzone to the pizza stone. Bake until well browned and the dough is cooked through, 12 to 15 minutes. Transfer to a cutting board, let sit for a couple of minutes, then cut into pieces and serve.

Vegetable and Chicken Calzones

Serves 2 to 3

For the filling in this calzone, I like slowly sautéing the onions, red peppers, and zucchini to caramelize and concentrate their flavors. Fresh oregano lends an earthy edge, the feta cheese and Parmesan provide richness.

3 tablespoons olive oil
1 small onion, cut in half and thinly sliced into half moons
½ red bell pepper, cored, seeded, and thinly sliced into strips
Kosher salt
1 small zucchini, cut in half lengthwise and thinly sliced into half moons
2 cups thinly sliced leftover chicken
2 tablespoons chopped fresh oregano
¼ cup chopped, pitted black olives (I like kalamatas)
6 ounces feta cheese, crumbled
⅓ cup freshly grated Parmesan cheese
Freshly ground black pepper
1 pound pizza dough (p. 255), stretched into a 12-inch round

1. Preheat the oven to 450°F and set a pizza stone on the middle rack.

2. Heat 2 tablespoons of the oil in a large skillet over medium-high heat until shimmering hot, about 1½ minutes. Reduce the heat to medium, add the onion and bell pepper, sprinkle with ¾ teaspoon salt, and cook, stirring, until browned in places and almost completely softened, 12 to 15 minutes.

3. Reduce the heat to medium-low, stir in the zucchini and cook until it just becomes tender, about 3 minutes. Stir in the chicken, oregano, olives, feta, and Parmesan and season generously with salt and pepper to taste. Set aside and let cool.

4. Arrange the sautéed vegetable mixture over half of the surface of the dough. Fold the empty side of the dough over the other so it forms a half moon shape. Using your fingers, crimp the dough so it forms a neat edge. Brush the top of the calzone with the remaining 1 tablespoon oil and sprinkle with ¼ teaspoon salt. Using a paring knife, make a couple of slits on the top of the calzone so that steam can escape.

5. Using a pizza peel, transfer the calzone to the pizza stone. Cook until the calzone is well browned, 12 to 15 minutes. Transfer to a cutting board, let sit for a couple of minutes, then cut into pieces and serve.

CHIX PICKS

Try a sear-roasted bird like Sear-Roasted Chicken with Lots of Garlic (p. 82) or Sear-Roasted Chicken with Tomatoes and Rosemary (p. 78), adding any of the sauce from the latter to the vegetables while they're sautéing.

Spanish Chicken Croquettes with Red Pepper Purée

Serves 2 to 3 as a main course

In Spain, tapas are a way of life: a reason for getting out and about, being with friends, and having a little something to drink and eat. Most every bar and café offers up all sorts of these small appetizer portions of food as accompaniments to a glass of wine or beer. *Croquetas*, or croquettes, have long been my favorite.

Spanish *croquetas* are smaller than their American counterparts. They have a creamy interior that is often studded with meat (generally some type of ham). Here, I fill the croquettes with chicken. I like to serve these with a red pepper relish, a nod to the flavors of the Iberian peninsula.

2 cups whole milk
¼ cup (½ stick) unsalted butter, plus more for greasing
I cup all-purpose flour
I cup diced leftover chicken
Large pinch of ground nutmeg
Kosher salt and freshly ground black pepper
2 jarred roasted red peppers, drained
3 tablespoons extra-virgin olive oil
I tablespoon sherry vinegar or balsamic vinegar
2 teaspoons chopped fresh thyme
2 large eggs, beaten
I½ cups Garlic-Thyme Breadcrumbs (p. 205)
Canola or sunflower oil for frying (6 to 8 cups)

1. Heat the milk in a medium-size saucepan over medium-low heat.

2. Melt the butter in a large saucepan over medium heat. Add ½ cup of the flour, mix well, and cook until it becomes a light golden color, 3 to 4 minutes. Add the warm milk and cook, stirring occasionally, until it comes to a light boil and thickens, about 15 minutes. Stir in the chicken and nutmeg and season with salt and pepper to taste (about ½ teaspoon of each).

3. Grease a 9 by 13-inch baking dish with butter and pour the chicken mixture into the dish. Refrigerate until solid, about a couple of hours.

4. Meanwhile, combine the red peppers, olive oil, vinegar, and thyme in a food processor and process until they form a smooth paste. Add a couple of tablespoons of water to loosen the purée if you like. Season with salt and pepper to taste (about ½ teaspoon of each), process once more, then refrigerate until ready to use, up to 2 days.

5. Set the remaining ½ cup flour, the eggs, and breadcrumbs in separate shallow bowls. Drop scoops of the chicken mixture (about 2 tablespoons each) onto a large baking sheet. Form into an oval shape, then lightly dredge in the flour, dip in the eggs, press to coat with the breadcrumbs, and set on a large plate. Repeat with the rest of the filling. You should have about 16 croquettes.

6. Preheat the oven to 300°F. Line another large baking sheet with paper towels. Fill a large saucepan or medium pot with oil so it's about 2 inches deep and heat over medium heat to 350°F, about 5 minutes.

7. Fry the croquettes in batches, taking care not to crowd the oil, until they're well browned, about 4 minutes total. With a slotted spoon, transfer them to a large baking sheet lined with paper towels and keep warm in the oven until all of the croquettes are fried.

8. Serve immediately with the red pepper purée for dipping.

CHIX PICKS

Try a mild roast chicken with Mediterranean flavors for this dish, like Sear-Roasted Chicken with Lots of Garlic (p. 82) or Roast Chicken with Rosemary-Mustard Crust and Browned Onions (p. 30).

Stacked Huevos Rancheros with Chorizo and Chipotle Salsa

Serves 4

Huevos rancheros contain some form of eggs—scrambled, poached, fried, etc.—jazzed up with some spice, chiles, and tortillas. I like scrambling the eggs with chorizo and thinly sliced chicken, then layering with crisp corn tortillas. Though deep-frying the tortillas produces ethereal results, I pan-fry and then finish crisping them in the oven—this browns the tortillas without the hassle of deep-frying.

If you want to prepare this dish for a brunch, make the salsa up to a day ahead and brown the tortillas a couple of hours beforehand—you can reheat them in a moderate oven just before serving.

8 small corn tortillas
1/4 cup olive oil
1/2 pound chorizo, cut into 1/2-inch dice
1 small yellow onion, finely diced
1/2 green bell pepper, cored, seeded, and finely diced
1 jalapeño, seeded and finely diced
Kosher salt
2 cups diced leftover chicken
1 teaspoon chili powder
10 large eggs, beaten well
Freshly ground black pepper
6 ounces extra-sharp Cheddar cheese, shredded (1 1/2 cups)
1 cup Tomato-Chipotle Salsa (p. 244)
1/2 cup chopped fresh cilantro

> ## CHIX PICKS
>
> For these eggs, try a roast chicken with plenty of spice. Any spice-rubbed chicken will do but Roast Chicken with Southwestern Rub and Cornbread and Jalapeño Stuffing (p. 48) or a roast chicken basted with Smoky Chipotle Butter (p. 61) would be particularly nice.

1. Preheat the oven to 375°F.

2. Heat a large, heavy skillet (I use a cast-iron pan) over medium heat for 2 minutes. Brush the tortillas on both sides with 2 tablespoons of the oil. Cook the tortillas two at a time in the skillet until they bubble and color light brown, about 2 minutes. Flip and cook the other side in the same manner. Repeat with the remaining tortillas.

3. Transfer the tortillas to a baking sheet and finish crisping them in the oven for 20 minutes.

4. Meanwhile, heat the remaining 2 tablespoons oil in the skillet over medium-high heat until shimmering hot, about 2 minutes. Add the chorizo, onion, bell pepper, and jalapeño. Sprinkle generously with salt (about ½ teaspoon) and cook, stirring occasionally, until the onion softens and browns in places, about 8 minutes (the chorizo should be nicely browned). Add the chicken and chili powder and cook, stirring well, until heated through, about 2 minutes.

5. Sprinkle the eggs with salt and pepper (about ½ teaspoon of each), whisk again, and add to the skillet. Cook, gently scrambling the eggs, until just set and cooked through, 3 to 4 minutes. Season with salt and pepper to taste.

6. To assemble, set a tortilla on each of 4 plates. Spoon a generous helping of the eggs on top. Sprinkle with half the Cheddar, salsa, and cilantro. Set the remaining tortillas on top and repeat with the remaining eggs, cheese, salsa, and cilantro and serve immediately.

Chicken, Asparagus, and Caramelized Onion Quiche

Serves 6 to 8

Of all the egg dishes in this book, this is definitely the one to call on if company's coming and you want to impress. The flavors—asparagus, Parmesan, and onions—are simple but elegant and make a great centerpiece for a brunch or light lunch.

Butter for greasing
One 9-inch Basic Pie Crust (p. 188)
  or store-bought pastry crust
All-purpose flour
4 tablespoons olive oil
1 large Spanish onion, thinly sliced
  (about ½ pound)
Kosher salt
½ pound fresh asparagus, bottoms snapped off,
  cut on the diagonal into 1-inch pieces
1½ cups thinly sliced leftover chicken
¼ cup low-salt chicken broth
5 large eggs, beaten
¾ cup whole milk
1 cup shredded sharp Cheddar cheese
½ cup freshly grated Parmesan cheese
½ teaspoon freshly ground black pepper

> ## CHIX PICKS
>
> Sear-Roasted Chicken with Spring Onions and Asparagus (p. 86) is a great match here, as you can fold in any leftover asparagus or onions. Or try a roast chicken with some sweetness like Balsamic-Glazed Rosemary Chicken with Bacon and Pearl Onions (p. 36)—any leftover onions or bacon from that dish will make a nice addition to the quiche.

1. Preheat the oven to 425°F. Grease a 9-inch pie plate or 10-inch quiche dish with butter.

2. Roll the dough into a 10-inch round (or one slightly larger if you're using the quiche dish) on a lightly floured work surface. Carefully transfer to the pie plate (or quiche dish) and mold to fit the plate's bottom and sides. Prick the dough all over with the tines of a fork and crimp the edges between your thumb and forefinger so they form a neat pattern along the top edge of the plate. Bake the crust until browned and crisp, 10 to 12 minutes. Let cool on a rack.

3. Meanwhile, heat 2 tablespoons of oil in a large, heavy sauté pan over medium-high heat until shimmering hot, about 1½ minutes. Add the onion, sprinkle with 1 teaspoon salt and cook, stirring, until it wilts and becomes translucent, about 5 minutes. Reduce the heat to medium-low and continue to cook, stirring occasionally, until the onion softens and turns a light caramel color, about another 20 minutes. Make a well in the center of the pan. Add the remaining 2 tablespoons of the oil and the asparagus, sprinkle with ½ teaspoon salt and cook, stirring, until it starts to soften and brown, about 3 minutes. Add the chicken and chicken

broth, cover with the lid askew, and cook, stirring, until the broth is almost completely cooked off and the asparagus is tender, about 2 minutes. Remove from the heat and let cool to room temperature. Reduce the oven temperature to 375°F.

4. In a large bowl, whisk together the eggs, milk, Cheddar, Parmesan, and asparagus mixture and season with ½ teaspoon salt and the pepper.

5. Gently pour the egg mixture into the crust and bake until the eggs just set and brown on top, about 35 minutes.

6. Let cool to room temperature for 10 minutes, then cut into wedges and serve.

Spanish Tortilla with Chicken, Roasted Red Peppers and Spinach

Serves 6 to 8

Tortilla española is a staple Spanish tapa, an all-day snack or appetizer served up at local bars and restaurants. Unlike the thin flour or corn wrappers that Americans think of as tortillas, a Spanish tortilla is a thick egg-and-potato cake, a cross between a frittata and a crustless quiche. Here, I've jazzed up the Spanish version with sautéed spinach, red peppers, and chicken.

6 tablespoons olive oil
1 large russet potato, peeled, cut in half lengthwise, and thinly sliced into half moons
Kosher salt
1 large Spanish onion, finely diced
6 ounces baby spinach
1 jarred roasted red pepper, cut into thin strips
2 cups thinly sliced leftover chicken
Freshly ground black pepper
8 large eggs, beaten

1. Preheat the oven to 425°F.

2. Heat 2 tablespoons of the oil in a large (8- to 10-inch-wide) ovenproof nonstick skillet over medium heat until shimmering hot, about 2 minutes. Add the potato, sprinkle with 1 teaspoon salt, toss well, and cook, stirring, until browned and tender, about 10 minutes. Transfer to a large plate.

continued

3. Add 2 more tablespoons of the oil and the onion to the pan, sprinkle with 1 teaspoon salt, and cook, stirring often, until it softens completely and browns in places, about 8 minutes. Stir in the spinach, red pepper, and chicken and cook, stirring, until the spinach just wilts. Remove from the heat and let cool for a couple of minutes.

4. In a large bowl, whisk ¾ teaspoon salt and 1 teaspoon black pepper with the eggs. Add the spinach mixture and the potatoes and gently toss.

5. Wipe the skillet out with a paper towel, add the remaining 2 tablespoons oil and heat over medium heat for 30 seconds. Add the egg mixture, reduce the heat to medium-low, and cook, gently scraping a spatula along the bottom of the skillet so the eggs don't burn, until they've just set, about 6 minutes.

6. Transfer the skillet to the oven and bake until browned and puffed on top and cooked through (a paring knife inserted into the center should come out clean), 12 to 15 minutes. Let cool for at least 10 minutes, then cut into wedges and serve. Or let cool, refrigerate, and reheat in the microwave or oven until hot.

CHIX PICKS

A roast chicken with garlic and herbs complements the flavors in this tortilla. Try Roast Chicken with Rosemary-Garlic Croutons (p. 44) or Sear-Roasted Chicken with Lots of Garlic (p. 82).

Frittata with Red Onions, Zucchini, and Chicken

Serves 6

A frittata is an Italian version of an omelet. Traditionally frittatas are flipped on the stovetop using a plate, but I prefer finishing them in a hot oven to avoid the challenge of the flip; moreover, the intense heat of the oven puffs up and browns the frittata.

1/4 cup olive oil
1 medium red onion, cut in half and thinly sliced into half moons
Kosher salt
3 1/2 ounces shiitake mushrooms, stemmed and caps thinly sliced
1/2 pound zucchini, (about 2 small) quartered lengthwise and thinly sliced across
Freshly ground black pepper
2 cups thinly sliced leftover chicken
1/2 cup freshly grated Parmesan cheese
2 teaspoons chopped fresh thyme
8 large eggs, beaten

CHIX PICKS

A mildly flavored roast chicken with plenty of herbs pairs well with this frittata. Try Bistro Roast Chicken with Lemon and Thyme (p. 34) or Roast Chicken with Rosemary-Mustard Crust and Browned Onions (p. 30), substituting any leftover onions for the red onions.

1. Preheat the oven to 450°F.

2. Heat 2 tablespoons of the oil in a large nonstick skillet over medium heat. Add the onion, sprinkle with 1/2 teaspoon salt, and cook, stirring, until softened and lightly browned, about 6 minutes. Add the shiitakes, sprinkle with another 1/2 teaspoon salt and cook, stirring, until they start to soften and brown, about 3 minutes. Reduce the heat to medium, add the zucchini, sprinkle with 1/2 teaspoon salt and a few generous grinds of black pepper and cook, stirring, until it becomes tender and browned, about 5 minutes. Stir in the chicken, Parmesan, and thyme, and cook 2 more minutes. Transfer the mixture to a large bowl and toss well. Let cool for a couple of minutes.

3. Meanwhile, wipe the skillet clean with a paper towel. Stir the eggs into the large bowl with the zucchini mixture. Heat the remaining 2 tablespoons of oil in the skillet over medium heat for 30 seconds. Add the eggs and cook, gently stirring, until they start to set around the edges, about 5 minutes.

4. Transfer to the oven and cook until the eggs set and are puffed and browned on top (a paring knife inserted in the center should come out clean), 8 to 10 minutes.

5. Slide the frittata onto a large cutting board, let rest for 5 minutes, then cut into wedges and serve.

Index